ART AND COPYRIGHT

Art and Copyright

by
SIMON STOKES
MA (Oxon), SM (MIT), LLM (Wales)
Solicitor; Partner, Tarlo Lyons, London

·HART·
PUBLISHING

OXFORD – PORTLAND OREGON
2001

Hart Publishing
Oxford and Portland, Oregon

Published in North America (US and Canada) by
Hart Publishing c/o
International Specialized Book Services
5804 NE Hassalo Street
Portland, Oregon
97213-3644
USA

Distributed in the Netherlands, Belgium and Luxembourg by
Intersentia, Churchillaan 108
B2900 Schoten
Antwerpen
Belgium

Hart Publishing is a specialist legal publisher based in Oxford, England.
To order further copies of this book or to request a list of other
publications please write to:

Hart Publishing, Salter's Boatyard, Folly Bridge,
Abingdon Road, Oxford OX1 4LB
Telephone: +44 (0)1865 245533 or Fax: +44 (0)1865 794882
e-mail: mail@hartpub.co.uk
WEBSITE: http//www.hartpub.co.uk

British Library Cataloguing in Publication Data
Data Available
ISBN 1–84113–225–X (hardback)

Typeset by Hope Services (Abingdon) Ltd.
Printed and bound in Great Britain on acid-free paper by
Biddles Ltd, www.biddles.co.uk

Acknowledgements

This book draws on my work with the Institute of Art and Law in Leicester since 1996. I would like to thank the Institute's Director, Ruth Redmond-Cooper, for giving me the opportunity to deepen my interest in art and copyright.

Tarlo Lyons has provided much needed support on occasion. My secretaries in the last year, Natalie Reynolds and Helen Barnes, helped with the typing of the manuscript. Lucy Awad, trainee solicitor, checked the footnotes and helped with proof-reading. Helen Dewar, the firm's librarian, tracked down a large number of cases and press cuttings.

Jonathan D.C. Turner, Barrister, of 4 Field Court provided updates on the progress of two copyright cases where he was Counsel and which are discussed in this book: *Designers Guild* and *Antiques-portfolio*. Simon Martin, Partner, Bell Gully, Auckland, provided assistance with some New Zealand materials.

I owe my interest in art to my parents and in particular to my father Roger Smith, an artist, and childhood visits to the Walker Art Gallery.

The greatest debts are to my wife for her encouragement and support in a project of (seemingly) ever increasing scope, and to my daughter Hannah, for her generally cheerful disposition throughout.

Simon Stokes
Clerkenwell
15 April 2001

Table of Contents

Frequently Cited Material

Bently and Sherman	L. Bently and B. Sherman, "Copyright Aspects of Art Loans" in N. Palmer (ed.), *Art Loans* (Kluwer, London, 1996)
Blakeney	M. Blakeney, "Protecting Expressions of Australian Aboriginal Folklore under Copyright Law" [1995] 9 *EIPR* 422
Bowrey	K. Bowrey, "Who's Writing Copyright's History?" [1996] 6 *EIPR* 322
Chilvers	I. Chilvers, *A Dictionary of Twentieth Century Art* (Oxford University Press, Oxford, 1999)
Coombes	R. Coombes, *The Cultural Life of Intellectual Properties* (Duke University Press, Durham, N.C. and London, 1998)
Copinger	K.M. Garnett et al., *Copinger and Skone James on Copyright* (14th edn., Sweet & Maxwell, London, 1999)
Cornish	W.R. Cornish, *Intellectual Property* (unless otherwise noted, all references are to the 4th edn., Sweet & Maxwell, London, 1999)
Dietz	A. Dietz, "Term of Protection in Copyright Law and Paying Public Domain: A New German Initiative" [2000] 11 *EIPR* 506
DuBoff and King	L.D. DuBoff and C.O. King, *Art Law in a Nutshell* (3rd edn., West Group, St. Paul, Minn., 2000)
Dworkin and Taylor	G. Dworkin and R. Taylor, *Blackstone's Guide to the Copyright, Designs and Patents Act 1988* (Blackstone Press, London, 1989)
Edwards and Waelde	L. Edwards and C. Waelde (eds.), *Law and the Internet* (2nd edn., Hart Publishing, Oxford, 2000)

Evatt	E. Evatt, "Enforcing Indigenous Cultural Rights: Australia as a Case-Study", in UNESCO and Institute of Art and Law, *Cultural Rights and Wrongs* (Institute of Art and Law, Leicester, 1998)
Golvan	C. Golvan, "Aboriginal Art and Copyright: An Overview and Commentary Concerning Recent Developments", [1999] *EIPR* 599
Gredley and Maniatis	E. Gredley and S. Maniatis, "Parody: A Fatal Attraction? Part 1: The Nature of Parody and its Treatment in Copyright", [1997] 7 *EIPR* 339
Gringras	C. Gringras, *The Laws of the Internet* (Butterworths, London, 1997)
Gurry	F. Gurry, *Breach of Confidence* (Clarendon Press, Oxford, 1984)
Hansmann and Santilli	H. Hansmann and M. Santilli, "Authors' and Artists' Moral Rights: A Comparative Legal and Economic Analysis (1997) 26 *J Legal Stud* 95
Hughes	J. Hughes, "The Philosophy of Intellectual Property", (1988) 77 *Georgetown Law Journal* 287
Hutcheon	L. Hutcheon, *A Theory of Parody: The Teaching of Twentieth Century Art Forms* (Methuen, London, 1995)
Isaac	B. Isaac, *Brand Protection Matters* (Sweet & Maxwell, London, 2000)
Jaszi	P. Jaszi, "Towards a Theory of Copyright: The Metamorphoses of 'Authorship' " (1991) *Duke Law Journal* 455
Joyce	C. Joyce, W. Patry, M. Leaffer and P. Jaszi, *Copyright Law* (5th edn., LEXIS Publishing, New York, NY, 2000)
Kearns	P. Kearns, *The Legal Concept of Art* (Hart Publishing, Oxford, 1998)
Kerly	D. Kitchin, D. Llewelyn, J. Mellor, R. Meade and T. Moody-Stuart, *Kerly's Law of Trade Marks and Trade Names* (13th edn., Sweet & Maxwell, London, 2001)

Laddie et al.	H.I.L. Laddie, P. Prescott, M. Vitoria et al., *The Modern Law of Copyright and Designs* (unless otherwise noted, all references are to the 3rd edn., Butterworths, London, 2000)
Laddie	H.I.L. Laddie, "Copyright: Over-strength, Over-regulated, Overrated?" [1996] *EIPR* 253
Lai	S. Lai, *The Copyright Protection of Computer Software in the UK* (Hart Publishing, Oxford, 2000)
Millinger	D.M. Millinger, "Copyright and the Fine Arts" (1980) 48 *Geo Wash L Rev* 354
Morcom	C. Morcom, A. Roughton, J. Graham, *The Modern Law of Trademarks* (Butterworths, London, 1995)
Nimmer	M. B. Nimmer and D. Nimmer, *Nimmer on Copyright* (M. Bender, New York, 1998)
Pollaud-Dulian	F. Pollaud-Dulian (ed.), *The Internet and Authors' Rights* (Sweet & Maxwell, London, 1999)
Rahmatian	A. Rahmatian, "Non-assignability of Authors' Rights in Austria and Germany and its Relation to the Concept of Creativity in Civil Law Jurisdictions Generally: A Comparison with UK Copyright Law", [2000] 5 *Ent LR* 95
Ricketson	S. Ricketson, *The Berne Convention for the Protection of Literary and Artistic Works: 1886: 1986* (Centre for Commercial Law Studies, Queen Mary College, London; Kluwer, London, 1987)
Rose	M. Rose, *Authors and Owners* (Harvard University Press, Cambridge, Mass., 1993)
Rushton	M. Rushton, "Economics and Copyright in Works of Artistic Craftsmanship", *Paper prepared for presentation at the Shepherd and Wedderburn Centre for Research into Intellectual Property and Technology (SCRIPT) at the University of Edinburgh, 30 October 2000* (available at <http://law.ed.ac.uk/script/rushton.htm>)
Russell-Clarke	M. Howe QC, *Russell-Clarke on Industrial Designs* (Sweet & Maxwell, London 1998)
Saunders	D. Saunders, *Authorship and Copyright*, (Routledge, London, 1992)

Sherman and Strowel   B. Sherman and A. Strowel (eds.), *Of Authors and Origins* (Clarendon Press, Oxford, 1994)

Sherman   B. Sherman, "From the Non-original to the Ab-original: A. History", in B. Sherman and A. Strowel (eds.), *Of Authors and Origins* (Clarendon Press, Oxford, 1994)

Spence   M. Spence, "Passing Off and the Misappropriation of Valuable Intangibles", (1996) 112 *LQR* 472

Stamatoudi and Torremans   I.A. Stamatoudi and P.L.C. Torremans (eds.), *Copyright in the New Digital Environment* (Sweet & Maxwell, London, 2000) Vol. 8 in the Perspectives on Intellectual Property Series

Sterling   J.A.L. Sterling, *World Copyright Law*, (Sweet & Maxwell, London, 1999)

Thomas   D. Thomas, *Copyright and the Creative Artist* (Institute of Economic Affairs, London, 1968)

Vaver   D. Vaver, "Intellectual Property: The State of the Art", (2000) 116 *LQR* 621

Vinje   T. Vinje "Should We Begin Digging Copyright's Grave?" [2000] 12 *EIPR* 551

Yen   A.C. Yen, "The Interdisciplinary Future of Copyright Theory", in M. Woodmansee and P. Jaszi (eds.), *The Construction of Authorship* (Duke University Press, Durham, N.C. and London, 1994)

Journals and Law Reports

ARTL   *Art, Antiquity and Law* (Institute of Art Law, Leicester/Kluwer)

ECDR   European Copyright and Designs Reports

EIPR   *Europan Intellectual Property Review* (Sweet & Maxwell)

EMLR   Entertainment and Media Law Reports

Ent LR	*Entertainment Law Review* (Sweet & Maxwell)
FSR	Fleet Street Reports
RIDA	*Revue Internationale du Droit d'Auteur*
RPC	Reports of Patent Cases

Other Abbreviations

| CDPA | Copyright, Designs and Patents Act 1988 |

Table of Cases

Table of Legislation

INTERNATIONAL

NATIONAL

Statutory Instruments

1

Introduction

1.1 BACKGROUND AND SCOPE

THE INTERNET AND the increasing commercial activities of museums and galleries mean that copyright has increasing importance in the art world. Artists are also becoming more aware of their rights and arguments about the appropriation of artists' works by others are arising more frequently.[1] There is also a growing debate about the extent to which existing law protects innovative works of modern art and the works of traditional cultures. At the same time the law of cultural property is now an established legal discipline, as increasingly is art law.[2]

This book aims to explore the UK law of copyright and related rights as applied to art as broadly defined[3] with a stress on the "fine arts"[4].

---

[1] See, for example, J. Napack, "Chinese artists may sue Venice Biennale," *The Art Newspaper*, September 2000 at 3: it was reported that certain Chinese artists and their art school were considering suing the artist Cai Guo Qiang for copyright infringement over his alleged 1999 appropriation of their 1965 Socialist Realist work "Rent Collector's Courtyard". Cai's work "Venice Rent Collector's Courtyard" won the International Prize at the 1999 Venice Biennale. In the UK the copyright infringement arguments surrounding the Turner Prize entry "The Loves of Shepherds 2000" hit the headlines late in 2000 and brought the issue of art and copyright to the fore. This case is discussed in Chap. 6.

[2] Art law is already an established legal discipline in the USA and the first holistic treatment of art law in the UK by Paul Kearns was published in 1998 (P. Kearns, *The Legal Concept of Art* (Hart Publishing, Oxford 1998) ("Kearns")). The Institute of Art and Law in the UK (in Leicester) was founded in 1995.

[3] No other attempt is made to define "art" for the purposes of this book. It will be clear in any event from the discussion of the law that follows that the legislature and the UK courts define "art" for the purposes of copyright protection in various ways, the category of "artistic works" in the CDPA being crucial. For an early and very useful discussion of the legal protection of "art" under UK law see P.H. Karlen, "What is Art? A Sketch for a Legal Definition" (1978) 94 *LQR* 383. See also Kearns. Photographs, given their importance in modern art and their categorisation as "artistic works" in the CDPA, are included for the purposes of this book. Films or video works, however, do not receive detailed treatment but are discussed in Chap. 6, section 6.3.4.

[4] The *Concise Oxford English Dictionary* (8th edn., Oxford University Press, Oxford, 1990) defines the "fine arts" as those "appealing to the mind or to the sense of beauty . . . especially painting, sculpture and architecture." In fact, with limited exceptions, UK

The protection of utilitarian or mass-produced items, except to the extent these comprise art—"ready-mades", for example—is not considered in detail.[5] Nor are works of architecture. The law of industrial design, for example, already receives detailed treatment in a number of works.[6] It is submitted that the growing relationship between the "fine arts" and copyright, including the development of artists' moral rights, the permitted scope of appropriation in copyright law, the copyright protection of modern art, and the challenges of digitisation and the Internet, points to the need for a UK text exploring this area. Although this book is not specifically concerned with the law of jurisdictions other than the UK, the international nature of the area means that it is often helpful to note the approach taken in other major jurisdictions. In particular, cases from other common law jurisdictions are noted and especially those from the USA, where there is a considerable amount of case law and scholarship in this field. Also in light of the attempts to harmonise copyright law in the EU and the long tradition of moral rights protection in continental Europe, these areas are also considered in some detail.

1.2 COPYRIGHT AND ART

Artists, like any other "authors", may be entitled to the protection of their works under the law of copyright and related rights. Most legal

copyright law now makes no express distinction between works of fine art and other artistic works in affording copyright protection but imposes limits on the copyright protection for industrial/utilitarian designs. But historically a distinction between the fine arts and the applied arts was maintained, at least in the classes of work protected (see L. Bently and B. Sherman, *The Making of Modern Intellectual Property Law* (Cambridge University Press, Cambridge, 1999)). Other jurisdictions also have made or do make such distinctions (for example early French (revolutionary) copyright law limited protection to the fine arts, but in 1902 protection was extended to sculptors and decorative designers irrespective of the merit of their work). The quality of the work can also be relevant in US law (see for example L. Bently and B. Sherman, "Copyright Aspects of Art Loans" in N. Palmer (ed.), *Art Loans* (Kluwer, London, 1996) ("Bently & Sherman")) and in particular, as discussed in Chap. 4, it is an issue in the US approach to moral rights.

   [5] "Ready-made" is the name given by Marcel Duchamp to a type of work he created which consists of a mass-produced article isolated from its functional context and displayed as a work of art (I. Chilvers, *A Dictionary of Twentieth-Century Art* (Oxford University Press, Oxford, 1999) ("Chilvers")), and see generally Chap. 6.

   [6] For example, C. Fellner, *Industrial Design Law* (Sweet & Maxwell, London, 1995); U. Suthersanen, *Design Law in Europe* (Sweet & Maxwell, London, 2000); and M. Howe Q.C., *Russell-Clarke on Industrial Designs* (Sweet & Maxwell, London, 1998) ("Russell-Clarke").

systems recognise two elements to such protection: economic rights (which in the UK are the rights to control copying (reproduction), publication, performance, broadcasting and adaptation[7]) and which are also generally referred to as "copyright" or "copyrights", and moral rights (in the UK the right to be identified as "author", to object to derogatory treatment of a work, the right to object to false attribution and the right to retain privacy with regard to certain photographs and films[8]).

Living artists or the estates of recently deceased artists are likely to benefit from moral rights, which only the artist or that person's estate can exercise. This is in distinction to the economic rights which can be freely transferred in whole or part by way of assignment.[9] In this sense copyright is an intangible property right like other intellectual property rights (patents, registered designs, trade marks, rights in confidential information, and so on) but with the added dimension that the creator, the author/artist, retains moral rights in the work irrespective of who owns the actual copyright. It is important to note that copyright is a purely negative right. It is primarily a right to stop others copying a work in which copyright subsists—it does not prevent someone else independently creating a similar work,[10] nor does it necessarily mean the copyright owner has the right to exploit their work themselves.[11]

Copyright and related rights are national rights—there is of course no universal law of copyright. In particular, the Anglo-American system of copyright law has tended to stress the economic aspects of copyright, whereas Continental, civil laws which stress "authors' rights" (*droit d'auteur*) have generally afforded greater protection to the artist/author, especially in the context of moral rights. However, from the nineteenth century onwards, there have been a series of

---

[7] S. 16, CDPA.

[8] Chap. IV, CDPA.

[9] At least in the UK: the position may well be different in civil law jurisdictions—see A. Rahmatian, "Non-assignability of Authors' Rights in Austria and Germany and its Relation to the Concept of Creativity in Civil Law Jurisdictions Generally: A Comparison with U.K. Copyright Law" [2000] 5 *Ent. LR* 95 ("Rahmatian").

[10] However absolute monopoly rights such as patents and registered designs can protect against this.

[11] For example take the publishers of an illustrated book. The publishers will own the copyright in the printed edition (see e.g. s.8 CDPA) but the author may retain the literary copyright in the text and the illustrator the artistic copyright in the illustrations: to exploit the book the publishers need the consent ("licence") of both the author and the illustrator, albeit that once the book is published the publishers will be able to enforce against pirates their copyright in the printed edition and any other copyright they may have in the work.

attempts to protect works internationally, the most important being the Berne Convention for the Protection of Literary and Artistic Works which dates back to 1886. In recent years the European Commission has devoted considerable effort to harmonising and strengthening the law of copyright across the EU, and this has generated an increasing amount of legislation. This has also meant that UK copyright law must increasingly address copyright concepts imported from authors' rights systems.

Broadly speaking common law "copyright" systems have tended to emphasise the protection of the "work", allowing the "author" of such works to be either an individual or a legal entity, such as a limited company; in contrast the civil law "authors' rights" systems have tended to emphasise the individual creator of the work and do not as a rule consider legal entities to be eligible as "authors"—only an individual can be an author of a "work" as the work is an emanation of that person's personality.[12]

Another distinction between authors' rights systems and the UK law of copyright is the concept of originality. In general, in both systems copyright is afforded only to "original" works: in UK law skill and labour alone will, with limited exceptions, confer "originality", whereas under authors' rights systems there must be creativity on the basis that the work reflects the personality of its creator. In fact, following the landmark Supreme Court *Feist* case,[13] US law now also requires "some minimal degree of creativity".[14]

It is also important to be aware from the outset of the so-called "idea/expression dichotomy" in copyright law.[15] Simply put, copyright

---

[12] Copinger, para. 1–05. The "personality theory" approach to copyright is discussed in Chap. 2.

[13] *Feist Publications* v. *Rural Telephone Service Co* 499 US 340, 113 L Ed 358 (1991) (Sup Ct) (at 369).

[14] The concept of "originality" is considered further in Chap. 3.

[15] Not all authors admit the existence of such a "dichotomy" in UK law, which has no express statutory basis—Laddie et al. call it the "idea/expression fallacy" (see H.I.L. Laddie, P. Prescott, M. Vitoria *et al.*, *The Modern Law of Copyright and Designs* (3rd edn., Butterworths, London, 2000) ("Laddie et al.") at 3.74) but it nevertheless appears in copyright cases on a regular basis (a few examples include *per* Nichols LJ in *ENTEC (Pollution Control) Ltd* v. *Abacus Mouldings* [1992] FSR 332, *George Ward (Moxley) Ltd* v. *Richard Sankey Ltd and Another* [1988] FSR 66, *Bradbury, Agnew & Co* v. *Day* (1916) 32 TLR 349; also see the cases cited below and also n.16 below). In any event, as Lord Hoffmann recently observed in *Designers Guild* v. *Russell Williams* [2000] 1 WLR 2416 at 2422 (HL), the distinction does find a place in the Agreement on the Trade-related Aspects of Intellectual Property (TRIPS) ([1994] OJ L.336/213) to which the UK is a party (in Art. 9.2). It is therefore submitted that this distinction is a useful and necessary

does not protect ideas, only the form in which they are expressed. As Lord Salmon once put it: "it is trite law that there can be no copyright in an idea".[16] So, for example, no one could copyright pointillism as an artistic style, but Seurat's paintings (if in copyright) would themselves be protected from copying as original artistic works. This dichotomy appears in copyright infringement cases from time to time where the style, technique or other elements of a design or painting have been reproduced but there has been no literal copying.[17] It is then frequently necessary to determine whether what has been copied is (protected) expression or merely an idea not capable of copyright protection.

Finally, copyright and related rights are distinct from the ownership rights (i.e. personal property) in a work of art or other work (such as a literary manuscript) which may benefit from copyright protection.[18] Indeed the US Copyright Act makes this expressly clear.[19] The sale or even the commissioning of a work of art will not necessarily transfer the copyright in the art work to the buyer/commissioner.[20] This, of

starting point when considering whether there has been infringement of an artistic work. Certainly it must be used with care—as Lord Hailsham commented (citing Prof. Joad of "Brains Trust" fame) "it all depends on what you mean by ideas" (*L.B. (Plastics) Ltd v. Swish Products Ltd* [1979] RPC 551 at 629 (HL) which Lord Hoffmann also referred to in *Designers Guild* (at 2422)). Laddie et al. in any event are prepared to restate the principle on the basis that whilst there is no copyright in general ideas, an original combination of ideas may constitute a substantial part of a copyright work (at 4.43) (citing Lord Hailsham in *Swish Products* (at 629) (see above), and Astbury J in *Austin v. Columbia Gramaphone Co* [1917–23] MCC 398 at 408 and again in *Vane v. Famous Players Film Co Ltd* [1923–28] MCC 374 at 398). The dichotomy is discussed in more detail in Chap. 3.

[16] *L.B. (Plastics) Ltd v. Swish Products Ltd* [1979] RPC 551 at 633 (HL). For a discussion of how the UK and USA have developed and applied this principle with emphasis on software copyright see S. Lai, *The Copyright Protection of Computer Software in the United Kingdom* (Hart Publishing, Oxford, 2000) ("Lai").

[17] See for example, *per* Morritt LJ and Lord Hoffmann in *Designers Guild v. Russell Williams*, discussed in Chap. 3.

[18] There are limited exceptions to this rule e.g. pre-CDPA photographs—see Copinger para. 5–02.

[19] S. 202: [o]wnership of a copyright . . . is distinct from ownership of any material object in which the work is embodied. This section was introduced following *Pushman v. New York Graphic Society Inc.* 287 NY 302, 308, 39 NE 2d, 249, 251 (1942) which held that transfer of ownership of an unpublished work transferred the common law copyright in the work as well (D. M. Millinger, "Copyright and the Fine Arts" (1980) 48 *Geo Wash L Rev* 354 ("Millinger") at 365).

[20] If such an assignment of copyright is sought this should be agreed in writing. Copyright (as opposed to moral rights) is transferable by assignment—this must be in writing (s.90(3) CDPA) and signed by the owner. Copyright is also transmissible on death by testamentary disposition. Note that the bequest of "an original document or other material thing" recording or embodying an unpublished artistic or other work shall

course, is of particular relevance to art loans where the borrower may well wish to benefit from the economic rights in the work by producing cards, catalogues and merchandise and may accordingly need to seek permission from the copyright owner.[21] Whether the work is protected by copyright, and who owns the copyright, may be difficult questions to answer. For example, when Churchill College, Cambridge, acquired some of Sir Winston Churchill's personal papers a few years ago with a controversial £12 million grant from the National Lottery,[22] it acquired physical title to the papers but not the copyright: copyright in Churchill's personal papers was kept by the Churchill trustees; copyright in the State papers (which were also given to the College by the Government at the same time) was kept by the Crown.

For many years copyright was the Cinderella of intellectual property law, overshadowed in importance by patents and trade marks. However the advent of digital technology means copyright now has centre stage—those seeking to protect and exploit their works on CD-ROM, DVD (digital video/versatile disk), other new media and the Internet increasingly need to rely on copyright. There is a continuing debate about whether the economic rights need to be broadened to cope with the challenges of the new digital technologies. This also brings to the fore another aspect of copyright: the conflicting relationship between owners, who wish to control the economic rights to their commercial benefit, and users, who claim the benefit of what is called "fair use" in the USA and "fair dealing" in the UK. Users wish to be able, free of charge, to publish and reproduce works in connection with non-commercial purposes (such as study or research) or for public-interest purposes (such as reporting current events). These and other issues are explored in chapters three and six.

Artists, museums, galleries and publishers are also increasingly looking to other intellectual property laws for protection as well as copyright. This area is considered in chapter eight.

include the copyright in the work unless the contrary is indicated in the testator's will or codicil, in so far as the testator was the owner of the copyright immediately before his death (s.93 CDPA). Commissioned artistic works are considered in Chap. 7.

[21] Note also that once an artist has sold their work and transferred possession of it to a third party they have no right under English law (absent a contractual right of access) to e.g. gain access to the work to photograph it or otherwise copy it, despite the fact they still retain the copyright in it. The position appears similar in the USA (Millinger, at 363–4).

[22] To be more correct, the National Heritage Memorial Fund purchased the papers using monies generated by the National Lottery.

Finally, in discussing art and copyright it is important to keep in mind the range of disciplines and perspectives now being brought to bear on the study of copyright law. The approach taken in this book follows in the main the "self-contained" legal approach to copyright law—readers interested in a detailed consideration of recent economic and sociological approaches to "authorship" and the cultural aspects of intellectual property are referred elsewhere.[23] Having said this, it will become apparent as this book progresses that notions of authorship and varying assumptions about the function of copyright remain important currents, albeit not always stated ones, in copyright law.[24]

[23] Prof. Sterling speaks of the "self-contained" approach in his *World Copyright Law* (Sweet & Maxwell, London, 1999) ("Sterling") at 39. For a consideration of copyright and "authorship" see, for example, B. Sherman and A. Strowel (eds.), *Of Authors and Origins* (Clarendon Press, Oxford, 1994) ("Sherman and Strowel"). In particular, Sherman, in his paper in Sherman and Strowel, "From the Non-original to the Ab-original: A History" ("Sherman"), criticises the "increasingly self-referential nature of copyright law" (at 114). He is of the view that in order to understand and explain copyright law not just the rules and principles underlying the law must be examined, but also it is necessary "to engage in more abstract, relexive, and historical examinations of the subject" (at 129). See also P. Jaszi, "Toward a Theory of Copyright: The Metamorphoses of 'Authorship'" (1991) 42 *Duke Law Journal* 455 ("Jaszi"), for an exploration of the extent to which copyright has received a constructed idea of "authorship" from literary and artistic culture and how this "authorship construct" has been mobilised in legal discourse. For a discussion of the two main theories underpinning copyright law (copyright as an economic incentive which advances social welfare versus the legal vindication of a person's right to property in the fruit of their labour (natural law theory)) (which are discussed in Chap. 2) and the need for an interdisciplinary approach to the subject which gives due weight to the natural law theory, see A. C. Yen, "The Interdisciplinary Future of Copyright Theory" in M. Woodmansee and P. Jaszi (eds.), *The Construction of Authorship* (Duke University Press, Durham, NC, and London, 1994) ("Yen"). Finally, an introduction to the various perspectives from which copyright has been approached (e.g. by legal historians, historians of publishing and a variety of scholars with various perspectives on authorship) is K. Bowrey, "Who's Writing Copyright's History?" [1996] 6 *EIPR* 322 ("Bowrey"): she comments on (1) Edelman (a Marxist perspective), whose *Ownership of the Image. Elements for a Marxist Theory of the Law*, translated by E. Kingdom (Routledge and Kegan Paul, London, 1979) is discussed by Kearns (in Chap. 3), (2) others (such as Mark Rose) influenced by Foucault's writings on authors, publishers and copyright, and (3) commentators from a cultural studies and legal perspective including Jane Gaines (author of *Contested Culture. The Image, The Voice and The Law* (University of North Carolina Press, Chapel Hill, NC, 1991)) and R. Coombes (a legal scholar and anthropologist who takes an interdisciplinary approach—see in particular her book *The Cultural Life of Intellectual Properties* (Duke University Press, Durham, NC, and London, 1998) ("Coombes")).

[24] For example, Peter Jaszi has argued that the Romantic conception of authorship (which he describes as "the Wordsworthian vision of the 'author-genius' with privileged access to the numinous" (Jaszi. at 459), referring to Woodmansee, "The Genius and the Copyright: Economic and Legal Conditions of the Emergence of the 'Author'", 17 *Eighteenth-Century Stud* 425 (1983–1984)) continues to have an abiding influence. Jaszi

So whilst this book primarily approaches art and copyright from the perspective of a practising lawyer, the author has endeavoured to alert the reader to writing on this area from a range of viewpoints, not just those of the practitioner. As will become clear as the book progresses, copyright is too important a matter to be left to practitioners alone.

It has been endeavoured to state the law relating to the UK as at 1 January 2001. In addition the adoption in April 2001 of the so-called Digital Copyright Directive is also noted.

cites the example of computer software copyright as being often justified on the grounds that programs are no less inspired than poems and that the imaginative processes of the programmers is fundamentally akin to that of the conventional author (at 463).

2

The Copyright System: Its Justification and History

2.1 INTRODUCTION

BEFORE SETTING OUT a detailed analysis of how copyright protects artistic works, it is worthwhile looking at both the justifications for copyright and the history of copyright law. In order to understand the current law it is necessary to have some background to how copyright has evolved.

It has been argued that copyright law initially developed in the UK without much recourse to philosophical or other justifications.[1] Indeed a leading copyright historian has categorised the historical development of copyright law as the development of a series of fragmented rules rather than principles—"there is no set of clearly defined principles for copyright".[2] Nevertheless an understanding of some of the main justifications for, and principles underlying, copyright is necessary to understand current debates about the scope of copyright, including its application to new situations, such as the protection of aboriginal art, digitisation and certain aspects of contemporary art discussed later in this book.[3] Intellectual property rights such as copyright

---

[1] See M. Rose, *Authors and Owners* (Harvard University Press, Cambridge, Mass., 1993) ("Rose"), chap. 3, who discusses the genesis of the first UK copyright statute, the Statute of Anne: "[p]robably the truth is that the exact status of authorial property was not something to which anyone had given a great deal of thought prior to the parliamentary consideration of [the Statute of Anne]—and it is unlikely that the matter was examined in any great detail during the deliberations over the statute" (at 48).

[2] L. R. Patterson, *Copyright in Historical Perspective* (Vanderbilt University Press, Nashville, Tenn., 1968) at 222.

[3] For a general discussion of the justifications for intellectual property in the much discussed and controversial area of intellectual property protection for brands see B. Isaac, *Brand Protection Matters* (Sweet & Maxwell, London, 2000) chap. 8 ("Isaac").

affect what people do and say and how they earn a living. So the introduction, continuation and expansion of copyright clearly require considerable justification.[4]

2.2 JUSTIFICATIONS FOR COPYRIGHT[5]

The main justifications for copyright fall into three broad areas. The
first justification is on the basis of economics; the second is on the basis
of public policy; the third is on the basis of moral rights.[6]

2.2.1 The Economic/Utilitarian Justifications for Copyright

In Anglo-American copyright law economic arguments have been
prevalent. It has been strongly argued, for example, that "the purpose
of copyright is basically to ensure a continuing profit to the originator
or creator of a copyrighted work".[7] Therefore the grant of exclusive

---

[4] See J. Waldron, "From Authors to Copiers: Individual Rights and Social Values in
Intellectual Property Law" (1993) 68 *Chicago-Kent LR* 841 at 887 (as discussed in
M. Spence, "Passing Off and the Misappropriation of Valuable Intangibles" (1996) 112
LQR 472 ("Spence") at 479).

[5] One way to try to make sense of the various "justifications" for copyright is to view
them as "rhetorics". The shape of copyright law can on one analysis be seen as the outcome of interest-group politics operating through the institutions of the law—the chief
"actors" being: consumers of copyright "goods", the distributors of copyright "goods"
(publishers, booksellers, etc) (who frequently will take the economic, entrepreneurial
risk) and the creators of copyright "goods". These actors employ various "rhetorics" at
various times to support their interests and these in turn "can take on lives of their own
and become independent factors in the development of intellectual property law" (See
C. Joyce, W. Patry, M. Leaffer and P. Jaszi, *Copyright Law* (5th edn., LEXIS Publishing,
New York, 2000) ("Joyce") at 61). Another approach is to look at the "norms" at work
in copyright laws, the "principles that lead to rules of action in concrete cases" (P. E.
Geller, "Must Copyright Be For Ever Caught Between Marketplace and Authorship
Norms" in Sherman and Strowel at 159). Geller categorises these norms as marketplace
norms (which reflect the economic/utilitarian pre-occupations of Anglo-American copyright law (see below)) and authorship norms which "dictate rules to empower authors
to control the use by others of their self-expression" (at 159) which are historically
prevalent in *droit d'auteur* copyright systems (see also below).

[6] For an overview see Copinger at para. 2–04. Copinger distinguishes four major principles underpinning the copyright system: natural law, just reward for labour, stimulus
to creativity and social requirements. In the author's view two of these principles merge
together: "natural law" and "just reward for labour", being both classed as "moral
rights" arguments.

[7] D. Thomas, *Copyright and the Creative Artist* (Institute of Economic Affairs,
London, 1968) at 27 ("Thomas").

rights to the author is an incentive for the author to create. It is also a very significant incentive to entrepreneurs such as publishers who rely on the copyright protection afforded to authors. Economic and public-policy arguments are also embodied in the copyright clause of the US Constitution: this granted the federal government the right "to promote the Progress of Science and useful Arts, by securing for limited Times to Authors and Inventors the exclusive Right to their Writings and Discoveries".[8]

Putting it another way, the economic rationale for copyright has both a "static" and a "dynamic" element: "static" in that the owner has a positive benefit as a result of ownership of the property right, and "dynamic" in that the right acts as an incentive to invest in creating the work on the basis that only the author or his or her assigns can exploit it.[9]

To quote Anthony Trollope, "[t]ake away from English authors their copyrights, and you would very soon take away from England her authors".[10]

Of course it can be debated whether in the fine arts the economic basis of copyright has much relevance: it is trite to say that Picasso, for example, would doubtless still have created his works regardless of the existence or otherwise of copyright. It is originals of his works (as opposed to (unsigned) copies) that command enormous prices, and Picasso was able to exploit the market for his works in his lifetime. However in the applied arts and areas such as lithography, photography and engravings where the copy (as opposed to the original) has economic value in its own right the economic justification has greater force. As Denis Thomas stated some years ago:

> "It has been suggested that copyright has no effect on true artistic creativity. However, it is presumably a factor in the world of the popular arts, with its

---

[8] Art. 1, para. 8, cl. 8. See for example the comments of the Supreme Court in *Mazer* v. *Stein* 347 US 201 (1954), 74 S Ct. 460, 98 L Ed. 630 (1954): "[t]he economic philosophy behind the clause . . . is the conviction that encouragement of individual effort by personal gain is the best way to advance public welfare through the talents of authors and inventors in 'Science and useful Arts.' Sacrificial days devoted to such creative activities deserve rewards commensurate with the services rendered."

[9] This analysis has been developed by W.M. Landes and R.A. Posner, see the much-cited Landes and Posner, "Trademark Law: An Economic Perspective" (1987) 30 *Journal of Law & Economics* 265, discussed, for example, in Isaac at 219. See also N.M. Landes and R.A. Posner, "An Economic Analysis of Copyright Law" (1989) 18 *J Legal Stud.* 325. In fact the approach of neoclassical economists such as Landes and Posner is somewhat different from earlier "classical" economic approaches: it is much more heavily free market-based and sees far less scope for "fair use" type doctrines except where there is market failure (see Joyce at 68–9).

[10] His *Autobiography*, quoted in Copinger at para. 2–04.

chance of quick returns for the entrepreneur alert for changes of mood and fashion, especially among the young. Nor can it be assumed that serious works of art would be entirely unaffected: though artists would continue to express themselves, as they have done throughout history, under all kinds of economic and social constraints, the publishers, impresarios and galleries needed to bring their own works before the public might be less inclined than under copyright protection to take the financial risk."[11]

In fact the economic argument for copyright protection, in one guise or another, has a long history in English law. For example, according to David Saunders,[12] in the seventeenth century case *Roper* v. *Streeter*[13] the "court recognised investment and expense as justifying a claim to a property [right] in copyright".

2.2.2 Public Policy Arguments

It is generally regarded as being for the public good that authors should be encouraged to publish their works to ensure as wide a dissemination of knowledge and culture as possible. The existence of copyright encourages this and in economic terms can help make such dissemination viable. However copyright protection raises conflicts here: it is one thing to encourage the production of copyright works, but, if unregulated, copyright may act as a fetter on those who need to copy the works for desirable purposes such as private study or research, or for critical comment. So arguments for exceptions to copyright protection on the basis of "fair use" or "fair dealing" also come to the fore in this regard. These are discussed in Chapters 3 and 6.

2.2.3 Moral Rights

There are two major theories underpinning arguments that an author has an intrinsic, just or moral right to their creative efforts. These are based on the idea of a "just reward" for labour, and that under natural law that authors have an exclusive right of property in their labours.

---

[11] Thomas at 27.
[12] D. Saunders, *Authorship and Copyright* (Routledge, London, 1992) ("Saunders") at 29.
[13] (1672) Skinner 233; 90 ER 107.

Just reward theory

At its most basic this theory can be summed up by Jesus' injunction: "[f]or the labourer is worthy of his hire".[14]

A variant of this is the desert theory or, as it is sometimes called, the "value-added" labour theory.[15] According to Becker (as summarised by Isaac), "this is a moral theory which seeks to justify the grant of a proprietary right to the creator of intellectual property on the basis that the 'effort' in creating the thing 'deserves' to be recognised and rewarded such that the creator can prevent imitation of his work".[16] Also it is argued that, as the author will have created something of benefit to society, he is entitled to receive in return a benefit from society, namely a property right.[17] Certainly the desert argument is to be distinguished from the natural law argument discussed below.

However, it has also been pointed out that the difficulty with the desert theory is in determining what sort of efforts are worthy of protection and what protection is given.[18] For example: "[m]any of the best value intangibles are the results of moments of inspiration that involve little or no apparent effort on the part of the person claiming the intangible. The work of the perspiring, but not the inspired, 'creator' would be protected by law".[19]

Thus the desert principle is not without its problems: in terms of effort, the labours of the artisan may outweigh those of the inspired artistic genius.

It can be argued that a variant of the desert theory is the "reap/sow" principle, or "unjust enrichment" argument as it is also called (i.e. that it is unjust to reap where you have not sown), although this also has

---

[14] Luke 10:7 (Authorised version): see Isaac, 222–3.

[15] For example, by J. Hughes in "The Philosophy of Intellectual Property" (1988) 77 *Georgetown Law Journal* 287 ("Hughes").

[16] Isaac at 223, citing G. Becker, "Deserving to Own Intellectual Property" (1993) 68 *Chicago-Kent Law Review* 609.

[17] Isaac at 223, again citing Becker. For example in the US case of *Mazer* v. *Stein* 3347 US 201 (1954) it has been argued (by Hughes), that the Supreme Court was saying that the enhancement of the public good through the efforts of intellectual labour made the creators *worthy* of their reward (see comments of Supreme Court cited in n. 8 *supra*) .

[18] Isaac at 223. See also E.C. Hettinger, "[a]lthough intellectual laborers often deserve rewards for their labor, copyrights, patents and trade secrets may give the laborer much more or much less than is deserved" (in "Justifying Intellectual Property", (1989) 18 *Philosophy & Public Affairs* 31).

[19] Spence 4 at 487. Spence gives other arguments against the desert theory as well (at 487–9)—given these difficulties Spence sees it as the least important theory in the discussion of intellectual property rights generally (at 488–9).

utilitarian aspects.[20] This has been used as a basis for preventing misappropriation or unfair competition. A well-known example of this principle is the US case of *International News Service* v. *Associated Press*.[21]

This principle frequently appears in UK copyright law from time to time[22]:

> "Free trade does not require that one should be allowed to appropriate the fruits of another's labour, whether they are tangible or intangible. The law has not found it possible to give full protection to the intangible. But it can protect the intangible in certain states, and one of them is when it is expressed in words or print. The fact that that protection is of necessity limited is no argument for diminishing it further, and it is nothing to the point to say that either side of the protective limits a man can obtain gratis whatever his ideas of honesty permit him to pick up."[23]

Indeed it was recently referred to by the House of Lords in a case involving artistic works, *Designers Guild Limited* v. *Russell Williams (Textiles) Ltd*[24]: "[t]he law of copyright rests on a very clear

---

[20] The "rhetoric" of misappropriation has roots in the longstanding legal doctrines of quasi-contract and restitution (see Joyce at 67).

[21] (1918) 248 US 215 (Sup. Court). In this case the Court held that the defendant could be enjoined from using the plaintiff's wire service news items during the period for which the information constituted "hot" news and had commercial value: strictly speaking what was restricted here was not copying but the use of information to the extent necessary "to prevent that competitor from reaping the fruits" of the the plaintiff's efforts. See A. R. Miller and M. H. Davis, *Intellectual Property* (2nd edn., West Publishing Co., St. Paul, Minn., 1990) at 418, and Isaac at 227.

[22] It is also the basis of the famous copyright maxim "what is worth copying is . . . worth protecting" (*per* Peterson J in *University of London Press Ltd* v. *University Tutorial Press Ltd* [1916] 2 Ch. at 610, cited with approval by Lord Reid in *Ladbroke Ltd* v. *William Hill Ltd* [1964] 1 All ER 465 at 471). Laddie J has spoken of the "almost evangelical fervour" of the UK courts in applying the commandment "thou shalt not steal" the results of the plaintiff's labours. "If that has necessitated pushing the boundaries of copyright protection further out, then that has been done. This has resulted in a body of case law on copyright which, in some of its further reaches, would come as a surprise to the draughtsmen of the legislation to which it is supposed to give effect" (*Autospin (Oil Seals) Ltd* v. *Beehive Spinning (A Firm)* [1995] RPC 683). Indeed this comment of Laddie J highlights a major difficulty with the misappropriation justification: there are no inherent checks and balances in its application (unlike the utilitarian argument where the incentive to create is balanced by granting copyright for a limited term and the development of fair use and other limiting doctrines such as the idea/expression dichotomy, and the natural law argument where a public domain element needs to be preserved on the basis of Locke's famous proviso)—see Joyce at 67 and n. 26 below.

[23] *Per* Lord Devlin in *Ladbroke* v. *Hill* [1964] 1 WLR 273 at 291; see W.R. Cornish, *Intellectual Property* (4th edn., Sweet & Maxwell, London, 1999) ("Cornish") at 363.

[24] [2000] 1 WLR 2416.

principle: that anyone who by his or her own skill and labour creates an original work of whatever character shall, for a limited period, enjoy an exclusive right to copy that work. No one else may for a season reap what the copyright owner has sown".[25]

Natural Law/Personality Bases

These bases are the ones most often raised by those seeking to protect authors' rights, as opposed to those exploiting creative works for profit. They have a number of aspects. One is the often-cited statement about property by John Locke in his *Second Treatise of Civil Government* (1690):

> "[E]very man has a Property in his own Person. This no Body has any Right to but himself. The Labour of his Body and the Work of his Hands, we may say, are properly his. Whatsoever then he removes out of the State that Nature hath provided, and left in, he hath mixed his Labour with, and joyned to it something that is his own, and thereby makes it his Property."[26]

Thus through labour an individual converts the raw material of nature into private property whether tangible or intangible. This argument features in the key eighteenth-century literary property cases between booksellers[27]:

> "Extended into the realm of literary production, [this] theory of property produced the notion put forward by the London booksellers of a property founded on the author's labour, one the author could sell to the bookseller. Though immaterial, this property was no less real and permanent, they argued, than any other kind of estate."[28]

[25] *Per* Lord Bingham of Cornhill at 2418A.

[26] As quoted in Rose at 5. It is important to note, however, Locke's famous proviso— "[l]abour being the unquestionable Property of the Labourer, no Man but he can have a right to what that is joyned to, *at least where there is enough and as good left in common for others [emphasis added]*" (para 27, *Second Treatise*). Gordon has restated the proviso as follows: "creators should have property in their original works, only provided that such grant of property does no harm to other persons' equal abilities to create or to draw upon the pre-existing cultural matrix and scientific heritage. All persons are equal and have an equal right to the common" (W.J. Gordon, "A Property Right in Self Expression Equality and Individualism in the Natural Law of Intellectual Property" (1993) 102 *Yale LJ* 1533 at 1563–4).

[27] Such as *Millar* v. *Taylor* (1769) 4 Burr. 2303, 98 ER 252 in which the Court of King's Bench ruled that literary property was a common-law right and that copyright was perpetual, and the House of Lords in *Donaldson* v. *Becket* (1774) 2 Bro. PC 129, (1774) 4 Burr. 2408, 17 Cobbett P. Hist. 954 which reversed *Millar* v. *Taylor* and declared that copyright was limited in term in accordance with the Statute of Anne (see Rose at 5 and generally).

[28] Rose at 6.

It has been argued that Locke's theory of a right of property deriving from personal labour was from the start embedded in American copyright law,[29] and that "the concept of English copyright law is a true picture of Locke's theory up to the present day. Copyright subsists in a literary, dramatic, musical or artistic work if some, albeit limited, work or effort has gone into the creation of the work".[30] Certainly in English law there was early judicial acknowledgement that it was just to grant copyright to authors of literary works, and also that authors had what we now call "moral rights", as Lord Mansfield made clear in *Millar* v. *Taylor*: "it is just, that an author should reap the pecuniary profits of his own ingenuity and labour. It is just, that he should judge when to publish. It is fit he should not only choose the time, but the manner of publication . . .".[31]

However in addition to the Lockean natural law strand, Anglo-American copyright law also lays particular stress on the economic basis for copyright protection—the distinctiveness, artistic merit or originality of expression is less relevant than protecting the economic value of the author's labour.[32]

Another theory underpinning copyright centres on artists' works as being nothing less than an extension of the artists' personality—the so-called "personality" theory. Kant defended copyright on this basis,[33] as did Hegel. It has been argued that the personality justification is the one best applied to the arts.[34]

The now unfashionable philosopher Herbert Spencer also argued in support of an argument for the peculiarly personal nature of an artist's work:

> "[A] production of mental labour may be regarded as property in a fuller sense than may be a product of bodily labour; since that which constitutes its value is exclusively created by the worker."[35]

[29] Saunders at 243, citing A.C. Yen "Restoring the Natural Law: Copyright as Labor and Possession" (1990) 51 *Ohio State Law Journal* 517.

[30] Rahmatian at 96. Rahmatian cites the test of originality for works to benefit from copyright under English law which depends on some, albeit a limited amount, of skill, labour and judgement being applied—see for example the House of Lords in *Ladbroke Ltd* v. *William Hill Ltd* [1964] 1 All ER 465, and see Chap. 3.

[31] (1769) 4 Burr. 2303, 98 ER 252.

[32] See, for example, Rahmatian at 97. It can be argued that Lord Mansfield's judgment in *Millar* v. *Taylor* mingles both the economic and personal rights of the author: "[i]n his presentation, the claims of propriety and property reinforced and validated each other: the personal interests moralised the economic claim, while the property claim gave legal weight to the personal interests" (Rose at 82).

[33] See Sterling at 43.

[34] See Hughes at 287.

[35] Thomas at 26, citing Spencer, *The Principles of Ethics* (1897), ii.

Indeed the link between copyright and the artist's personality is regarded as the basis for copyright protection in civil law (or *droit d'auteur* ("authors' rights")) jurisdictions:

"[I]n the civil law countries, the justification for the protection of a person's creation is not the potential economic value of the labour and effort which have gone into the work, but the fact that every person can claim protection for his/her personality and anything that flows from it."[36]

Indeed the first French authors' rights laws (13–19 January 1791 and 19 July 1793) reflected this principle, Le Chapelier, when presenting one of these early French revolutionary laws stating: *"[l]a plus sacrée, la plus personnelle de toutes les propriétés est la fruit de a la pensée d'un ecrivain".*[37] These laws were of broad scope (granting a property right protecting the works of authors, composers, painters and engravers for their entire life) and exerted a great influence on the laws of France's neighbours.[38]

The use of natural law arguments to justify intellectual property rights is not without its critics: if all labour or creative effort resulted in a grant of property rights would this not prevent others from drawing on the common pool or public domain of works and ideas?[39] Also it has been argued that the Lockean theory fails properly to explain why property ought to be created in the item created: simply because a book is an author's creation is this a sufficient reason to make it the author's property?[40] What of creations which are 99 per cent inspiration and

---

[36] Rahmatian at 97. According to Sterling, in French law the test for subsistence of copyright is whether the work shows "the mark of the author's personality" and in German law the subsistence of the author's right relates to the personal act of creation by the author (Sterling at 43).

[37] Rahmatian at 98. This point is also made by Sam Ricketson: "there was a conscious philosophical basis to the French laws that saw the rights protected as being embodied in natural law" (S. Ricketson, *The Berne Convention for the Protection of Literary and Artistic Works: 1886:1986* (Centre for Commercial Law Studies, Queen Mary College/Kluwer, London, 1987) ("Ricketson") at 5.

[38] See Ricketson at 6.

[39] Nevertheless Locke's theory continues to be a fertile basis for analysis especially in the context of copyright: for example Gordon, in applying a Lockean natural law analysis to the idea/expression dichotomy, has stated that Locke's "proviso" "prohibits a creator from owning abstract ideas because such ownership harms later creators" (Gordon n. 26 *supra*, at 1581). For a discussion of the "proviso" see n. 26 *supra*.

[40] S. Breyer, "The Uneasy Case for Copyright: a Study of Copyright in Books, Photocopies and Computer Programmes" (1970) 84 *Harvard LR* 281 at 289 (cited in Saunders).

1 per cent perspiration, for example, where little labour is expended?[41] Other objections have also been raised.[42]

A strong argument against over-reliance on natural rights justifications for copyright is the nature of artistic works. In reality "authorship" is not a solitary activity in which one person creates an entire work from his or her imagination alone. As Bard and Kurlantzick have argued, all artists are part of an artistic community which shapes their vision: artistic works do not just reflect the artists' personality, they embody a mixture of their personality, the influence of contemporary society and the works of other artists (living and dead). Indeed this fact argues strongly for the recognition of a strong public domain element to copyright.[43]

2.2.4 Copyright Scepticism

The extent to which copyright, based on any or all of the above justifications, is viewed as necessarily desirable, is perhaps surprising.[44] Certainly there are continuing debates about the appropriate duration of copyright protection—indeed many of these are conducted on strictly economic grounds: what is the optimal duration to stimulate creativity without stifling the rights of others to create derivative works? At what point do the marginal benefits from increasing the term or scope of copyright protection (such as the additional revenues generated which help to encourage more works) equal the marginal costs incurred from increasing the protection (such as the cost of creating works, the possibility of restricted public access to works and the

---

[41] "The labor justification cannot account for the idea whose inception does not seem to have involved labor" (Hughes).

[42] See for example Sterling at 41–2—various difficulties in applying Locke's property theory to copyright are explored. See also Hettinger n. 18 *supra*, at 31 for a critique of the Lockean and desert theories, among others.

[43] R.L. Bard and L.S. Kurlantzick, *Copyright Duration: Duration, Term Extension, The European Union and the Making of Copyright Policy* (Austin & Winfield, San Francisco, Cal., 1999). See also n. 26 above.

[44] The 1996 article by Laddie J (the revised text of a Memorial Lecture in honour of the distinguished copyright lawyer Stephen Stewart QC), "Copyright: Over-strength, Over-regulated, Over-rated?" [1996] 5 *EIPR* 253 ("Laddie") remains a trenchant critique of modern copyright law. See also his conclusion in *Autospin (Oil Seals) Ltd* v. *Beehive Spinning (A Firm)* [1995] RPC 683 for some similar criticisms. (See also n. 22 *supra*).

increased administrative costs of administering and enforcing copyright protection)?[45]

However there are also those who actively challenge the application of copyright law of whatever duration, especially to utilitarian works. As noted above, although not a defined term in UK copyright law, a strong "public domain" (i.e. the work in question is either not protected by copyright at all (for example it falls into the "idea" side of the idea/expression dichotomy) or copyright in it has expired) is important in allowing the "inspiration" so important to artistic success to flourish.[46] Hugh Hansen in a witty and original article speaks of the players on the copyright stage: first, the secular priesthood of copyright lawyers all firmly believing that creators are entitled to copyright in their works; secondly, the "agnostics and atheists" "imbued with the culture of the public domain".[47]

Indeed Rushton and others have argued that copyright protection for certain works, in particular "works of artistic craftsmanship", is not justified by economic analysis. This is on the basis that law ought to help promote economic efficiency—on this basis the law should be wary of creating property rights for every conceivable creative work.[48] Rushton sees works of artistic craftsmanship as less deserving of copyright protection than works of fine art.[49]

[45] This is the classic, albeit simplified, benefit-cost analysis in economics: see M. Rushton, "Economics and Copyright in Works of Artistic Craftsmanship", paper prepared for presentation at the Shepherd and Wedderburn Centre for Research into Intellectual Property and Technology (SCRIPT) at the University of Edinburgh, 30 October 2000 (available at http://www.law.ed.ac.uk/script/rushton.htm) ("Rushton").

[46] To quote Laddie J, "[t]he whole of human development is derivative. We stand on the shoulders of the scientists, artists and craftsmen who preceded us. We borrow and develop what they have done; not necessarily as parasites, but simply as the next generation. It is at the heart of what we know as progress" (Laddie at 259). The limits of appropriation, in the context of parody and other uses of someone else's work, are discussed later in this book.

[47] H.C. Hansen, "International Copyright: An Unorthodox Analysis" (1996) 29 *Vanderbilt Journal of Transnational Law* 579.

[48] Rushton at 15.

[49] For example, according to Rushton such works inevitably have functional aspects (which ought not to be protected by copyright); they are attractive to consumers for a number of reasons, not least often because of their attribution to a particular "artist-craftsman" (so granting copyright to such works will not necessarily stimulate the creation of new works at all), a strong "public domain" or "tradition" is important for creativity in the applied arts, it will often be expensive for copiers to succeed in making acceptable copies of a work of artistic copyright (hence on economic grounds copyright protection is not required) and moral rights in the applied arts are less important: the law of passing off should suffice (Rushton at 12–14).

Others see the continuing expansion of intellectual property law into areas such as the protection of functional designs, the patenting of computer software and micro-organisms as indicating that intellectual property has come to be more of an end in itself than as a means to promote innovation.[50] Whenever a new intellectual property right is argued for (such as *sui generis* database rights discussed in Chapter 3) or the expansion of an existing right is called for (such as extending the exclusive rights granted to copyright owners to include "transmission right" to protect the exploitation of works on the Internet, as discussed in Chapter 5) then at the very least some attempt at a cost-benefit analysis ought to be undertaken. Nor should intellectual property be treated as an absolute value—ranged against it are values of at least equal importance—these include, as Professor David Vaver has argued, "the right of people to imitate others, to work, to compete, talk, and write freely, and to nurture common cultures" and the way intellectual property should be reconciled with these societal values has changed and will continue to change over time.[51] Vaver goes on, "[such] adjustments occur for social and economic reasons; they are not ordained by natural law. Where a particular line should be drawn can certainly not be answered by circularities like 'Intellectual property is property' ".

Certainly, it should be noted, as Professor Vaver does, that the historical trend has been for intellectual property rights to become more intense and all-encompassing.[52] In its early years, for example, Vaver notes that copyright law simply prevented *literal* copying: so, for example, when the copyright owner of a painting complained that *tableaux vivants* mimicking it were being staged in London without his permission, a claim of copyright infringement failed.[53] This has now

---

[50] D. Vaver, "Intellectual Property: The State of the Art" (2000) 116 *LQR* 621 at 636 ("Vaver"). See also his earlier article, "Intellectual Property Today: Of Myths and Paradoxes" (1990) 69 *Canadian Bar Review* 98, in which he argued that copyright, with its minimal standards for eligibility, is less concerned with authors, art and literature than with protecting the mass media ("art and literature [in comparison to the 'army of standardized industrial products—fungible pop records, soap operas, formula films, pulp books' . . ."] occupy so small a field that it is hard to see how copyright law significantly encourages their creation" (at 109) and copyright he adds can even be used as a tool of censorship (he cites for example the US case where J.D. Salinger was able to prevent a biographer from using letters of his available to the public in an archive: *Salinger v. Random House Inc.* (1987) 811 F. 2d 90 (CA 2 Cir, 1987)).

[51] See Vaver at 636 (citing an earlier work of his, *Intellectual Property: Copyright, Patents, Trade-marks* (1997) at 5–6).

[52] *Ibid.*, 625–6.

[53] *Hanfstaengl v. Empire Palace* [1894] 2 Ch. 1 (CA), affirmed *sub nom. Hanfstaengl v. Baines & Co* [1895] AC 20 (discussed in Vaver at 625).

changed.[54] Likewise it has been argued that the concept of "originality" as the basis for protection in copyright law has mutated, from an understanding that "original" should embody an element of novelty akin to patent law, to simply that it involves some independent skill and labour on the part of the author.[55] So, as we will see later in this book, copyright law protects equally a simple engineering drawing or "logo", a photograph of a work of art and a painting by an accomplished artist such as John Piper. Whether this is in the interests of society as a whole is another matter—as Laddie J once memorably put it, ". . . you can have too much of a good thing and I suggest we have got too much copyright".[56]

Another approach is that of Marxist historians who have argued that the emergence of copyright and notions of originality were a conversion of ideas into things: property. Art became property and this basis was reinforced by stressing the creative genius of the artist and hence introducing a moral basis (moral rights) to plagiarism as equivalent to theft.[57] Nevertheless the artist fails to benefit from the copyright system as the artist's rights are frequently transferred to business interests, to "Capital", either by virtue of their employment or by assignment: it is Capital not Labour that ultimately benefits from copyright, albeit that copyright is dressed up in the language of authors' rights.[58]

Finally there are those, like John Perry Barlow, who, in the light of the rapid growth of the Internet and digitisation and the difficulties of preventing the digital piracy of works, see the very notion of copyright as outdated: "intellectual property law cannot be patched, retrofitted

---

[54] See *Bradbury, Agnew & Co* v. *Day* (1916) 32 TLR 349 which held that the earlier cases (see n. 53 *supra*) were no longer good law in light of s.1(2) of the Copyright Act 1911 (" 'copyright' means the sole right to produce or reproduce the work or any substantial part thereof in any material form whatsoever").

[55] See for example *per* Lush LJ in *Dicks* v. *Yates* (1881) 18 Ch. D 76 (CA): "I take it to be established law that to be the subject of copyright the matter must be original, it must be a composition of the author, something which has grown up in his mind, the product of something which if it were applied to patent rights would be called invention". This is in distinction to the House of Lords in *Walter* v. *Lane* [1900] AC 539 where simply the original effort in transcribing the notes of a speech done by a shorthand writer was sufficient to justify copyright protection. Both these cases are discussed by Laddie at 259–60.

[56] *Ibid.* 260.

[57] See A.B. Kernan, "Art and Law", *Princeton Alumni Weekly,* 12 October 1998, 34 at 69 (cited by David Vaver in his 1990 article at n. 50).

[58] This is admittedly a gross oversimplification of the Marxist analysis—for a more detailed discussion see for example Bowrey at 325 (citing Edelman).

or expanded to contain digitized expression any more than real estate law might be revised to cover the allocation of the broadcasting spectrum".[59] He sees encryption as the technical solution for most intellectual property protection.

2.2.5 Some Concluding Comments

There are a variety of justifications for copyright. No one argument is likely to prevail in any jurisdiction or at any particular time: the justifications are, in the words of the leading English copyright text *Copinger*, "cumulative and interdependent . . . although different countries give varying emphasis to each of them".[60] However, the general view is that in the development of modern copyright laws the economic and public policy justifications are given greater weight in Anglo-American laws, whilst in civil law and especially continental jurisdictions, moral rights arguments are given primacy.[61] In fact the European Court of Justice in *Phil Collins*[62] has defined the specific subject matter of copyright and performers' rights as being to ensure the protection of the moral *and* economic rights of their holders.[63]

Also the perceived difficulty of adequately protecting works on the fringes of, or outside, traditional concepts of copyright or property rights, for example databases or "semiconductor topographies", has

---

[59] J.P. Barlow, "The Economy of Ideas: Everything You Know about Intellectual Property is Wrong", *Wired*, March 1994.

[60] Copinger at para. 2–04. Laddie for example simply sees three "sacred" principles as justifying the existence of copyright: (i) The Eighth Commandment ("Thou shalt not steal"), (ii) that matter created by the brain should be treated as property and finally (iii) the principle of reward—copyright serves as an incentive to allow and encourage artists and the like to spend time in creative activities as their "investment" of time and money will be protected at law and this is in the public good: Laddie at 253–4.

[61] Saunders speaks of the "great divide" between the traditions of "copyright" as developed in English law and the *droit moral* in *droit d'auteur* systems of author's right protection (Saunders at 236–7); see also Copinger at para. 2–04.

[62] *Phil Collins* v. *Imtrat Handelsgesellschaft mbH*, Joined Cases C–92/92 and C–326/92 [1993] ECR I–5145.

[63] At para. 20 (emphasis added). Although outside the scope of the present work, it is worth noting that *Phil Collins* made clear that copyright and moral rights potentially affect trade in goods and services and also competitive relationships within the European Community. Hence, although governed by national law, such rights are subject to the requirements of the EC Treaty and fall within its scope of application (at para. 22). In particular the exercise of copyright in an anti-competitive manner could fall foul of Arts. 81 and 82 of the EC Treaty (see for example *Magill*, Case No. 89/205/EC *ITP, BBC and RTE* v. *Commission* [1995] ECR I–743; [1995] FSR 530).

led to the growth in so-called *sui generis* rights—rights "of their own nature", not linked juridically to other specific rights. Indeed it has been suggested that authors' rights generally should be classified as *sui generis*. But this has not found much favour, except in very limited circumstances.[64]

2.3 HISTORY OF COPYRIGHT[65]

Copyright arose out of monopoly privileges granted by the Crown to printers from the fifteenth century onwards. Alongside such printing privileges ("patents") direct from the Crown under the Royal Prerogative, the printing trade also developed its own system of regulation through the Stationers' Company in London (which in turn derived its authority from the Crown).

The modern notion of the creator-authors owning exclusive rights to print and publish their works played no part in the early years of copyright. It was not until the first copyright statute in the world, the 1709 Statute of Anne,[66] that authors of books or other writings (not works of art) and their assigns were granted a limited 14-year period of protection in the first instance. In the eighteenth century it was disputed whether literary copyright existed at common law independently from the 1709 statute—in the landmark case of *Donaldson v. Beckett*[67] the House of Lords held that upon publication of a work it did not. From then on the law of copyright became the sole creature of statute.[68]

Works of art were given protection later on: first by a series of statutes beginning in 1735 in favour of engravings[69]. The first of these, the Engraving Copyright Act of 1734,[70] was the first statute to give legislative protection to artistic works, granting a 14-year term of protection only for works both designed and engraved by the artist. This was because the force behind the Act, the celebrated artist and engraver William Hogarth, was invariably the designer as well as the engraver of

---

[64] See Sterling at 44 for a discussion of various theories (for example of Picard, Roubier and Dabin) in this regard.

[65] See J.H. Baker, *An Introduction to Legal History* (3rd edn., Butterworths, London, 1990) at 348–50, chap. 9 of Cornish and chap. 2 of Copinger.

[66] 8 Anne, c.19.

[67] (1774) 4 Burr. 2408, 2 Bro. PC 129.

[68] Common law copyright did survive for unpublished works but this was abolished by the Copyright Act 1911.

[69] Stat. 8 Geo.II, c.13; enlarged by 6 Geo.III, c.38, s.2; 17 Geo.III, c.57.

[70] Stat. 8 Geo.II, c.13.

his well-known works which were widely pirated.[71] Indeed in distinction from literary property and the genesis of the Statute of Anne (where the book trade as opposed to the authors was primarily seeking protection), it was the artists, as opposed to the printers and print-sellers, who sought legislative protection against piracy.[72] The later Act of 1766[73] redressed the position and allowed engravers who engraved to the designs of others themselves to benefit from copyright protection. Prints taken by lithography or other mechanical processes gained protection through the International Copyright Act of 1852.[74]

Further statutes beginning in 1787 gave very limited protection to fabric designs.[75] Sculptures were granted protection by statutes of 1798 and 1814.[76] Perhaps surprisingly it was not until 1862 that copyright was extended to paintings, drawings and photographs.[77]

The first comprehensive, modern statute was the Copyright Act 1911 which took account of the Berne Convention of 1886[78] and technological developments such as sound recordings, and the period of protection for most types of work was made at least the author's life plus

---

[71] See generally Copinger para. 2–19. In particular Hogarth's "A Harlot's Progress" was widely pirated. The Act became law on 25 June 1735 and so Hogarth delayed publication of the even better known "The Rake's Progress" until that date (D. Bindman, *Hogarth* (Thames and Hudson, London, 1981) at 61). Hogarth himself commented: "[a]fter having had my first plates Pirated on all sides and manner, I applied to parliament for redress which not only has so effectually done my business but has made prints a considerable article and trade in this country, there being more business of that kind done in this Town than in Paris or any where else" (quoted in S. Shesgreen (ed.), *Engravings by Hogarth* (Dover Publications Inc., New York, 1973) at p. xxvi).

[72] J. Feather, *Publishing, Piracy and Politics* (Mansell, London, 1994) at 70. Feather notes that in the 1735 petition by Hogarth, George Vertue and other artists and engravers for protection against unauthorised copying of their engraved prints, they sought similar protection to that already afforded to others "as the Laws now in being have preserved the Properties of the Authors of Books" (at 70).

[73] Stat 6 Geo.III, c.38.

[74] Stat 15 & 16 Vict. C.12, s.14.

[75] Stat. 27 Geo.III, c.38.

[76] Stat. 38 Geo. III, c.71 (busts or statues of humans or animals); 54 Geo.III, c.56. The term of protection in the first instance was 14 years from publication.

[77] Stat. 25 & 26 Vict., c.68. The term was the author's life plus seven years.

[78] This has been revised on numerous occasions and, along with the Universal Copyright Convention (UCC) of 1952, is one of the two main international copyright conventions. The Berne Convention ensured equality of protection between member states under which either the personal connection of the author with a member state, or first publication in a member state, was enough to secure copyright in any other member state, on the terms afforded by that state to its own authors (the so-called principle of national treatment): this is discussed further in Chap. 3 and generally see Ricketson.

50 years.[79] The Copyright Act 1956 took account of further technological developments and added three new forms of entrepreneurial copyright—in cinematograph films, broadcasts and the typographical format of published editions.

By the 1970s there was a consensus that further changes to the law were required to take account of photocopying, audio and video taping and computing. The use of copyright to protect industrial designs was also being reassessed. The UK also decided fully to adopt the continental concept of moral rights, and the copyright protection for unpublished works was set at life plus 50 years,[80] and other changes were also considered desirable. The result was the Copyright, Designs and Patents Act 1988 ("CDPA") which is the current copyright statute and which repealed the 1956 Act (which in turn repealed the 1911 Act).[81] The CDPA itself has been revised on a number of occasions to take account of a stream of European copyright directives—this has been done through Regulations (i.e. by statutory instrument) rather than by a new Act.

The influence of the harmonisation programme of the European Commission has been and will continue to be far reaching. Elements of the civil law authors' rights approach are now finding their way into UK law.[82]

---

[79] This remained the position in the UK until 1996 when, in response to European directive 93/8327 [1993] OJ L248, harmonising the term of copyright, it was made life plus 70 years.

[80] Under the 1911 and 1956 Acts, so long as a literary, dramatic or musical work, and certain artistic works, remained "unpublished" after the author's death, the 50-year term did not begin to run.

[81] The earlier Acts are still relevant in certain cases, for example to determine subsistence of copyright in a pre-CDPA work, etc: see the transitional provisions in the CDPA (see Sched. 1).

[82] See Copinger paras. 1–05, and 25–66 *et seq.* Laddie et al. criticises the way a number of EC copyright directives have been implemented into UK law (see Laddie et al. chap. 2—"Invalid Legislation") and points out some of the difficulties this potentially raises.

3

The Modern Law of Copyright

3.1 BACKGROUND

THE BERNE CONVENTION expressly recognises that artistic works are to be given protection in member states of the Berne Copyright Union. Article 2 of the Berne Convention states that "the expression 'literary and artistic works' shall include every production in the literary, scientific and artistic domain, whatever may be the mode or form of its expression, such as . . . cinematographic works . . .; works of drawing, painting, architecture, sculpture, engraving and lithography; photographic works . . .; works of applied art . . .".

In US law artistic works are protected by copyright and fall within the definition of "pictorial, graphic and sculptural works".[1]

When granting copyright protection most states do not discriminate between "good" and "bad" artistic works. So a work merely has to be an "artistic work" rather than above a particular threshold of quality. Indeed in the UK, as we will see below, artistic works are protected irrespective of their artistic quality. The exception to this rule is works of "artistic craftsmanship".

It is not surprising that the legislature and the judiciary have tended to shy away from making artistic copyright subject to the artistic merit

---

[1] Section 102(a), Copyright Act 1976. These are defined to include "two-dimensional and three-dimensional works of fine, graphic, and applied art, photographs, prints and art reproductions, maps, globes, charts, diagrams, models, and technical drawings, including architectural plans. Such works shall include works of artistic craftsmanship insofar as their form but not their mechanical or utilitarian aspects are concerned; the design of a useful article, as defined in this section, shall be considered a pictorial, graphic, or sculptural work only if, and only to the extent that, such design incorporates pictorial, graphic, or sculptural features that can be identified separately from, and are capable of existing independently of, the utilitarian aspects of the article" (s. 101). "Useful article" is further defined as "an article having an intrinsic utilitarian function that is not merely to portray the appearance of the article or to convey information. An article that is normally a part of a useful article is considered a 'useful article' " (s. 101).

of the work in question. The matter was very well put by Oliver Wendell Holmes (as Justice of the US Supreme Court) in *Bleistein* v. *Donaldson Lithographing Co.*[2] which affirmed copyright protection for a circus advertising poster depicting acrobats performing on bicycles:

> "It would be a dangerous undertaking for persons trained only to the law to constitute themselves final judges of the worth of pictorial illustrations, outside of the narrowest and most obvious limits. At one extreme some works of genius would be sure to miss appreciation. Their very novelty would make them repulsive until the public had learned the new language in which their author spoke. It may be more than doubted, for instance, whether the etchings of Goya or the paintings of Manet would have been sure of protection when seen for the first time."[3]

Also, as Rose has argued, "the prestige of items of 'high art' . . . is also invoked to legitimate the protection of humbler products".[4] It therefore can be argued that, for art to flourish, those who seek to be artists must receive the same treatment in copyright law as those who succeed as artists.[5] Also even a modest work of art deserves protection because it will have the stamp of the artist's personality on it. To quote Oliver Wendell Holmes in *Bleistein* v. *Donaldson Lithographing Co.*[6] again:

> "Personality always contains something unique. It expresses its singularity even in handwriting, and a very modest grade of art has in it something irreducible, which is one man's alone. That something he may copyright."[7]

However it is worth noting that in countries where copyright is based on the authors' rights system the requirement of "creativity" for a work to benefit from copyright protection can sometimes pose problems for the protection of artistic works—for example, in Germany *objets trouvés* and ready-mades have been denied copyright protection.[8]

---

[2] 188 US 239 (1903).

[3] At 251.

[4] Rose at 137. See for example *per* Rimer J in *SPE International Ltd* v. *Professional Preparation Contractors (UK) Ltd* [2000] EIPR N–19, where the originality of drawings for a mobile blast-cleaning machine is discussed in the same context as a picture by Mondrian (see section 6.3.3 below).

[5] Paraphrasing Goldstein: "for authorship to flourish, those who seek to be authors must receive the same welcome as those who succeed as authors"—see P. Goldstein, "Copyright" (1991) 38 *Journal of the Copyright Society of the U.S.A.* 109, at 115–16.

[6] 188 US 239. This echoes the "personality" basis for copyright discussed in Chap. 2.

[7] At 299–300.

[8] BGH [1986] GRUR at 458, *Oberammergauer Passionspiele*: see Bently & Sherman at 249 and 257.

It is further worth noting that in UK law if the work in question is blasphemous, offensive or immoral it may be the case that copyright protection will not be granted or at the very least the courts will not enforce it.[9] Andres Serrano's highly controversial work, "Piss Christ", and works made out of once living human matter (such as the freeze dried foetus earrings the subject of a prosecution *inter alia* for outraging public decency in 1989[10]) have been suggested in this regard.[11]

3.2 UK LAW

In setting out the modern law of copyright in the UK under the Copyright, Designs and Patents Act 1988 ("CDPA") it is necessary to consider:

(a) The classes of work protected by copyright—the "subject-matter" of copyright;

(b) Criteria for protection i.e. they are original;

(c) Who is the author?

(d) The need for fixation/permanence of the work;

(e) Qualifying factors for protection;

(f) Duration of protection;

(g) Who is the first owner of the copyright?

(h) Scope of the copyright monopoly i.e. the economic rights;

(i) Other rights analogous to copyright.

---

[9] *Glyn* v. *Weston Feature Film* [1916] 1 Ch. 261; *AG* v. *Guardian (No.2)* [1988] 3 All ER 640. See also the recent CA judgment in *Hyde Park Residence Ltd* v. *David Yelland and others* [2000] 3 WLR 215 in which Aldous LJ gave examples of situations when the court would be entitled to refuse to enforce copyright as including work which was immoral, scandalous or contrary to family life, or injurious to public life, public health and safety or the administration of justice, or work which incites or encourages others to act in this manner (see R. A. Browes, "Copyright: Court of Appeal Considers Fair Dealing Defence and Rejects Common Law Defence of Public Interest" [2000] *EIPR* 289 at 291).

[10] [1990] 2 QB 619, as discussed at length in Kearns at 29–35.

[11] See Bently & Sherman at 246–7. Kearns also gives the example of Leonard McComb's statue of a naked youth, "Portrait of a Young Man", which was withdrawn from an exhibition in Lincoln Cathedral in 1990 after complaints that it was indecent for a place of worship, in a discussion of the application of the law of blasphemous libel to works of art (Kearns at 25–6).

3.2.1 The Classes of Work Protected by Copyright

Copyright can subsist only in certain classes of works, exhaustively defined by section 1 of the CDPA[12] as:

(a) "original"[13] literary works (includes any written work including a computer program),[14] dramatic and musical works;

(b) "original" artistic works[15]: a graphic work (which includes (a) any painting, drawing, diagram, map, chart or plan, and (b) any engraving, etching, lithograph, woodcut or similar work),[16] photograph, sculpture or collage, in each case *irrespective of artistic quality* [emphasis added]; a work of artistic craftsmanship; a work of architecture (i.e. a building or a model for a building);

(c) sound recordings, films, broadcasts and cable programmes; and

(d) the typographical arrangement of published editions.[17]

Of primary relevance to this book are "artistic works". It is important to note that UK law is quite specific in the categories of artistic works that are protected by copyright. If a work does not fall into one

---

[12] It is an unresolved point whether only one "copyright" can subsist in a given work—this issue arises from time to time primarily in engineering drawings and designs which often contain both diagrams and notation: for example in *Anacon Corporation* v. *Environmental Research Technology Ltd* [1994] FSR 659, Jacob J held that a circuit diagram for a piece of electronics could be both an artistic work and a literary work (i.e. a list of components together with special notation for their interconnection) as under s. 178 of the CDPA "writing" includes any form of notation or code. This finding was criticised by Laddie J in *Electronic Techniques (Anglia) Ltd* v. *Critchley Components Ltd* [1997] FSR at 412–13: the information concerned is communicated either graphically or by words. However the matter remains in debate: see also *Aubrey Max Sandman* v. *Panasonic U.K. Ltd & Matsushita Electric Industrial Co. Ltd* [1998] FSR 651 and *Mackie Designs Inc* v. *Behringer* [1999] RPC 717.

[13] The issue of originality is considered below.

[14] S.3, CDPA.

[15] S.4, CDPA.

[16] S.4(2), CDPA.

[17] This rather narrow copyright serves to protect the "image on the page" and protects the publisher (who is the owner of this right) who has incurred the costs of typesetting etc. from exact copying by photo-lithography or similar means: it protects the entire edition whether it contains a number of separate literary works or not (see *The Newspaper Licensing Agency Ltd* v. *Marks and Spencer PLC* [2000] 4 All ER 239 at para. 23 (*per* Peter Gibson LJ). Designs for typefaces themselves are protected by artistic copyright—see below.

of these categories it will not be protected by copyright.[18] So for example, contemporary art works such as "ready-mades" do not easily fall into any specific category.[19] So the categories of artistic work under the CDPA and what is likely to fall within the relevant category are subjects worth detailed consideration, in particular given the way contemporary art is developing—this along with the issue surrounding the originality of such works are considered in Chapter 6.

Graphic Works: Paintings, Drawings, Engravings, etc[20]

"Painting" has its ordinary usage for the purposes of copyright and it is a question of fact in any particular case whether what is being considered is or is not a painting.[21]

Drawing also has its ordinary usage and no particular artistic merit is required for graphic works: in *Kenrick v. Lawrence*[22] it was held that there could be copyright in a simple drawing of a hand for a voting card but the scope of the copyright protection was very limited (to the exact reproduction of that drawing) as no one could monopolise the drawing of a hand in general. Another often cited case illustrating that quite simple artistic works will qualify for copyright protection is *British*

---

[18] In practice, as one leading copyright judge recently put it, the law has been "bedevilled" by attempts to extend the scope of these definitions (*per* Laddie J in *Metix* v. *Maughan* [1997] FSR 718), and this is a feature of the lack of a developed law of unfair competition in the UK according to another judge (Whitford J in *Davis (J&S) (Holdings) Ltd* v. *Wright Health Group Ltd* [1988] RPC 410).

[19] As discussed in Bently & Sherman at 248–9. Bently & Sherman are of the view that the case for artistic copyright protection for ready-mades is stronger when the works are made with an artistic purpose in mind than where the work is simply "found" and "relocated with artistic meaning" as in Duchamp's *Readymades*. This issue is given greater consideration below and in Chap. 6 in particular.

[20] The term "graphic work" was new to the CDPA (s.4(2)) (but included paintings, drawings and engravings defined in s.3(1)(a) of the Copyright Act 1956 as artistic works) and graphic work is defined to include (a) any painting, drawing, diagram, map, chart, or plan, and (b) any engraving, etching, lithograph, woodcut or similar work. In *Anacon Corporation Ltd and Another* v. *Environmental Research Technology Ltd and Another* [1994] FSR 659, Jacob J said that the essential nature of a graphic work was that it was a thing to be looked at in some manner or other. "It is to be looked at in itself" (at 662) (here circuit diagrams were held to be artistic works and also literary works). As discussed in this case, the visual significance of artistic works is important both in assessing their originality and also where a case of copyright infringement arises (see also *Billhofer Maschinenfabrik GmbH* v. *T.H. Dixon & Co Ltd* [1990] FSR 105). See also below.

[21] *Merchandising Corporation* v. *Harpbond* [1983] FSR 32 (the facial make-up of the 1980s pop star Adam Ant was not a "painting" as a painting has to be on a surface of some kind).

[22] (1890) 25 QBD 93.

Northrop Ltd v. *Texteam Blackburn Ltd*[23] in which copyright was held to subsist in drawings for rivets, screws, bolts, etc. Other cases have afforded copyright protection to the label design for a sweet tin,[24] a signature,[25] the arrangement of a few decorative lines on a parcel label[26] and (recently) colour charts containing numbers used to produce patchwork bedspreads and cushion covers.[27] A trade mark (a "device mark") has also been held to be an artistic work (a drawing).[28]

It is worth speculating whether a random series of marks, say where an artist throws a pot of paint at a canvas, would qualify as a painting. If there is some order or selection behind the creation of the work (for example, through the selection of paint, canvas, etc.) there appears no reason why not.[29] However there is old authority that where what is produced is "meaningless" copyright protection may be refused.[30]

Rubber stereos for producing designs on transfer paper have been held to be "engravings",[31] an engraving being held to include both the images made from the engraved plate and the engraved plate used to

---

[23] [1974] RPC 57.

[24] *Taverner Rutledge* v. *Specters* [1959] RPC 355 (CA).

[25] According to an unreported decision cited in Copinger at para. 2–23.

[26] *Walker* v. *British Picker* [1961] RPC 57: see Cornish at 389.

[27] *Vermaat* v. *Boncrest Ltd, The Times*, 23 June 2000, [2000] EIPR N–151; (2000) 3 *Intellectual Property Lawyer*, 10. It was held that artistic copyright (as a graphic work) could potentially subsist in a drawing accompanied by words and figures that provided instructions to create an artistic work (on the basis of *Lerose Ltd and Another* v. *Hawick Jersey International Ltd* [1974] RPC 42 which held that "point patterns" for knitting machines were artistic works ("drawings" under s.3 of the 1956 Act)) (*Interlego AG* v. *Tyco Industries Inc* [1989] AC 217 distinguished). So clearly literary elements of a design can form part of an artistic work (and see also the cases on circuit diagrams discussed above at note 12).

[28] The mark consisted of the words "Karo Step" surrounded by a circle within four arcs of circles which met to form the four points which were filled in to give it the character of a star (*KARO STEP Trade Mark* [1977] RPC 255). Whitford J did however comment that a drawing could be so simple that it failed to be a "work" for copyright purposes (for example a straight line or a circle), for "work" carried with it the idea of the exercise of some degree of skill and labour (at 273).

[29] "Originality" ought not to be an issue as some skill and labour would be involved in selecting the materials and creating the work.

[30] *Fournet* v. *Pearson Ltd* (1897) 14 TLR 82, (CA) (unintelligible drunken scrawl) (see Sterling at 189). However the authority of this case must be doubted—it concerned an alleged literary work written by a drunken optician and published after the event "for scientific purposes": the test for a literary work was held by the judge at trial to be whether "it was something of enduring benefit to mankind". The Court of Appeal gave no consideration to the question of subsistence of copyright.

[31] *James Arnold and Co. Ltd* v. *Miafern and Others* [1980] RPC 397.

produce the engravings.[32] Certainly what is meant by the terms "engravings, etchings, lithographs, and woodcuts" depends upon how the processes concerned (engraving, etching, etc.) are defined.[33]

Photographs

"Photograph" is defined under the CDPA (section 4(2)) as "a recording of light or other radiation on any medium on which an image is produced or from which an image may by any means be produced, and which is not part of a film". Photography is a problem area for copyright law as in a sense every photograph is a copy of something, and unlike drawing or painting the actual recording of the image can require no skill or labour beyond the mere mechanical operation of a "point and shoot" camera—hence can photographs be "original" in order to qualify for copyright protection?

Certainly UK law is more generous in its protection of photographs than the *droit d'auteur* systems which according to Professor Cornish "tend only to give copyright to 'photographic works', that is the results of careful and distinctive arrangement (scene setting, lighting, angle, etc.), involving an element of aesthetic judgment which is personal to the photographer".[34] So, unlike UK law, such systems will exclude both snapshots and press photographs.[35] However in the UK, "the work of the humble snapshot-taker stands in the same category as Beaton and Cartier-Bresson".[36]

In any event, in UK law there is still scope for originality in a photograph: for example, the use of specialised techniques such as angle of shot, exposure and use of filters; the creation of a specific scene or style of subject; and merely being in the right place at the right time. These factors all contribute to the creation of an original work. Also only a low level of originality is required in UK law—that some, albeit

---

[32] At 403. Paul Baker Q.C. was also of the view that an engraving need not just be made by an engraving process (i.e. cutting into wood, metal or other material) (at 403)—however Copinger queries whether a mould or die as such would be an "engraving" (at 3–37) and this was also doubted by the Hong Kong Court of Appeal *per* Fuad JA in *Interlego AG v. Tyco Industries Inc.* [1987] FSR 409 at 453 commenting on a New Zealand case where "engraving" included the mould to make a "Frisbee" (*Wham-O Manufacturing Co. v. Lincoln Industries Ltd* [1985] RPC 127 (CA)). In any event where a mould is used a sculpture may be the result.

[33] See generally Copinger at 3–37.

[34] Cornish at 390.

[35] *Ibid*. The work may nevertheless benefit from more limited "neighbouring rights" protction. See also Kearns at 69–71.

[36] Cornish at 407.

limited, work or effort has gone into the creation of the work is enough. A photograph of an engraving from a picture, for example, has been held to be an "original" photograph worthy of copyright protection.[37]

Sculptures/Ready-mades/Collages

"Sculpture" is not defined by the CDPA, except that it includes "any cast or model made for the purposes of sculpture".[38] Hence a sculpture for the purposes of the CDPA is a sculpture in the ordinary sense of the term or any cast or model made for the purposes of sculpture. Can ready-mades be sculptures? It appears accepted that objects other than what one would traditionally class as such may be sculptures for the purpose of copyright protection—in a New Zealand case a carved wooden model of the "Frisbee" was held to be a sculpture, but the manufactured plastic flying discs themselves were considered utilitarian objects lacking "any expressive form of the creator and any idea which the creator seeks to convey"—according to the judge, "sculpture should in three-dimensional form express the idea of the sculptor".[39] However, in a later case models and casts for dental impression trays were held not to be sculptures as they were not made for the purposes of sculpture, were merely steps in the production process and it was never intended that they have any continuing existence.[40]

In any event the extension of "sculpture" to include what are properly industrial designs (for example, in *Breville Europe Ltd* v. *Thorn EMI Domestic Appliances Ltd*[41] plaster shapes made to produce die-casting moulds for the heating plates of a sandwich toaster were held to be a sculptures) appears to be receding. Recent case law certainly

---

[37] *Graves' Case* (1869) LR 4 QB 715 is the authority for this—this case is not without its critics and the matter is given further consideration in Chap. 6.

[38] S.4(2), CDPA.

[39] *Wham-O Manufacturing Co.* v. *Lincoln Industries Ltd.* [1985] RPC 127, at 157 (*per* Davison CJ) .

[40] *J&S Davis (Holdings) Ltd* v. *Wright Health Group Ltd* [1988] RPC 403.

[41] [1995] FSR 77 (a case in fact decided by Falconer J in 1985). The manner in which the work was made was held to be important, for example carving, modelling and casting are all part of the process of making a sculpture based on the ordinary dictionary meaning of sculpture (from the *Concise Oxford Dictionary*) as extended by s.48(1) of the 1956 Act (which extended sculpture to include "any cast or model made for the purposes of sculpture") (at 94); this approach was followed by Lloyd J in *Creation Records* v. *News Group Newspapers*, *The Times*, 29 April 1997, [1997] EMLR 445, who stated that the assembly of *objets trouvés* in that case could not be a sculpture on this basis.

suggests that the courts will tend to interpret "sculpture" in its ordinary sense—"a three dimensional work made by an artist's hand".[42]

In *Creation Records Ltd. and others v. News Group Newspapers Ltd*[43] it was argued that the scene of assembled objects in a swimming pool together with the members of the Oasis pop group which was to form the subject matter of an album cover photograph was itself an artistic work, either a sculpture, collage or work of artistic craftsmanship. The judge gave short shrift to it being a sculpture or a work of artistic craftsmanship as, citing *Breville*, no element in the composition had been carved, modelled or made in any of the other ways in which sculpture is made. Nor did it appear to involve the exercise of any craftsmanship.[44]

However the judge in *Creation Records* did discuss at greater length the possible meaning of "collage" under the CDPA. "Collage" was introduced into the CDPA in 1988 as a new category of artistic work. According to Lloyd J, the traditional understanding of that word is that it involves the use of glue or some other adhesive in the process of making a work of visual art, being derived from the French, although the *Concise Oxford Dictionary* (ninth edition) also defined it as "a collection of unrelated things". Lloyd J was firmly of the view that an essential element of a collage is the sticking of two or more things together; the collocation of random, unfixed elements (as in the photograph) was not a collage even if done with artistic intent.[45]

The judge's discussion of whether the composition in question was a "collage" is worth reading. Counsel for the plaintiffs had argued that section 4 of the CDPA ought not to be construed to deny copyright protection to novel works of art. So Lloyd J considered, in passing the possible copyright treatment of a number of contemporary art works difficult to categorise within the existing definitions of works protected

---

[42] *Metix (UK) Ltd and Another v. G.H. Maughen (Plastics) Ltd and Another* [1997] FSR 718, *per* Laddie J. The case concerned *inter alia* moulds for making cartridges (used to mix chemicals) which the plaintiffs claimed copyright in as works of sculpture. This was firmly rejected by the judge on the basis that, although it was not possible to say with precision what is and what is not a sculpture, the persons making the moulds did not appear to consider themselves (nor were they considered by anyone else) to be artists when they designed the moulds, and their only consideration in making the moulds was to achieve a precise functional effect rather than any aesthetic appeal. To describe the moulds as sculptures would be to go far beyond the meaning which the word "sculpture" has to ordinary members of the public, notwithstanding the frequent attempts made to widen the field covered by the Copyright Acts.

[43] N. 41 *supra*.

[44] At 448–9.

[45] At 450.

by copyright. These included Carl Andre's bricks, the stone circles created by Richard Long, Rachel Whiteread's house, the living sculptures of Gilbert and George and installation art generally. In the end he did not find it necessary or appropriate to determine the matter. However he did distinguish the record cover "compilation" or assembled scene from such works of art on the basis that the "compilation" was merely, indeed intrinsically, ephemeral, and was materially different from such works of art.[46]

A Work of Artistic Craftsmanship

The courts have had difficulty defining this category of work which expressly includes "artistic" in its definition. Its introduction into English copyright law in the 1911 Copyright Act[47] was a response to the Arts and Crafts Movement. It appears to cover the work of an artist-craftsman and includes such items as hand-painted tiles, stained-glass windows, wrought-iron gates and certain pieces of furniture.[48] As nine separate approaches to the definition of "work of artistic craftsmanship" are discernible from the leading case, *Hensher*,[49] the law is, to say the least, uncertain. For example, Lords Simon and Kilbrandon considered that the intention of the maker to create a work of art was highly significant.[50]

[46] At 449–50. Nor was it a "dramatic work" as it was inherently static, having no movement, story or action (at 448). The judge in fact rejected all attempts to claim that the "composition" assembled for the photograph was a work protected by copyright. However he did consider that there was an arguable case that the taking of the photograph and its publication were in breach of confidence (the composition had been made at a hotel under conditions of security and limited access). A similar circumstance might be if an artist kept his studio private and photographs of his works were taken without his permission—in addition to a copyright infringement action (assuming the works were protected by copyright) there might be an action for breach of confidence—this area is discussed in more detail in Chap. 8.

[47] S.35.

[48] See *George Hensher Ltd* v. *Restawile Upholstery (Lancs) Ltd* [1975] RPC 31, the leading case, in which the House of Lords considered the availability of copyright protection for the prototype model of a drawing room furniture suite comprising two chairs and a settee. The House unanimously determined that the prototype furniture did not fall within the definition of a "work of artistic craftsmanship" within s.3(1)(c) of the Copyright Act 1956. This case has been the subject of much comment: see for example D. Booton, "Art in the Law of Copyright: Legal Determinations of Artistic Merit under United Kingdom Copyright Law" [1996] 1 *ARTL* 125. See also Kearns, chap. 3.

[49] See n.48 *supra*.

[50] In *Hensher* Lord Simon was also of the view that "works of artistic craftsmanship" must be construed as a whole (and artistic and craftsman *not* construed in isolation (at 69)) and furthermore it could not be properly construed without bearing in mind the aims and achievements of the Arts and Crafts Movement with its emphasis on the applied or decorative (as opposed to the fine) arts, although craftsmanship is not limited to handicraft

Lord Reid, however, whilst regarding the intention of the designer as important, did not consider this conclusive, nor was the utility of the work a bar to protection. The work must clearly be made by craftsman-ship[51] and in determining whether it is "artistic" it is important to avoid philosophical concerns of aesthetics, not least as those ignorant about philosophy are entitled to have opinions about what is artistic.[52] Lord Reid was also of the view that a work was "artistic" if a substantial sec-tion of the public genuinely admired and valued it for its appearance and got pleasure or satisfaction, whether emotional or intellectual from look-ing at it, whether or not others considered it vulgar or common or mean-ingless.[53] Lord Morris said that to decide whether a work fell within the definition the work must itself be assessed in a detached and objective way to determine whether it has the character or virtue of being artistic, without giving decisive weight to the author's intention (although this was a possible pointer). It was a question of fact upon which the court should pay heed to the evidence adduced.[54] Viscount Dilhorne was also of the view that the functional appeal of a work was not a bar to protec-tion: for him it was simply a question of fact for the judge and "works of artistic craftsmanship" must be given its ordinary and natural meaning.[55]

nor is "artistic" incompatible with machine production (at 66). It did however presuppose special training, skill and knowledge for its production (at 66—Lord Simon cited *Cuisenaire* v. *Reed* [1963] VR 719 and *Cuisenaire* v. *S.W. Imports Ltd* [1968] 1 Ex. CR 493 at 514). Ultimately what was important was is the work by someone who in this respect was an artist-craftsman? (at 69), and, given the presence of craftsmanship, what was the intent of the creator and the result of their work? (at 70) ("artists have vocationally an aim and impact which differ from those of the ordinary run of humankind" (at 70)). See also the later Australian case of *Komesaroff* v. *Mickle and Others* [1988] RPC 204 (a product for creating moving sand pictures was held not to be a work of artistic craftsmanship as no craftsmanship on the part of the creator was employed in creating the product (*Cuisenaire* v. *Reed* was also applied, although *Hensher* was not cited)). Lord Kilbrandon was also of the view that the conscious intention of the craftsman was the primary test of whether his product is artistic or not: "the fact that many of us like looking at a piece of honest work, especially in the traditional trades, is not enough to make it a work of art" (at 71).

[51] At 53—Lord Reid was of the view that this suggests a durable handmade object and not something, for example, to be used merely as a step in a commercial operation which has no value in itself.

[52] At 54.

[53] At 54.

[54] At 57.

[55] At 62. Like Lord Reid he was also of the view that a work of craftsmanship is some-thing made by hand and not mass-produced (at 60). Note however that in light of the development of the Arts and Crafts Movement Lord Simon was of the view that "crafts-manship" was not limited to handicraft (but it did presuppose special training, skill and knowledge for its production) nor was "artistic" incompatible with machine production (at 66). (See n. 50 *supra*).

Cases subsequent to *Hensher* do little to clarify things. In *Merlet* v. *Mothercare plc*[56] Walton J denied protection to a baby raincosy as the creator, Mme Merlet, had designed it without any artistic consideration in mind but rather to protect her baby on a visit to Scotland from "the assumed rigours of a Highland summer";[57] also, following Lord Reid and others in *Hensher*, the onlooker gained no aesthetic satisfaction from contemplating the garment.[58] In *Shelley Films Ltd* v. *Rex Features Ltd*,[59] *Merlet* was distinguished and it was held to be arguable that copyright could subsist in a film set as a work of artistic craftsmanship.[60] *Creation Records Ltd and Others* v. *News Group Newspapers Ltd*[61] also considered *Shelley Films*: the assembly of "*objets trouvés*" photographed in *Creation Records* was held not to be a work of "artistic craftsmanship"—it was not the subject of or result of the exercise of any craftsmanship,[62] and it could be distinguished from a film set (as in *Shelley Films*) which clearly does involve craftsmanship in its creation. In the New Zealand case *Bonz Group (Pty) Ltd* v. *Cooke*,[63] Tipping J had to consider whether hand-knitted woollen sweaters and cardigans designed and knitted by different persons depicting among other things dancing lambs and golfing kiwis were entitled to protection as works of artistic craftsmanship: the judge held they were.[64] *Bonz* was recently

---

[56] [1986] RPC 115. Applied in *Guild* v *Eskandar* (Ch D, 2 February 2001; Rimer J)

[57] At 126–7.

[58] At 124. It was not permissible to consider the article in its intended use (i.e. mother, baby and raincosy together as an ensemble); to determine the question the article must be judged on its own merits (at 124).

[59] [1994] EMLR 134 (application for interlocutory relief).

[60] If the set were imaginatively conceived and implemented overall and the overall effect and intent were artistic (at 143).

[61] [1997] EMLR 444 (another application for an interlocutory injunction).

[62] See especially Lord Simon in *Hensher*, n. 48 *supra*.

[63] [1994] 3 NZLR 216.

[64] Consideration was given to *Hensher, Merlet, Cuisenaire* v. *Reed* and the earlier dress design case of *Burke and Margot Burke Ltd* v. *Spicers Dress Designs* [1936] Ch. 400 (which denied protection to a woman's dress on the basis that it was a work of artistic craftsmanship (skilled dressmakers derived their ideas from a design sketch made by a director of the plaintiff—a case doubted by Oliver J in *Radley Gowns Ltd* v. *Costas Spyrou* [1975] FSR 455 where it was found to be arguable that the original dress was a work of artistic craftsmanship)). Tipping J had difficulty with making the intention of the designer the determinative test—there had to be an objective element—there must be some artistic quality present. What was important was that the author was both a craftsman and an artist: a craftsman makes something in a skilful way and takes justified pride in their workmanship; an artist has creative ability who produces something with creative appeal. The idea of craftsmanship relates more to the execution of the work than its design, but "artistic" relates more to the design and it does not matter that the designer and craftsman are different persons (at 224).

applied in the UK in *Vermaat* v. *Boncrest Ltd*[65] which concerned sample patchwork bedspreads which were held not to be works of artistic craftsmanship; following *Bonz* it was necessary to consider whether they could fairly be said to be the work of both a craftsman and an artist, and in this case the bedspreads could not be viewed as artistic or creative enough to fall within the definition of a work of artistic craftsmanship.[66] The court did not consider the talents and intentions of the designer.[67]

It has been suggested that, possibly because of the lack of clear guidance in *Hensher*, few claims to works of artistic craftsmanship have been raised in the courts.[68] A leading text, Laddie, strongly rejects any test which may involve a question of taste, subjective quality or personal opinion as it exceeds the functions of a court of law to adjudicate on these matters and they are inconsistent with the very concept of the rule of law.[69] To overcome this Laddie proposes a test essentially similar to that of Lord Reid in *Hensher*.[70]

---

[65] *The Times*, 23 June 2000 (Ch. D, Evans-Lombe J), [2000] EIPR N–151; *Intellectual Property Lawyer*, Issue 3, July 2000. *Hensher* was considered by Evans-Lombe J but the approach of Tipping J in *Bonz* was the one he actually applied.

[66] As the works were made by seamstresses in India (to the designs of designers in England) they were held to be works of craftsmanship but, although pleasing to the eye, the works did not have sufficient artistry or creativity to qualify as "artistic".

[67] To add even further confusion, Uma Suthersanen, in her *Design Law in Europe* (Sweet & Maxwell, London, 2000) at 16–050, refers to a recent unreported case, *Hourahine* v. *Everdell & Mitchard*, which concerned pop-up greetings cards—these were held to be works of craftsmanship (on the basis of the effort put into constructing the card) but were not *artistic*—notwithstanding criticism of the Court of Appeal, for example by Lord Reid (at 55), the Court of Appeal in *Hensher* was nevertheless relied on to the effect that for a work to qualify as a work of artistic craftsmanship its utilitarian or functional appeal should not be the primary inducement to its acquisition or retention (*per* Russell LJ at 49) and the functional aspect predominated in this case.

[68] Laddie et al. at 4.31.

[69] Laddie et al. at 4.30 citing a number of cases where the courts have refused to adjudicate on questions that are not susceptible of judicial determination including *White* v. *Mellin* [1895] AC 154 at 165 (HL), *per* Lord Herschell (whether one trader's product was "better" than another) and *Harris* v. *Warren and Phillips* (1918) 35 RPC 217 at 221–2, *per* Eve J (relative merits of musical compositions and whether they constituted the mature art of their composers).

[70] Craftsmanship is seen as the working of materials by manual dexterity to produce the work and "artistic" relates to the visual appearance of the work, which must be significant in that persons wish to acquire and keep the work on especial account of its appearance (at 4.30). Laddie et al. sees such a two-part test as the only one actually workable.

Works of Architecture and Typefaces

Although not the subject of detailed consideration in this book, it should be noted that for copyright purposes "artistic works" also include a work of architecture, being a building or a model for a building.[71] This is in distinction from any plans, drawings and sketches for such works which are eligible for protection as artistic works in their own right (as graphic works).[72]

The CDPA assumes that typefaces are protected as "artistic works" although they are not expressly included in this category by section 4 of the CDPA.[73]

3.2.2 Criteria for Protection, i.e. Work must be "Original"

The standard required for a work to qualify as "original" is very low. An often cited case is *University of London Press Ltd* v. *University Tutorial Press Ltd*[74] which considered what was meant by "original" in the context of a literary work. According to the judge:

> "The word 'original' does not in this connection mean that the work must be the expression of original or inventive thought. Copyright acts are not concerned with the originality of ideas but with the expression of thought, and, in the case of a 'literary work,' with the expression of thought in print or writing. The originality which is required relates to the expression of the thought. But the Act [Copyright Act 1911] does not require that the

---

[71] CDPA, s.4(1)(c). "Building" includes any fixed structure, and a part of a building or fixed structure (s.4(2)). Copinger argues that, based on the Copyright Act 1911, a work of architecture needs to have an artistic character or design to benefit from copyright protection (at 3–44).

[72] So it is possible to infringe copyright in a building (as distinct from its plans) by, for example, copying the original building in an extension to a building (as in *Meikle* v. *Maufe* [1941] 3 All ER 144 which involved an extension to the Heal's building in Tottenham Court Road, London; at the time (in the middle of the Second World War) this case generated much controversy given that in the past architects had tended to view such copying as a compliment rather than insisting on their legal rights and also given the context of the immense amount of rebuilding (and hence "copying") foreseen after the war). In any event there are a number of specific exceptions to copyright infringement for buildings and models for buildings (e.g. s.62, CDPA (photographing, filming or drawing a building, etc) and s.65 (reconstructing a building)).

[73] See s.178 and ss.54–55 of the CDPA. Cases under the Copyright Act 1911 held that both individual letters and fonts were artistic works (for example, *Millar & Lang, Ltd* v. *Polak* [1908] 1 Ch. 433 and *Stephenson, Blake & Co.* v. *Grant, Legros & Co Ltd* (1916) 33 RPC 406).

[74] [1916] 2 Ch. 601.

expression must be in an original or novel form, but that the work must not be copied from another work—that it should originate from the author."[75]

Sherman has pointed out[76] that this case highlights that in copyright law "originality" centres on the relationship between the work created and its creator—the source of the work must be the individual involved; there must be something in the work which can be said to be distinctively the "author's". Given that all artistic works emanate from some sort of tradition (and therefore will inevitably draw on ideas or indeed expression from other works), Sherman sees copyright drawing "a line demarcating the acceptable (*original*) [*emphasis added*] works from those in which the external influences become so great that the effort of the subject is overshadowed or eclipsed".[77]

In any event it remains the case that some degree of skill and labour on the part of the author is required to qualify a work as "original",[78] but no more than trivial effort and skill are required for these purposes.[79] Also what counts in the context of artistic works is whether the skill and labour applied to the new work pertain to that which is *visually significant*: this is particularly important when the work is derived

---

[75] *Per* Peterson J at 608–9. The judgment also appears to acknowledge what is often called the idea-expression dichotomy in copyright: copyright does not protect ideas as such, but only their expression—see below and Chap. 1.

[76] Sherman at 118–20.

[77] *Ibid.*, at 120, n.33. For the importance of "authorship" see the recent case of *Vermaat* v. *Boncrest Ltd, The Times*, 23 June 2000, [2000] EIPR N–151; (2000) 3 *Intellectual Property Lawyer*, 10 discussed earlier at nn. 65 and 66 above, in which some sketches for textile product designs were held not to be graphic works under CDPA s.4(1)(a) as they were insufficiently precise and lacked the requirement of originality under s.1(1)(a) CDPA because they did not depict the design pattern specified by the second claimant, which would differentiate them from other similar textile products: as the sketches could not be differentiated from the work of others then there was no proof of authorship (see *Comment* by Jeremy Phillips in *Intellectual Property Lawyer*, Issue 3, July 2000).

[78] *Interlego AG* v. *Tyco Industries* [1989] 1 AC 217 at 262H.

[79] *Autospin (Oil Seals)* v. *Beehive Spinning (a firm)* [1995] RPC 683 at 694, cited in *SPE International Ltd* v. *Professional Preparation Contractors (UK) Ltd* [2000] EIPR N–19. Certainly the level of originality in the UK appears lower than that required in the USA where, as noted earlier, following the Supreme Court in *Feist Publications* v. *Rural Telephone Service Co* 499 US 340, 113 L Ed. 358 (1991) the work must possess at least *some minimal degree of creativity* (at 369). In Europe the position is different still—not only must origination be present, but the author's own personality must find its expression in the work. Also attempts at harmonisation by the European Commission (for example in the context of the Term Directive (93/98/EEC of 29 October 1993 [1993] OJ L290/9) where the concept of originality is applied to computer programs, databases and photographs) speak of "the author's own intellectual creation reflecting his personality" as the criterion for protection (see Art. 6 of and Recital 17 to the Term Directive). See generally Lai, 2.6–2.14.

from another work—mere "slavish" copying, even if it involves considerable skill, labour or judgement, cannot confer originality.[80] In cases of copying from another work there needs to be some element of material alteration or embellishment which suffices to make the totality of the work an original work.[81] Indeed the audience to which the artistic work is addressed appears relevant—certainly in cases involving engineering drawings what counts is whether the new work is visually significant to an engineer, not a layman.[82]

Given the low standard required for "originality", this hurdle to copyright protection in the UK is likely to be satisfied for most artistic works, including such relatively "unoriginal" works as photographs of paintings or objects in a gallery's collection.[83] Nevertheless, as discussed above mere mechanical copying will not be sufficient to confer "originality": in *The Reject Shop plc* v. *Manners*[84] the Court of Appeal rejected an argument that a slightly enlarged image produced using a photocopier was itself an original artistic work—there was no skill and labour involved in the copying sufficient to confer "originality of an artistic character".[85]

However problems may nevertheless arise in certain areas (for example in the context of appropriation art, ready-mades, minimalist art and photographs), and these are discussed further in Chapter 6.[86]

---

[80] *Interlego AG* v. *Tyco Industries and Others* [1989] 1 AC 217 at 262H as cited, for example, in *SPE International Ltd* v. *Professional Preparation Contractors (UK) Ltd*, Ch. D, High Court, 15 July 1999, Rimer J [2000] EIPR N–19. See also n.20 *supra*.

[81] *Interlego* v. *Tyco* at 263C. It must be stressed that using existing material as the basis for a new work will not necessarily prevent the new work benefiting from copyright protection—original thought is not required for "originality", although the law will protect against plagiarism of a work in copyright (see for example *Andrew Christoffer* v. *Poseidon Film Distributors Ltd* [2000] EIPR N–34 (here the source of the copyright work was Homer's Odyssey)).

[82] *Billhöfer Maschinenfabrik GmbH* v. *T.H. Dixon and Co. Ltd* [1990] FSR 105.

[83] See Chap. 6.

[84] [1995] FSR 870.

[85] *Per* Legatt LJ at 876.

[86] Note for example that in *Merchandising Corp. of America* v. *Harpbond* [1983] FSR 32 Lawton LJ was of the view that two straight lines drawn with grease-paint with another line in between them drawn with other colouring by itself could not attract copyright as it had no originality (at 47). However the main issue in this case was whether facial make up could be a "painting" for copyright purposes. Contrast Megarry J in *British Northrop Ltd* v. *Texteam Blackburn Ltd* [1974] RPC 57 at 68: a single straight line drawn with the aid of ruler was an artistic work.

3.2.3 Who is the Author?

For artistic and literary works the "author" for copyright purposes is the creator of the work in question.[87] "Author" is a term of art used throughout the CDPA.

3.2.4 The Need for Fixation/Permanence of the Work

In the case of a literary, dramatic or musical work, copyright will subsist in the work only if it is recorded in writing or otherwise.[88] There are no equivalent provisions for artistic works, although Bently & Sherman consider that it is arguable that a similar requirement may be demanded by the courts for artistic works.[89] Indeed on public policy grounds it has been argued that as copyright is in the nature of a monopoly there must be certainty in its subject matter to avoid injustice.[90] Certainly some element of fixation has on occasion been found necessary for artistic works in UK law.[91] For example, in addition to the "Adam Ant" case, which Bently & Sherman cite, in the Australian case *Komesaroff v. Mickle and Others*[92] works of "kinetic art" ("sand

---

[87] S.9(1), CDPA; the rule is different for sound recordings, films, broadcasts and published editions (in respect of protection for typographical arrangements).

[88] S.3(2), CDPA.

[89] They cite the *Merchandising Corp* "Adam Ant" case in which Lawton LJ said that a painting could not be an idea—it was an "object" (Bently & Sherman at 46).

[90] By Farwell LJ in *Tate* v. *Fullbrook* [1908] 1 KB 821 at 822–33. This case concerned infringement of a dramatic work (music hall "dramatic sketch"). The question arose whether scenic effects, stage "business" and the make-up of the actors were protected by copyright. They were held not to be as they could not be the subject of printing and publication, and in any event the scope of the monopoly granted by copyright had to be clear. Farwell LJ's dictum was approved by the Privy Council in *Green* v. *Broadcasting Corporation of New Zealand* [1989] 2 All ER 1056 at 1058 (dramatic "format" of the TV show "Opportunity Knocks" *inter alia* not certain enough to be protected by copyright, for example, the identity of performers would change from show to show, the material presented would change; nor was it a dramatic work as the format lacked the essential characteristic of having sufficient unity to be capable of performance). See also Laddie et al. at 3.33.

[91] US law for example requires fixation of original works of authorship "in any tangible medium of expression, now known or later developed, from which they can be perceived, reproduced, or otherwise communicated, either directly or with the aid of a machine or device" (s. 102, Copyright Act 1976). Millinger is of the view that the US requirements appear to deny copyright protection to conceptual art works of a temporary nature, for example, Christo's "Running Fence" and "Wrapped Buildings" which last only a few days or weeks (Millinger at 359).

[92] [1988] RPC 204 at 210.

pictures") were found to lack sufficient permanence to be classed as works of artistic craftsmanship[93]; no sand picture was static for any length of time. In *Davis (J&S) (Holdings) Ltd* v. *Wright Health Group Ltd*[94] Whitford J held that the models and casts in that case were not sculptures, as *inter alia* it was never intended they should have any continuing existence.[95] In *Creation Records* (discussed above in the contact of collages) an assembly of *objets trouvés* was *inter alia* not a collage as it was intrinsically ephemeral, existing for only a few hours.[96] However the general proposition that something which has a mere transient existence cannot be a "work of sculpture" was rejected by Laddie J in *Metix (UK) Ltd* v. *G.H. Maughan (Plastics) Ltd*.[97] So the position is unclear.

3.2.5 Qualifying Factors for Protection

It is important to note that the basis behind the international copyright system enshrined in the Berne Convention is the principle of "national treatment". This in effect means that in the UK, for example, a work originating in a foreign country will in the vast majority of cases be given the same protection as a work created in the UK.[98]

So it is in general the case that in the UK a work will be protected by copyright provided either (a) that the author is at the material time[99] a

---

[93] At 210.

[94] [1988] RPC 403.

[95] This case concerned plastic dental impression plates—the items in question were stages in producing these items rather than independent artistic works, so Whitford J's decision at 410–12 is not surprising. See also comments of Lord Simon in *Hensher* at n.50 above.

[96] Whether or not there was artistic intent in the creation of the assembly was held to be irrelevant.

[97] [1997] FSR 718. It was accepted in argument before Laddie J that a sculpture made from ice is no less a sculpture because it may melt as soon as the temperature rises.

[98] Set against "national treatment" is the argument for reciprocity in copyright protection i.e. that in the UK a work of foreign origin will be given only the protection to which that work is entitled in its country of origin. In recent years "reciprocity" provisions in intellectual property legislation have become more common, especially in the EU (where non-EU states must offer a similar level of protection for their authors to benefit from EU protection): see for example the Database Directive (96/9 [1996] OJ L077/20) and the copyright Term Directive (93/98 [1993] OJ L290/9). But the TRIPS Agreement (as does the Berne Convention with a few exceptions) requires national treatment (see H.C. Hansen, "International Copyright: An Unorthodox Analysis" (1996) 29 *Vanderbilt Journal of Transnational Law* 579).

[99] For literary, dramatic, musical and artistic works this is (in the case of unpublished works) when the work was made or, if the making of it extended over a period, a

"qualifying person", i.e. a British national or resident or domiciled in one of the countries of the Berne Union (i.e. states which are parties to the Berne Convention) or a country which is a party to the Universal Copyright Convention, or (b) that the work was first "published"[100] in one of these countries.[101] There is no requirement to register the work with the Stationers' Company or the UK Patent Office—no such formalities are necessary to secure copyright in the UK.[102] However it is desirable, for international protection and also to help enforce the owner's rights, to include a copyright notice on copies of a work along the lines of © [name of copyright owner], year of first publication.[103]

3.2.6 Duration of Protection

From 1 January 1996 copyright in new and existing literary and artistic works was extended as a result of EU harmonisation, and in general now lasts for the life of the author and expires at the end of the period 70 years from the end of the calendar year in which the author dies— this is the so-called 70-year *post mortem auctoris* rule. Until 1 January 1996 the term was 50 years *post mortem auctoris*.[104] Furthermore the introduction on 1 January 1996 of the new copyright term has been to "revive" copyright in works previously out of copyright in the UK but which on 1 July 1995 were protected under the copyright legislation of

---

substantial part of that period, and (in the case of a published work), when the work was first published or, if the author had died before that time, immediately before his death (s.154(4), CDPA). See n. 100 below for a discussion of what constitutes "publication".

[100] S. 175 of the CDPA states that "publication" means the issue of copies to the public, and includes, in the case of a literary, dramatic, musical or artistic work, making it available to the public by means of an electronic retrieval system. The exhibition of an artistic work does not constitute publication (s.175(4)(b)), and there are other specific rules for buildings and works incorporated in them and other works generally. Thus in general "publication" is only relevant to copies of an artistic work, not the work itself.

[101] Ss. 153–156, CDPA. The rules for foreign authors are potentially complex—see G. Dworkin & R. Taylor, *Blackstone's Guide to the Copyright, Designs and Patents Act 1988* (Blackstone, London, 1989) at 11–13.

[102] Indeed Art. 5(2) of the Berne Convention provides that the enjoyment and exercise of authors' rights shall not be subject to any formality.

[103] See Art. III(1) of the Universal Copyright Convention (UCC)—this will help to secure protection in UCC countries which are not part of the Berne Union.

[104] See The Duration of Copyright and Rights in Performances Regulations 1995 (SI 1995/3297). There are different rules for example for works of unknown authorship/-anonymous works, for example folklore and indigenous art.

any other state in the EEA.[105] The effect of this is likely to revive copyright in works by Paul Klee (d.1940) and Lucien Pisarro (d.1944), for example.

3.2.7   Who is the First Owner of the Copyright?

Under UK law, unless the work is created in the course of employment, the copyright in an artistic work will automatically vest in the author. Thus, even if a work is commissioned, copyright in general will vest with the artist/photographer etc., unless a written assignment of copyright is executed by the author.[106] The author may allow a copyright and collecting society such as DACS (The Design and Artists Copyright Society) to administer and protect their copyright on their behalf.[107]

3.2.8   Scope of the Copyright Monopoly, i.e. the Economic Rights

Under English law the copyright owner has a bundle of exclusive rights which he can prevent others from exercising. These so-called "restricted acts" include[108]:

(a)   the right to copy[109] the work (this includes (in respect of an artistic work) making a two-dimensional copy of a three dimensional work, and vice versa), and

(b)   the right to issue copies to the public.

---

[105] The EEA means the European Economic Area i.e. the EU (Denmark, Sweden, Finland, United Kingdom, Ireland, Austria, Germany, France, Italy, Greece, Spain, Portugal, Belgium, Luxembourg, the Netherlands) plus certain neighbouring states (Norway, Liechtenstein, Iceland). Germany already has a 70-year *post mortem auctoris* term. The "transitional" provisions in the 1995 Regulations dealing with the ownership and exploitation of "revived" copyright are complex.

[106] Under the 1956 Copyright Act the commissioner of, for example, a portrait for money or money's worth is the first owner of the copyright, subject to agreement to the contrary. In the case of a commission, ownership by the commissioner in equity may in limited cases result from the circumstances—this is discussed further in Chap. 7.

[107] DACS is not the owner by assignment of the copyright—it is simply the agent of the owner-artists it represents. It has not been afraid to commence criminal proceedings for breach of copyright—see *Thames & Hudson Ltd* v. *Design and Artists Copyright Society Ltd and others* [1995] FSR 153.

[108] S.16, CDPA.

[109] Copying in relation to a work means reproducing the work in any material form. This includes storing the work in any medium by electronic means (s.17(2)).

Copyright in a work is infringed by a person who, without the licence of the copyright owner, does, or authorises another to do, any of the acts restricted by copyright.[110] Thus a museum would infringe copyright if, in relation to a painting in its possession but in which it did not own the copyright, it took photographs of the work or allowed (i.e. authorised[111]) others to do so without the licence of the artist-copyright owner. Likewise, in the case of the Churchill papers referred to in Chapter 1, for example, their reproduction would require the consent (i.e. licence) of the relevant copyright owner and not of Churchill College, Cambridge.

It is important to note that for the purposes of copyright infringement copying involves the copying of the work as a whole or a substantial part of it, and either directly or indirectly.[112] The definition of what is meant by "a substantial part" is not a precise one: as we shall see later when considering the "idea/expression dichotomy", there is no one test and the phrase is susceptible to a number of meanings.[113] A recent attempt to define what "substantial" means in the context of the CDPA was made in *The Newspaper Licensing Agency* v. *Marks and Spencer Plc*,[114] where Peter Gibson LJ was of the view that the word

---

[110] S.16(2), CDPA. However, to infringe the act must be in respect of the work as a whole or a substantial part of it (s.16(3)). The test of "substantial" is of quality not quantity (see *Ladbroke (Football)* v. *Hill (William) (Football)* [1964] 1 WLR 273) and see below. Also see *Bauman* v. *Fussell* [1978] RPC 485 (CA) (painting derived from a photograph did not infringe the photograph—see in particular the dissenting judgment of Romer LJ) and *Krisarts* v. *Briarfine* [1977] FSR 577 (interlocutory judgment: the plaintiffs had an arguable case of copyright infringement where the defendants used paintings in which the plaintiffs held copyright to assist them in producing their own paintings of well-known views of London which were *not* slavish copies of the plaintiffs' copyright works) for some specific examples of how the courts have dealt with the copying of art. Infringing copyright may give rise to a civil liability (payment of damages to the aggrieved copyright owner, granting of an injunction and delivery up to prevent the infringement) as well as a possible criminal liability—see Chap. VI, CDPA.

[111] Thus museums should be cautious about allowing photography or filming of their collections. However in the light of *Durand* v. *Molino* [2000] ECDR 320 (which referred to *CBS Songs Ltd* v. *Amstrad Consumer Electronics Plc* [1988] AC 1013 (HL) where "authorise" was held to mean to grant or purport to grant expressly or by implication the right to do the act complained of (*per* Lord Templeman at 1054)), museums and galleries can take comfort that some degree of encouragement or actual authorisation or approval is required—merely "standing by" whilst the infringement takes place is not enough to constitute "authorisation" for copyright infringement purposes. The use of "no photography" notices and steps taken to enforce them ought to be more than sufficient.

[112] S.13(3), CDPA.

[113] Note also that whether there can be infringement by the reproduction of small parts of copyright works on a regular basis (none of which by itself amounts to taking a substantial part) is problematic: see *Electronic Techniques (Anglia) Ltd* v. *Critchley Components Ltd* [1977] FSR 401 at 407–11.

[114] [2000] 3 WLR 1256.

described something more than *de minimis*, something considerable in amount sufficient to make it worthy of consideration.[115] Anglo-American copyright law generally looks to "substantial similarity" to prove infringement. In the case of artistic works it is the visual similarity of the original and the copy that is important. The often-cited US Judge Learned Hand said that the plaintiff must show "that the ordinary observer, unless he set out to detect the disparities [between the two works], would be disposed to overlook them, and regard their aesthetic appeal as the same".[116]

Indeed it has been argued by Peter Karlen, in a critique of the application of the idea/expression dichotomy, that the copyright protection afforded to art enables the artist to restrain plagiarists from using the material world to recreate in the audience the imaginative experiences first created by his or her work. So for example, the owner of copyright in a sculpture can prevent others who have seen the work from "shaping any part of the universe, using any materials, to simulate the sculpture".[117]

Leaving aside Peter Karlen's view of the scope and rationale for copyright protection, to better understand the scope of the copyright monopoly in UK law it is necessary to analyse how the UK courts have applied the idea/expression dichotomy, albeit that in the UK this concept has no statutory basis.

3.2.9   The Idea/Expression Dichotomy in UK Law

Although there is no statutory basis for the idea/expression dichotomy in the UK, unlike in the USA,[118] the often-cited fact that copyright does not protect ideas as such but only their expression receives judicial consideration and guarded support from time to time in UK law.[119] Indeed

---

[115] At 1265G.

[116] *Peter Pan Fabrics, Inc* v. *Martin Weiner Corp*, 274 F 2d 487, 489 (2d Cir. 1960): for the US position generally see P. Karlen, "Intellectual Property in Intellectual Creations", *Copyright World*, April 1999, 14 ("Karlen").

[117] See Karlen 17 and 18.

[118] See s.102(b) of the Copyright Act 1976: "[i]n no case does copyright protection for an original work of authorship extend to any idea, procedure, process, system, method of operation, concept, principle, or discovery, regardless of the form in which it is described, explained, illustrated, or embodied in such work". See discussion in Chap. 1.

[119] See Chap. 1. According to W. J. Gordon (in her "Touring the Certainties of Property and Restitution : A Journey to Copyright and Parody", *Oxford Electronic*

it has been used to help determine whether there has been copying of a "substantial part" of a copyright work. One of the more recent cases to consider the scope of copyright protection for aesthetic, artistic designs, *Designers Guild Ltd* v. *Russell Williams (Textiles) Ltd*,[120] gave express consideration to the idea/expression dichotomy. This case concerned the copying of fabric designs (derived from an original artistic work) in which the copying involved was not literal or exact: the style, technique and ideas behind the plaintiff's work were copied. The plaintiff succeeded at first instance, lost in the Court of Appeal and then had the trial judge's order restored in the House of Lords.

Morritt LJ in the Court of Appeal expressly referred to the idea/expression dichotomy: "copyright subsists, not in ideas, but in the form in which the ideas are expressed".[121] For there to be copyright infringement in his view, the expression of an idea, rather than the idea itself, must be copied. He later went on to cite an observation by Professor Cornish that there is no clear boundary between what amounts to a substantial part of a copyright work and what does not.[122] Nevertheless, according to Professor Cornish, the idea/expression dichotomy is a useful and necessary concept, albeit that it was too vague a distinction to offer again more by way of general guidance.[123] To quote Professor Cornish again, "the answer in a particular case can only lie in the tribunal's innate sense of fairness".

Journal of Intellectual Property Rights, October 1999 (http://www.oiprc.ox.ac.uk/EJWP1399.html) (also to be published as part of the University of Montreal volume on certainty and the law, *Des Certitudes du Droit*, to be published by Editions Themis, Montreal, in 1999) ("Gordon"), at 21–2), because no firm definition has ever evolved of what constitutes an "idea", the idea/expression dichotomy all depends on how the judge determines what constitutes an idea: "[b]y characterising something as an 'idea', a judge is essentially ruling that it is something that cannot be commodified for purposes of private ownership, but rather should be commonly shared. No certain rule can capture this enquiry".

   120 [1998] FSR 803 (Ch.D), [2000] FSR 121 (CA), [2000] 1 WLR 2416 (HL).
   121 At 128.
   122 A well-known dictum in this regard by Judge Learned Hand in the US case *Nichols* v. *Universal Pictures Corporation* 45 F 2d 119 (1930) (in the context of a play) (quoted by Morritt LJ at 130) was cited by Prof. Cornish in support (and is also discussed by Laddie et al. (at 4.45) in an analysis of the distinction between a work protected by copyright and a general idea which is not): "upon any work . . . a great number of increasing patterns of increasing generality will fit equally well, as more and more incident is left out. The last may perhaps be no more than the most general statement of what the [work] is about, and may at times consist only of its title; but there is a point in this series of abstractions where they are no longer protected, since otherwise the [author] could prevent the use of his 'ideas', to which, apart from their expression, his property never extended . . . Nobody has ever been able to fix that boundary, and nobody ever can" (at 121).
   123 At 130 citing W. Cornish, *Intellectual Property* (3rd edn., Sweet & Maxwell, London, 1996) at para. 11–06 *et seq.*

As *Designers Guild* is the latest artistic copyright infringement case to be heard before the House of Lords, and it gives express consideration to the idea/expression dichotomy, it is now considered in more detail.

Facts

The plaintiff, the Designers Guild Ltd, is a designer and manufacturer of wallpapers and fabrics. In September 1995 it launched a new range of fabric designs under the name "Orientalis". One of those designs ("Ixia") was a striped pattern with flowers scattered over it in a somewhat impressionistic style. It was a successful design, achieving sales of £171,000 in its first year. The Ixia fabric design was produced from a design painted by Helen Burke, a designer employed by the plaintiff. It was inspired by the "handwriting and feel" of Matisse.

In September 1996 the defendant Russell Williams (Textiles) Ltd exhibited at trade fairs in Belgium and the Netherlands a striped design ("Marguerite") with scattered flowers, also in a somewhat impressionistic style.

The plaintiff took the view that the defendant's Marguerite design had been copied from Ixia and commenced proceedings on 24 December 1996. The defendant accepted subsistence and ownership of copyright in the painting but denied infringement. The issue at trial was therefore whether, for the purposes of sections 16 and 17 of the CDPA, the defendant had copied from the Ixia design and thereby *indirectly* copied a substantial part of the painting.

High Court

The judge found that there was copying by the defendant. Furthermore there was copying of a substantial part of Ixia. Looking at Ixia as a whole the Judge[124] found that the defendant had adopted the "essential features and substance" of the original.[125]

---

[124] Lawrence Collins, Q.C., sitting as a Deputy Judge of the Chancery Division: [1998] FSR 803.

[125] At 828. This test is referred to in Copinger at 7–82.

Court of Appeal

The judge at first instance gave greater consideration to whether there was copying than to whether what was copied was protectable expression, i.e. whether a substantial part of Ixia was copied. The Court of Appeal concentrated on the latter point.[126] The Court found that although the designers of Marguerite copied the idea of Ixia and adopted the same techniques, they did not copy a substantial part of the expression of the idea.[127] When Morritt LJ analysed the similarities between the two works he found that Marguerite adopted the same idea as Ixia (a combination of flowers and stripes) and in three respects the same techniques (brushwork, formation of the design and the resist effect used); nevertheless the same techniques produced "different visual effects" in Marguerite and the subject matter of their use (stripes and flowers) were not copied from Ixia into Marguerite.[128]

House of Lords

The House of Lords was unanimous in overturning the Court of Appeal's decision. In particular the approach of Morritt LJ, in analysing individual features of the two works to determine substantial copying rather than comparing the two works *as a whole*, was criticised.[129] The question was "did *Marguerite* incorporate a substantial part of the skill and labour expended by the designer of *Ixia* in

---

[126] For example Morritt LJ gave six pointers for assessing whether a substantial part has been copied (at 131): "(1) the part to be considered is the part of the work which has been copied; (2) *the copying which is relevant is the copying, not of the idea, but of the expression of the idea* [emphasis added]; (3) substantiality is a qualitative not a quantitative test; (4) the antithesis of "substantial" is "insignificant"; (5) no weight is to be attributed to that which is commonplace or well-known or derived from some other source when considering whether the part which has been copied is "substantial"; and (6) *the object of the law of copyright is to protect the product of the skill and labour of the maker not to confer on him a monopoly in the idea it may express* [emphasis added]".

[127] At 135. Morritt LJ stressed that what the law was seeking to protect here was the product of the skill and labour of the designer—in this case to allow a finding of copyright infringement would be to cast the net of copyright protection too wide and to create a monopoly in ideas.

[128] At 134.

[129] Morritt LJ was of the view that some dissection of the work allegedly copied was necessary in order to focus on the relevant aspects of the work which had been copied (at 131). This approach was rejected by the House of Lords (for example, *per* Lord Scott of Foscote at 2434, *per* Lord Hoffmann at 2421–2, *per* Lord Bingham of Cornhill at 2418).

producing *Ixia*?"[130] Also the Court of Appeal's attempt to approach the issue of substantiality afresh, where the trial judge had not misdirected himself, was also criticised.

Lord Hoffmann gave detailed consideration to the application of the idea/expression dichotomy in UK law, which he felt must be handled with care.[131] In particular he stressed that every element in the expression of an artistic work ("unless it got there by accident or compulsion") would in fact be the expression of an idea on the part of the artist: "[i]t was the artist's choice to paint stripes rather than polka dots, flowers rather than tadpoles, use one colour and brush technique rather than another, etc".[132] The expression of these ideas was clearly protected by copyright, both as a cumulative whole and also to the extent to which they formed a "substantial part" of the work. Substantiality depended upon quality rather than quantity.[133] In his view there were numerous authorities for the proposition that the "part" which is regarded as substantial can be a feature or combination of features of the work, abstracted from it rather than forming a discrete part of it. For example, the original elements in the plot of a literary work such as a play may be a substantial part of the work, so that copyright may be infringed by a work which fails to reproduce a single sentence of the original. If one were to ask what was being protected in such a case, it was difficult to give any answer except that it was an idea expressed in the copyright work.

Based upon an analysis of the cases applying the idea-expression dichotomy, Lord Hoffmann discerned two distinct propositions. The first was that a copyright work can express certain ideas which are not protected because they have no connection with the literary, dramatic, musical or artistic nature of the work.[134] The other proposition was

---

[130] *Per* Lord Scott of Foscote: he spoke approvingly of the test proposed in the second edition of Laddie et al. (at 92–3, para. 2–108) where infringement of copyright by an *altered copy* is concerned (this was the case here) "[h]as the infringer incorporated a substantial part of the independent skill, labour etc contributed by the original author in creating the copyright work?" Lord Scott considered this a useful test "based as it is on an underlying principle of copyright law, namely, that a copier is not at liberty to appropriate the benefit of another's skill and labour" (at 2431G).

[131] At 2422D–2423E.

[132] At 2422F.

[133] Citing *Ladbroke (Football) Ltd* v. *William Hill (Football) Ltd* [1964] 1 WLR 273 (HL), *per* Lord Reid at 276, Lord Evershed at 283, Lord Hodson at 288 and Lord Pearce at 293.

[134] He cited as an example the fact that although a literary work may describe a system or invention this does not entitle the author to claim protection for his system or invention as such. The same was true of an inventive concept expressed in an artistic

that certain of the ideas expressed by a copyright work may not be protected because, although they may be ideas of a literary, dramatic or
artistic nature, they are not original, or are so commonplace as not to
form a substantial part of the work.[135]

In conclusion, in cases of artistic copyright, the more abstract and
simple the copied idea, the less likely it was to constitute a substantial
part of a copyright work. According to Lord Hoffmann, originality, in
the copyright sense of the contribution of the author's skill and labour,
tended to lie in the detail with which the basic idea was presented:
"copyright law protects foxes better than hedgehogs".[136]

Comment

Designers Guild is a difficult copyright infringement case. In a straw
poll of the author's office the vast majority agreed with Morritt LJ that
the designs in question just did not look "sufficiently similar" for there
to be copyright infringement.[137] The judgment of Lord Hoffmann may
be helpful in clarifying the current application of the "idea/expression"

work (*Kleeneze Ltd.* v. *D.R.G. (U.K.) Ltd.* [1984] FSR 399 was cited by Lord Hoffmann
in support: this case involved the copying of the concept of a letterbox draught excluder,
which was held not to be infringement). But what of a literary work that describes an
artistic work in sufficient detail to allow someone else to reproduce it in two or three
dimensions? Does the same analysis apply? When considering some previous authorities
it is submitted arguably not, on the basis that it is the function of copyright to protect the
skill and labour of the writer which is then copied in creating the artistic work—see *per*
Laddie J in *Autospin (Oil Seals) Ltd* v. *Beehive Spinning (A Firm)* [1995] RPC 683 who
doubted the *obiter* statement of Lord Oliver in *Interlego AG* v. *Tyco Industries Inc.*
[1988] RPC 343 at 373: "infringement of copyright by three dimensional copying is
restricted to artistic copyright. To produce an article by following written instructions
may be a breach of confidence or an infringement of patent, but it does not infringe the
author's copyright in his instructions". Laddie J also doubted *Brigid Foley Ltd* v. *Elliott*
[1982] RPC 433 (which concerned a (failed) allegation that a knitting guide was infringed
by making knitted garments to its instructions). Both these cases concerned instructions
in *artistic works* as opposed to literary works being copied, according to Laddie J, and
therefore were not relevant when infringement of a literary work was considered.

[135] Lord Hoffmann cited *Kenrick & Co.* v. *Lawrence & Co.* (1890) 25 QBD 99. So
applying this to *Designers Guild*, the mere notion of combining stripes and flowers was
not a substantial part of the plaintiff's work. "At that level of abstraction, the idea,
though expressed in the design, would not have represented sufficient of the author's skill
and labour as to attract copyright protection" (at 2423D).

[136] At 2423E. Lord Hoffmann was of the view that here the elements copied went well
beyond the banal and that the trial judge was justified in deciding that they formed a substantial part of the originality of the work.

[137] At 133. Morritt LJ of course did not reach a concluded view on *"so subjective and
unanalytical approach alone"* (at 133). He went on to conduct the analysis of the designs
referred to earlier.

dichotomy in UK law, but it should be noted that their Lordships all took different approaches to the issue of "substantiality". The common thread was that the works should be compared as a whole in assessing copying of a substantial part, and all (apart from Lord Millett) stressed that what copyright protected was the skill and labour of the original designer.

3.2.10 Defences to Copyright Infringement[138]

There are certain limited exceptions/defences to copyright infringement which include:

(a) Fair dealing with an artistic or literary work for the purposes of research or private study, criticism or review, or (other than a photograph) reporting current events does not infringe copyright.[139]

---

[138] The rationale for these defences stems from a not always recognised desire to preserve some element of the "public domain": copying is not necessarily wrongful—it is how we learn, develop new creative works and it is the essence of a common culture— "[t]he trick is to find some means to distinguish wrongful from fair copying. Some of those means are case-by-case, like 'substantial similarity' and 'fair use'. Some are system-wide rules, like the provisions limiting the duration of copyrights and patents" (Gordon, n. 119 *supra*, at 29). Unlike in US law there is no general "fair use" defence in UK law nor a general "public interest defence"—a specific statutory exception in Chap. III of Part I of the CDPA must be relied on, as these set out what is and is not permitted and they set out in detail the extent to which the public interest overrides copyright (see for example Aldous LJ in *Hyde Park Residence Ltd* v. *Yelland* [2000] 3 WLR 215 (CA) at 228H; *Yelland* has been criticised, see, for example, R. Burrell, "Defending the Public Interest" [2000] 9 *EIPR* 394). However Laddie et al. still sees a limited role for fair use as developed in the nineteenth century as a factor a court may take into account when determining whether a substantial part of a copyright work has been taken in assessing infringement in borderline cases, especially where the defendant's work was not competing with the plaintiff's but rather was to "enlighten the public" (at 4.54), suggesting that the concept of "fair use" may fall within the exercise of a rule of reason or proportionality by the courts. However Laddie et al. notes that "[t]he fair use doctrine seldom applied to artistic works because it would not often be the case that there was any countervailing benefit of public enlightenment to be gained by permitting copying of works of that kind" (at 4.54)—see *Bradbury* v. *Hotten* (1872) LR 8 Exch. 1 at 5, 7 (the defendant introduced nine pictures from *Punch* owned by the plaintiffs into his "comic life of Napoleon III" which was held to be an infringement—Kelly CB put the matter thus: "where one man for his own profit puts into his work an essential part of another man's work, from which that other may still derive profit, or from which, but for the act of the first, he might have derived profit, there is evidence of a piracy upon which a jury should act" (at 6)).

[139] Ss.29–30, CDPA. The general view is that to benefit from a fair dealing defence the copying must be "fair", and in assessing fairness, the amount or proportion of the work

(b) In the case of sculptures, models for buildings and works of artistic craftsmanship permanently situated in a public place or in premises open to the public, the copyright in such a work is not infringed by *inter alia* making a graphic work representing it, or making a photograph or film of it, but a three-dimensional reproduction would amount to an infringement.[140]

(c) To copy an artistic work for the purpose of advertising the sale of it—this is clearly of importance to auction houses.[141] This exception would apply both to a hard-copy catalogue and also to an on-line electronic sale catalogue.

(d) Where the author of an artistic work is not the copyright owner, he does not infringe the copyright by copying the work in making another artistic work, provided he does not repeat or imitate the main design of the earlier work.[142]

(e) The incidental inclusion of a work protected by copyright in an artistic work, sound recording, film, broadcast or cable programme does not infringe copyright.[143]

copied will be important, as will be whether usage competes with the copyright owner (see Dworkin and Taylor at 76). The method by which the copyright material was obtained (for example, in the case of unpublished works) can also be relevant, but is generally irrelevant once the work in question is in the public domain (*Time Warner Entertainments Company LP v. Channel Four Television Corporation plc and Another* [1994] EMLR 1 (CA)). By way of example, in a recent case (where the defendant Carlton TV used in a programme criticising chequebook journalism a 30-second extract from a programme broadcast by the plaintiff in Germany which featured an exclusive interview with Mandy Allwood and her boyfriend Paul Hudson) such use was considered by the Court of Appeal to be fair dealing for the purposes of criticism or review. According to the Court of Appeal in this case, the test of whether an extract from a copyright work had been used by another "for the purposes of criticism or review" was an objective one; but the user's subjective intentions or motives were relevant to whether the material's use satisfied the test of fair dealing on which that defence also depended (*Pro Sieben Media AG v. Carlton UK Television Ltd and Another*, *The Times*, 7 January 1999).

[140] S.62, CDPA. This exception is clearly important where works of sculpture or artistic craftsmanship are permanently on public display. However, there is nothing to stop the exhibition organiser/gallery owner from restricting such copying as a term of condition of entry to the art gallery where the works are on public display.

[141] S.63, CDPA.

[142] S.64, CDPA. This is considered in detail in Chap. 9.

[143] S.31, CDPA. By way of example, should Sister Wendy Beckett or some other art critic be filmed walking through the Tate with the odd incidental shot of works still in copyright, this would appear to be incidental inclusion. However, if she was then filmed in front of a work whilst commenting on it this would clearly not be incidental inclusion—however it would be likely to be fair dealing for the purposes of criticism or review. See also *IPC Magazines Ltd* v. *MGN Ltd* [1998] FSR 431—incidental inclusion was considered to mean that the inclusion was casual, inessential, subordinate or merely background (at 441).

The fair dealing defence is given greater consideration in Chapter 7 when the use of artistic works to illustrate books is considered.

3.2.11 Other Rights Analogous to Copyright or Related to It (other than Moral Rights)

Copyright, more than any other intellectual property right, has been expanded in the UK to cover a wide range of objects and activities, and to protect both economic and moral interests, adding to the complexity of the subject. Moral rights and *droit de suite* are dealt with separately in Chapter 4, and what follows is a discussion of certain other aspects of copyright, domestic and foreign, of relevance to artists, publishers and galleries.

Industrial Designs[144]

The protection of utilitarian or mass-produced items by copyright was an important and controversial feature of UK copyright law until the CDPA[145]; the effect of the CDPA was to exclude the vast majority of industrial designs from copyright protection.[146] This was done by effectively removing copyright protection from designs other than for

---

[144] Detailed consideration of this difficult and controversial area is outside the scope of this book. For more information the following works are recommended: C. Fellner, *Industrial Design Law* (Sweet & Maxwell, London, 1995); U. Suthersanen, *Design Law in Europe* (Sweet & Maxwell, London, 2000); and M. Howe Q.C., *Russell-Cooke on Industrial Designs* (Sweet & Maxwell, London, 1998) (the leading practitioner text). Copinger, Laddie et al. and Cornish also contain useful discussions of this area and the relationship between copyright and the law of industrial design.

[145] The "high water mark" was *British Leyland Motor Corp* v. *Armstrong Patents Co. Ltd* [1986] RPC 279 (HL) which upheld that copying of functional industrial articles constituted infringement of artistic copyright in their design drawings by (indirectly) reproducing those drawings in three dimensions—see M. Howe Q.C., *Russell-Clarke on Industrial Designs* (Sweet & Maxwell, London, 1998) at 5.56.

[146] "It was clearly the intention of the framers of the CDPA that copyright protection was no longer to be available to what can compendiously be described as ordinary functional commercial articles" (*per* Pumfrey J in *Mackie Designs Inc* v. *Behringer* [1999] RPC 717 at 723). However as *Mackie Designs* illustrates, design right (as opposed to copyright) is primarily available only to European "authors" or those with a connection (for example, residence) here (see s. 217 of CDPA and Design Right (Reciprocal Protection) (No.2) Order 1989)—in this case circuit diagrams originating in the USA did not benefit from design right protection, and an argument that they were protected by copyright in any event failed due to the application of s. 51 of the CDPA (see below).

artistic works and typefaces,[147] and limiting the term of copyright protection for designs "made by an industrial process" and derived from an artistic work to 25 years from first marketing.[148] In short, the intention behind the CDPA was to leave copyright as the preserve of what might properly be called artistic works.[149] A concern frequently raised

[147] S. 51, CDPA. For these purposes "design" means the design of any aspect of the shape or configuration (whether internal or external) of the whole or part of an article, other than surface decoration (s.51(3)). S, 51 was recently considered in *BBC Worldwide Ltd* v. *Pally Screen Printing Ltd* [1998] FSR 665, which highlights some of the difficulties of the relationship between copyright and design protection. On an application for summary judgment, the copying of the Teletubbies TV characters to make T-shirts and other clothing benefited from a defence under s. 51. In particular there was no evidence that the three-dimensional Teletubby characters were artistic works—had this been proven then the case would have been decided differently. A claim in passing off (to the effect that members of the public would regard the defendant's products as those of the plaintiff or in some way associated with them and therefore there was deception) failed as well. (See also Chap. 8.)

[148] S. 52, CDPA. Under The Copyright (Industrial Process and Excluded Articles) (No.2) Order 1989 (SI 1989 No. 1070) an article will essentially fall within s.52 as "made by an industrial process" if (a) it is one of more than 50 such articles or (b) it consists of goods manufactured in lengths or pieces, not being hand-made goods. Also Art. 3 of these regulations provide that s.52 does not however apply to works of sculpture (other than casts or models used or intended to be used as models or patterns to be multiplied by any industrial process); wall plaques, medals and medallions; and printed matter primarily of a literary or artistic character (listed to include among other things book jackets, dress-making patterns, greetings cards, labels, maps, plans, and playing cards).

[149] Copinger at 13–29 (citing Hansard, HL, Vol.491, cols 185.186). Copinger distinguishes a work of fine art (such as a painting) from an "industrial" design on the basis that a work of fine art performs no particular function other than to be enjoyed as an object in itself (at 13–02). US law follows the approach in *Mazer* v. *Stein* 347 US 201, 74 SCt. 460, 98 L Ed. 630 (1954), where the Supreme Court upheld the copyright protection for a statue used as a lamp base on the basis that the statue was capable of existing as a copyright-protected work of art separate from the lamp (see s.101, Copyright Act quoted in n. 1 above). According to DuBoff and King, current US law will deny copyright protection to the shape of industrial products even if they are aesthetically satisfying unless that shape is physically *or conceptually* separate from the product. Even then, the protection extends only to those aspects of the shape and not the article itself. See generally DuBoff and King at 168–169. The test for "conceptual separability [sic]" is clearly a difficult one to apply in practice. Reading the US cases and analysis one is reminded of the differing approaches taken by the House of Lords in *Hensher*. For example, in a dissenting judgment in *Carol Barnhart Inc* v. *Economy Cover Corp.* 773 F 2d 411 (2d Cir. 1985) Judge Newman stated that "[f]or the design features to be 'conceptually separable' from the utilitarian aspects of the useful article that embodies the design, the article must stimulate in the mind of the beholder a concept that is separate from the concept evoked by its utilitarian function" (the so-called "temporal displacement test"). See also R. Denicola, "Applied Art and Industrial Design: A Suggested Approach to Copyright in Useful Articles" (1983) 67 *Minn. LR* 707 whose test for "conceptual separability" was applied in *Brandir International Inc* v. *Cascade Pacific Lumber Co* 834 F 2d 1142 (2d Cir. 1987) (see Joyce at 198). Denicola argued that rather than concentrating exclusively on the *results* of the creative effort expended, it is the *process* of creation that distinguishes industrial from applied art—the intention of the artist to create art as opposed to

against copyright protection for "useful" articles is that the designer will receive protection which will exceed any expression of its aesthetic elements and encompass the technological applications of the utilitarian article. This may foreclose competitors from using designs of general application, and if a monopoly should be granted this ought to be patent protection.[150]

Industrial designs may, however, still benefit from registered design protection under the Registered Designs Act 1949,[151] from the (new) unregistered "design right" under the CDPA[152] and copyright is still relevant to protect the surface decoration of three-dimensional designs

industrial design was paramount (see generally R. M. Polakovic, "Should the Bauhaus be in the Copyright Doghouse? Rethinking Conceptual Separability" (1993) 64 *University of Colorado Law Review* 871 ("Polakovic") for a discussion and critique of Denicola's approach as well as a suggestion for a two-step test for conceptual severability). The US courts have had particular difficulty with designs in the "Bauhaus" tradition where industrial design and art merge (see *Esquire, Inc.* v. *Ringer* 591 F 2d 796 ((1978) light fitting exemplifying modern abstract sculpture denied copyright protection (see Polakovic at 873–4)).

[150]   See Polakovic n. 149 *supra*, at 889.

[151]   This Act protects new "designs" being "features of shape, configuration, pattern or ornament applied to an article by any *industrial* [emphasis added] process, being features which in the finished article appeal to and are judged solely by the eye" (s.1(3), Registered Designs Act 1949). The protection must be applied for and the design "registered" at the UK Patent Office to gain this protection before (in general terms) the design is used or otherwise published (s.1(4)). Certain designs are excluded from registration, being more properly the subject of copyright protection alone, namely works of sculpture (except casts or models used or intended to be used as models or patterns to be multiplied by any industrial process), wall plaques or medals, and printed matter primarily of a literary or artistic character (Rule 26, Registered Designs Rules 1989 (SI 1989 No 1105)). The exclusive right given by design registration relates to controlling the manufacture, import or sale of articles to which the design (or a substantially similar design) has been applied (s.7, Registered Designs Act 1949). For a case dealing with how the UK courts have treated similar issues to those in the US "conceptual separability [sic]" cases noted above in the context of registered designs see *Interlego AG* v. *Tyco Industries Inc*. [1988] 3 All ER 949.

[152]   Design right arises in an "original design", comprising "any aspect of the shape or configuration (whether internal or external) of the whole or part of an article" which is not "surface decoration" (s.213, CDPA)—hence surface decoration is properly the subject of copyright (or registered design protection) and can include both decoration lying on surface (for example, a painted finish) and decorative features of the surface (for example, beading, engraving) and can also serve a functional as well as a decorative purpose (see *Mark Wilkinson Furniture Ltd* v. *Woodcraft Designs (Radcliffe) Ltd* [1998] FSR 65 at 72–3, and Russell-Clarke at 4.30). Where a design (for example, a work of artistic craftsmanship, can benefit from both design right and copyright, copyright takes precedence (s.236, CDPA). The exclusive (i.e. economic) right of the design-right owner is to reproduce the design for commercial purposes by making articles to the design or making a design document recording the design for the purpose of enabling such articles to be made (s.226, CDPA). Thus taking a photograph of a design which is not an artistic work would not infringe copyright or design right.

(and copyright remains of some importance to designs created before 1 August 1989 when the CDPA came into force).[153] Registered designs and design right and their relation to copyright should therefore be borne in mind when considering the intellectual property right protection of mass-produced or manufactured objects.[154] Registered design protection can freely overlap with copyright and unregistered design right.[155] Unless they are works of artistic craftsmanship, clothing designs will fall within design protection, as opposed to copyright protection (except for any surface decoration aspects of the design).[156]

Such issues may need to be considered when a museum decides to reproduce articles in its collection for merchandising purposes (for example, by copying ceramics, design objects or even making an object (for example, a vase) to a design in a well-known drawing or painting in its collection which is in copyright). It should be noted that registered design and design right protection are of a much more limited duration than copyright.[157]

For completeness it should be noted that the UK must implement an EC Directive harmonising the legal protection of designs by 28 October 2001,[158] and a proposal for a Community Design Regulation is currently going through the EU legislative process.[159]

---

[153] Under the transitional provisions in the CDPA—see generally M. Howe Q.C., *Russell-Clarke on Industrial Designs* (Sweet & Maxwell, London, 1998), chap. 5.

[154] Interesting issues also arise when fictional characters, in particular cartoon characters, are concerned, where there are frequently overlaps between copyright and design protection: see H. Porter, "U.K. Design Copyright and Cartoon Characters" [2000] 11 *EIPR* 542. This area is particularly relevant to merchandising activities (see Chap. 8 below).

[155] See Russell-Clarke at 1.04–1.09.

[156] See *Jo-Y-Jo Ltd* v. *Matalan Ltd* (unreported, 31 March 1999, Rattee J): comment by S. Clark, "*Jo-Y-Jo Ltd* v. *Matalan Retail Ltd*—Threadbare Protection for Clothing Designs?" [1999] 12 *EIPR* 627.

[157] Provided it is renewed, registered design protection may extend for up to 25 years from the date of registration; unregistered design ("design right") lasts for 15 years from the end of the calendar year in which the design was first recorded in a design document or an article was first made to the design, whichever first occurred, or if articles made to the design are made available for sale or hire within five years from the end of that calendar year, 10 years from the end of the calendar year in which that first occurred (s.216, CDPA). Also as discussed above there is a more limited period of copyright protection in respect of the exploitation of an artistic work by making by an industrial process and marketing articles which are copies of the work (see s.52, CDPA) (see n. 148 *supra*).

[158] Directive 98/71 [1998] OJ L289/28. The Directive deals with registered designs ("design rights"): unregistered design rights and copyright protection remain unaffected (see Arts. 16 and 17). "Design" in the Directive means the appearance of the whole or a part of a product resulting from the features of, in particular, the lines, contours, colours, shape, texture and/or materials of the product itself and/or its ornamentation (Art. 1). "Product" means any industrial or handicraft item, including *inter alia* parts intended to

Publication and Database Rights

Two relatively recent additions to UK copyright law as a result of European directives, namely publication right and database rights, are also of relevance to the protection of artistic works.

From 1 December 1996 a new right, "publication right", equivalent to copyright (but excluding moral rights protection), protecting unpublished literary, artistic and other works in which copyright has expired, was introduced into the CDPA.[160] The first owner of the publication right is the person who "publishes" such a work for the first time within the European Economic Area (EEA), being a national of an EEA state.[161] The right lasts for 25 years from the end of the calendar year in which

be assembled into a complex product (i.e. a product composed of multiple components which can be replaced permitting disassembly and reassembly of the product), packaging, get-up, graphic symbols and typographic typefaces, but excluding computer programs (Art. 1). Design right shall not subsist in features of appearance of a product which are solely dictated by its technical function or which are necessary for interconnection purposes (Art. 7) (although this does not mean the design must have an aesthetic quality (Recital 14)). Based on these definitions there appears to be a potential overlap between "design right" under the Directive and works of artistic craftsmanship under s.4(1)(c), CDPA (a number of the Law Lords in *Hensher* equated a work of craftsmanship as one involving "handicraft") and possibly other artistic works under UK law (depending upon how "handicraft item" is interpreted), provided such works are "new" and have individual character (Art. 3(2)).

[159] See C. D. Thorne, "European Community Design Regulation" [2000] 12 *EIPR* 583.

[160] See the Copyright and Related Rights Regulations 1996 (SI 1996 No. 2967) ("Regulations"). Of course the fact that copyright must have expired means that works which never benefited from copyright protection in the first place cannot then benefit from publication right. The purpose behind the Directive concerned (Council Directive 93/98/EEC [1993] OJ L290 (the Term Directive)) was to harmonise this area as a number of countries had a publication right (in particular the *editio princeps* of Germany on which the Directive is mainly based (Copinger at 17–02)).

[161] "Publication" is defined to include any communication to the public, and includes exhibiting or showing the work in public or other communication to the public as well as more traditional means of publication (for example, issuing copies to the public) (reg. 16(2)). The Regulations therefore appear to envisage that an *unpublished* work will cease to be "unpublished" once it is exhibited in public, for example; however, the EC Directive upon which the Regulations are based (Art. 4 of Council Directive 93/98/EEC (the Term Directive)) can be interpreted differently so that "publication" (in the context of an unpublished work) simply means issuing copies to the public as opposed to exhibiting the work (see, for example, Art. 3(3) of the Berne Convention and see Laddie et al. at 11.26 to 11.30; Copinger also acknowledges this possibility (see 7–04 note 22) but relies on the strict language of the Regulations rather than the Directive in its analysis), so it is submitted that the matter remains unclear. Laddie et al. discusses how a court would treat the Regulations given their view that they fail properly to implement the Directive and therefore may be *ultra vires* and to that extent invalid: in their view a court could treat them as amended in order properly to reflect the Directive (see Laddie et al. at 11–32 and, generally, Laddie et al.chap. 2).

the work is first published. Those with historic collections of artistic works, such as museums, galleries and private collectors, need to bear this right in mind and exercise caution when allowing others to "publish" their unpublished works, by for example exhibiting them in public or allowing photography, lest they lose the publication right.[162] Database rights came into force on 1 January 1998.[163] Databases,[164] in addition to possible copyright protection,[165] gained the benefit of a *sui generis* database right protection.[166] There are no formalities for database right protection, but the maker of the database must have a connection with an EEA state.[167] The fair dealing and moral rights provisions in the CDPA do not apply to database right.[168] Database right

---

[162] For a detailed consideration of publication right see H. Simpson and D. Booton, "The New Publication Right: How it will Affect Museums, and Galleries" (1997) 2 *ARTL* 283. See also Copinger, chap. 17, and Laddie et al., chap. 11.

[163] Under the Copyright and Rights in Databases Regulations 1997 S.I. No. 3032 ("Regulations") implementing Directive 96/9/EC [1996] OJ 077 on the legal protection of databases. The intention was to harmonise the law across the EC protecting compilations of mere data or factual information, and the right is economic in origin. For example, the "maker of the database" (a crucial definition for ownership, and hence enforcement) is in general the person who takes the initiative in obtaining, verifying or presenting the contents of a database and assumes the risk of investing in that obtaining, verification or presentation (reg. 14). For a discussion of database right and copyright generally see Laddie et al., chap. 30 and Copinger, chap. 18.

[164] A "database" is a collection of independent works, data or other materials which (a) are arranged in a systematic or methodical way, and (b) are individually accessible by electronic or other means (s.3(1) and s.3A(1), CDPA). So for example a "virtual art gallery" on a website or on CD-ROM could qualify for database right protection regardless of the copyright position of the individual images/pictures in the gallery (which could be owned by persons other than the database right owner). See Chap. 5 for a fuller discussion.

[165] Copyright protection for a database as an original literary work is still available on the basis that the selection or arrangement of the contents of the database constitutes the author's own intellectual creation (a higher originality requirement than was previously the case (see s.3A(2), CDPA)). "Old" (pre-28 March 1996) databases which were in copyright on 31 December 1997 continue to enjoy copyright even if they fail to satisfy the new originality requirement (reg. 29).

[166] For 15 years from the making of the database or making it available to the public, whichever is longer, the owner of the database right can prevent the extraction or re-utilisation of all or a substantial part of the contents of the database (regs. 16 and 17, subject to the transitional provisions in reg. 30); a substantial change to the contents of a database (for example, updating) can in certain circumstances effectively extend the term of protection to a further 15 years from the date of the change (reg. 17(3)). Absent agreement otherwise except in the case of works created during the course of employment, the first owner of database right will be the maker of the database (regs. 14(2) and 15). To benefit from database right protection there must have been a substantial investment in obtaining, verifying or presenting the contents of the database (reg. 13(1)).

[167] Reg. 18.

[168] There are more limited "fair dealing" type restrictions on database right in reg. 20.

protection is most likely to be encountered in the context of artistic works, for example, where the intellectual property protection of CD-ROMS or websites is concerned. This area is further discussed in Chapter 5.

Rental and Lending Rights

Another recent innovation is the extension of the rental and lending rights in section 18 of the CDPA (i.e. the right to restrict the rental and lending of copies of a work to the public) to artistic works. This is in consequence of the 1992 EC Directive on Rental and Lending Right.[169] At first glance the Directive appears to restrict the lending of *original* artistic works as well as copies. But the Council Working Group involved in the Directive wanted to avoid this result and so Recital 13 was included:

> "Whereas it is desirable . . . to exclude from rental and lending . . . certain forms of making available as for instance. . .making available for exhibition . . .; whereas lending within the meaning of this Directive does not include making available between establishments which are accessible to the public."

So the better view is that the Directive does not apply to the renting or lending of art works for the purposes of exhibition.[170] However a recent Austrian case suggests that this is without prejudice to any national rights which expressly provide for the payment of royalties if works are exhibited.[171] In this case the defendant, a non-profit organisation, organised an exhibition of artistic works of members of the plaintiff (a copyright collecting society) which was sponsored by the Bank of Austria. This was held to be a "for profit" exhibition for which royalties were payable by the defendant.

In any event when implementing the Directive the UK government expressly excluded from rental and lending rights the making available (of a work) for the purpose of exhibition in public.[172]

Exhibition/Display Right[173]

The Berne Convention does not contain any requirement of a right to display artistic works in public, although the exhibition of a work of

---

[169] Directive 92/100 [1992] OJ L346/61.
[170] See generally Bently and Sherman at 273–4.
[171] *Re Copyright Collecting Society*, Sup. Ct., 23 November 1999, [2000] EIPR N–63.
[172] S.18A(3)(b), CDPA.
[173] See Bently and Sherman at 274–6.

art in an inappropriate place might infringe the moral right of integrity.[174] So, for example, under UK law whilst the public perform-ance of a film without consent can infringe copyright, exhibiting an original work of art or indeed a copy in public will not do so. Few countries have such a right: in France the better view is that there is such a right (as part of the general right to control the public presentation of a work) and in Canada there is a well developed exhi-bition right. In the USA and Germany the copyright owner appears to have this right, but it cannot be exercised where the work is exhibited with the permission of the owner of the art work. Nevertheless the German government still pays royalties to artists where their works are exhibited in public galleries.[175]

In Canada, owners of copyright in artistic works created after 8 June 1988 have the right to:

> "present at a public exhibition, for a purpose other than sale or hire, an artis-tic work created after the coming into force of this paragraph, other than a map, chart or plan or cinematographic production that is protected as a photograph."[176]

Although overshadowed by *droit de suite* in Europe, some have argued for the development of display right as a means of providing financial incentives for visual artists. But this development appears unlikely in the near future, if at all.[177]

Droit de Suite/Domaine Public Payant

Also there are moves to harmonise *droit de suite* (right of an artist or their estate to a share in the resale price of their works) across Europe and they are discussed in Chapter 4 below. But the introduction across Europe of a *domaine public payant* system ("paying public domain"), where royalties are paid upon exploitation of works, after their copy-right has expired, into a joint fund (to benefit needy authors or to pro-mote the arts in general), has so far received little support.[178]

---

[174] Ricketson at 470. See generally Chap. 4.

[175] J.L. Duchemin, "Thoughts on the Exhibition Right" (1993) 156 *RIDA* 14 at 48.

[176] S.3(1)(g), Copyright Act, RSC, 1985 c.C–42.

[177] See Hansmann and Santilli at 117. See also Note, "Copyright Royalties for Visual Artists: A Display-based Alternative to the Droit de Suite", (1991) 76 *Cornell LR* 510.

[178] Italy has an established *domaine public payant*; France has engaged in a number of experiments; Germany extended its copyright period to the author's life plus 70 years rather than confer such a right—see Cornish, at 365. Indeed an attempt to "fill the gap"

Yet there remain advocates of paying public domain, such as the German Writers Union, which has recently proposed a modernised form of paying public domain.[179] This is on the basis that earlier authors, whose works are often successful only long after their death, should help finance the creative activities of current, living authors.[180] Indeed it has been argued that *droit de suite* and *domaine public payant* ought to operate in tandem, as *droit de suite* generally favours artists' heirs and not living artists.[181]

The argument for domaine public payant is certainly a challenging one for countries such as the UK which have a chequered history of state funding for the arts and communal funds for artists. The principle behind the introduction of such a system is that artists should be viewed as members of an artistic community spanning both the past and present. Artists whose works are successful only long after their death will by way of a (fictitious in legal terms) "testament", effectively contribute to the financing and development of the creativity of later living artists. These living artists are in effect paid in advance and will make a payment back in due course by income from their works after their death.[182] So in a sense the dead care for the living.

between the 50-year and 70-year *post mortem auctoris* periods by a special version of paying public domain—that the last 20 years of protection *post mortem auctoris* should not profit authors' heirs but should be established as an authentic right of the community of the living generation of authors—failed during the run-up to the adoption of the so-called Term Directive (Council Directive 93/98 of 29 October 1993 harmonising the term of protection of copyright and certain related rights [1993] OJ L290/9)—see A. Dietz, "Term of Protection in Copyright Law and Paying Public Domain: A New German Initiative" [2000] *EIPR* 506 ("Dietz") at 507.

[179] See *ibid.*

[180] *Ibid.*, at 510.

[181] Indeed the introduction of *droit de suite* is often criticised on this ground—see *ibid.*, at 508. See also the highly publicised opposition of various artists to the proposed introduction of *droit de suite* across Europe ("Artists against *droit de suite*"—the group includes David Hockney, Sir Anthony Caro, Georg Baselitz and others) on the ground that its introduction is likely negatively to affect the first price an artist gets for his or her works, by handicapping the primary, i.e. first sale, market and it is also seen as violating artists' human rights—it cannot be waived and is to be imposed at a fixed rate (see "Artists enter the fray", *The Art Newspaper*, December 2000 at 75).

[182] Dietz n. 178 *supra*, at 507.

4

Moral Rights And Droit de Suite

4.1 MORAL RIGHTS[1]

AS DISCUSSED IN Chapter 1 the cultural value of authorship is embedded in the development of both the Anglo-American and authors' rights (*droit d'auteur*) copyright systems. In copyright systems based on authors' rights it has long been the case that the personality of artists as expressed in their creations benefits from protection as a proprietary right alongside the economic interests in their exploitation. The argument is that any author, whatever he creates, embodies some part of himself in his works, and this gives rise to an interest which deserves protection in the same manner as other personal rights such as reputation and confidences.[2] To mistreat the work of art is to mistreat the artist, to invade his privacy and impair his personality.[3] Another argument advanced in support of moral rights is the belief that "authors" are "almighty creators who pour particular meanings into their creations and therefore inherently have undisputed authority over the uses and interpretations of those creations".[4]

The general justifications for moral rights are based on the natural law/personality theories which were discussed in Chapter 2.

Moral rights can also be justified on economic and public policy grounds. The European Commission, for example, has stated that by protecting the authorship and authenticity of a work, moral rights also

---

[1] For a comparative legal and economic analysis of moral rights see H. Hansmann and M. Santilli, "Authors' and Artists' Moral Rights: A Comparative Legal and Economic Analysis" (1997) 26 *J Legal Stud.* 95 ("Hansmann and Santilli").

[2] Ricketson at 456.

[3] Jaszi at 497, citing J. Merryman and A. Elsen, *Law, Ethics, and the Visual Arts* (2nd edn., 1987) at 145.

[4] L.A. Beyer, "Intentionalism, Art and the Suppression of Innovation: Film Colorization and the Philosophy of Moral Rights" (1988) 82 *NW ULR* 1011 at 1027 (as discussed in Jaszi at 497).

serve consumer interests as they can assist consumers in verifying that they have received the authentic product they are seeking and not any different or pirated goods.[5] Hansmann and Santilli also argue that moral rights have economic implications: a work of art will sell for more if it can be attributed to the artist (hence the value of the right of paternity). Furthermore the reputation of an artist is based on the entire *corpus* of their work and so the right of integrity is important in helping preserve the artist's reputation (and so preserving the value of the artist's work).[6] These are variants of an argument often advanced to justify trade mark rights.[7]

The first country to protect moral rights was France, although it was not until the early part of this century that the French courts began to speak about a *droit moral* or moral rights as such.[8] Because of their traditional stress on the economic aspects of copyright the common law systems traditionally viewed moral rights as quite alien.[9] Professor Cornish points out that the separate "moral rights" element of copyright has been progressively enhanced on the continent over the past century.[10] In particular both France and Germany give at least equal recognition to moral rights and economic rights, although the basic assumptions in each case are different. French law renders moral rights perpetual as well as (in some sense) inalienable; German law gives both moral rights and economic rights the same duration.[11]

---

[5] See Follow-Up to the Green Paper on Copyright and Related Rights in the Information Society COM(96)568 final, 20 November 1996, at 27.

[6] Hansmann and Santilli at 108–9.

[7] Trade mark rights operate in the public interest by protecting consumers against confusion, and in economic terms they help lower the search costs for consumers and encourage quality control by trade mark owners (see, for example, Landes and Posner, "The Economics of Trademark Law" (1988) 78 *Trademark Reporter* 276–7, also their "Trademark Law: An Economic Perspective" (1997) 30 *J Law & Econ.* 265, and N. J. Wilkof, "Trade Marks and the Public Domain: Generic Marks and Generic Domain Names" [2000] 12 *EIPR* 571.

[8] Ricketson at 457–9.

[9] Ricketson at 459. That is not to say there was no equivalent protection—there was the possibility of common law actions in defamation and passing off and the Fine Arts Copyright Act 1862 afforded a limited form of protection in respect of unauthorised changes and alterations of artistic works (Ricketson at 459).

[10] Cornish at 444.

[11] The German position according to Prof. Cornish is due to "the Hegelian perception of the work as the fulfilled expression of the author's personality" (Cornish at 444). According to Sam Ricketson there are two major approaches to the nature of moral rights—the monist approach or the dualist approach. The monist approach prevails in Austrian and German law—the economic and moral rights are inextricably linked and interdependent and therefore should be of the same duration. The dualist approach which is followed in France and similar legal systems view such rights as separate and distinct (see Ricketson at 458).

Following the Paris text of the Berne Convention,[12] moral rights are generally considered to include the right to be identified as author (right of paternity (sometimes also termed the right to attribution[13])) and to object to certain types of derogatory acts in relation to one's work (right of integrity):

"(1) Independently of the author's economic rights, and even after the transfer of the said rights, the author shall have the right to claim authorship of the work and to object to any distortion, mutilation or other modification of, or other derogatory action in relation to, the said work, which would be prejudicial to his honour or reputation.

(2) The rights granted to the author in accordance with the preceding paragraph shall, after his death, be maintained, at least until the expiry of the economic rights, and shall be exercisable by the persons or institutions authorised by the legislation of the country where protection is claimed. However, those countries whose legislation, at the moment of their ratification of or accession to this Act, does not provide for the protection after the death of the author of all the rights set out in the preceding paragraph may provide that some of these rights may, after his death, cease to be maintained.

(3) The means of redress for safeguarding the rights granted by this Article shall be governed by the legislation of the country where protection is claimed"[14]

In fact authors' rights countries tend to go further and, in addition to these two rights, moral rights in such countries may well include some or all of the following:[15]

(a) right to decide upon first publication or other release (the so called "right of disclosure" in French law[16]), including the right to refuse to supply the original; in an early French case the artist Whistler was held entitled not to deliver to the commissioner a portrait with which he was dissatisfied, even after exhibiting it.[17] In a later case an artist was able to prevent the publication of his youthful works after having stored them away.[18]

---

[12] Art. 6*bis*.
[13] For example, by DuBoff and King at 204, 208–11 in discussing the US law in this area.
[14] Art. 6*bis* Berne Convention.
[15] Cornish 444, 452–3.
[16] Art. L. 121–2 CPI (Intellectual Property Code).
[17] *Eden* v. *Whistler* D.P. 1900 I 497: according to Cornish the artist had to return his fee and undertake not (further) to exhibit the portrait himself (Cornish at 452).
[18] *Bouvier* v. *Cassigneul*, Cass.Crim. 13 December 1995 (1996) RIDA 306.

(b) right of the author to insist on completion of the original where that depends on the execution of others: this is a rather extreme sanction and the French case of *Renault* v. *Dubuffet*[19] which concerned a sculpture which Renault had to complete once execution had begun has been much criticised.[20]

(c) right to correct or withdraw works of which the author no longer approves. French law, for example, recognises this right but it is subject to the author indemnifying the publisher against loss, and so according to Professor Cornish it appears to be exercised rarely.[21] However it should be noted that this right seems available only to authors of published works and not to visual artists.[22]

(d) right to object to the destruction or removal of the original: to some extent this overlaps with the right of integrity—as was the case with the famous refrigerator decorated by Bernard Buffet on all its panels—its owner was prevented from breaking it up in order to sell it[23]; nevertheless according to Professor Cornish even French law is unclear about whether the right extends to prevent destruction. Nevertheless in addition to Bernard Buffet's there have been other cases where the French courts have objected, for example, to the destruction of a church sculpture considered blasphemous[24] or to the dismantling of a work of art, again in a religious setting, where the organisers of the exhibition considered the work unsuitable for its setting.[25] This goes further than Article 6*bis* of the Berne Convention where the general view is that the right of integrity does not extend to the destruction of works.[26]

---

[19] [1983] ECC 453.

[20] Cornish cites the criticism of the leading authors Françon and Ginsburg (1985) 9 *Col–VLA JLA* 381 (Cornish at 452): taking the right to its logical conclusion it could in theory mean the commissioner would have to maintain the work once executed.

[21] Intellectual Property Code, Art. L. 121–4; Cornish at 452. In French law the right is termed that of "withdrawal and repentance" (see A. Françon, "Protection of Artists' Moral Rights and the Internet" in F. Pollaud-Dulian (ed.), *The Internet and Authors' Rights* (Sweet & Maxwell, London, 1999) ("Pollaud-Dulian (ed.)").

[22] See Cour de Paris, judgment of 19 April 1961, J.C.P. 111N. 12183 (1961) (French case denying right of withdrawal to Vlaminck)—see Hansmann and Santilli n. 1 *supra*, at 139.

[23] Judgment of 6 July 1962 (*l'affaire Bernard Buffet*, CA, Paris, Recuil Dalloz D. 1962 570).

[24] "*Bezombes*", CA Paris, 25 November 1980 (1981) 108 RIDA 162.

[25] *Hong* v. *Saltpetriere Chapel Assn.*, CA, Paris, 1 Ch., 10 April 1995; (1995) 166 RIDA 316.

[26] Ricketson at 470.

Until 1 August 1989 when the CDPA came into force, moral rights as such were not expressly recognised by UK copyright law, although limited protection was afforded by the law of defamation, passing off, contract and section 43 of the Copyright Act 1956 (false attribution of authorship)[27]. The CDPA incorporates the rights of paternity and integrity into English law, and also added the right to object to false attribution and the right to privacy of certain photographs and films.[28] However, in distinction from the *droit d'auteur* systems, under UK law authors can waive their moral rights, and this is standard practice in many publishing contracts.[29]

Unlike copyright, moral rights cannot be assigned by the author but, as noted above, they may be waived by an instrument in writing signed by the person giving up the right. However, infringements of the moral right of paternity can arise only after the right has been "asserted" by the author. This is a controversial requirement. In order to exercise their moral rights, authors should not only assert their rights in contracts with publishers/art dealers, but also, to ensure that third parties are bound by the rights, include on all copies of their work an express statement asserting the right of paternity. There is a special provision as regards the public exhibition of artistic works: the name of the author on the original, or the authorised copy, or the frame of the work is usually sufficient to assert the right.[30] All the moral rights bar that of false attribution continue to subsist for as long as copyright subsists in the work; the right in relation to false attribution subsists for 20 years after a person's death.[31] However, no moral rights apply if the author died before 1 August 1989 (the date of commencement of the CDPA 1988).[32]

[27] Laddie et al. (2nd edn.), at 1007.

[28] Chap. IV, CDPA: breach of moral rights is actionable as a breach of statutory duty (see Laddie (2nd edn.) at 1008).

[29] S.87, CDPA.

[30] So that, for example, the artist's signature on a painting or his name on the original frame would amount to an assertion of the author's right of paternity in connection with the public exhibition of that painting (see s.78, CDPA). Indeed even if subsequently the identification of the artist is removed or obscured, the moral rights remain asserted—see s. 78(4)(c), which is discussed in Laddie et al. (2nd edn.) at 1012: they recommend that a purchaser of a work of art should require a warranty (coupled with an appropriate indemnity) that there was no such identification (if there is none apparent).

[31] S.86, CDPA.

[32] Sched. I, para. 23 to the CDPA. Also the paternity and integrity rights do not apply to anything done before 1 August 1989 nor (in respect of "existing" works (i.e. works made before 1 August 1989)) to anything done after that date by or with the licence of the copyright owner (Sched. I para. 23(3)(b) where the author was not the first owner), nor to anything which by virtue of an assignment or licence granted before 1 August 1989 could be done without infringing copyright (Sched. I, para. 23(3)(a)) (see Laddie et al.

The right of paternity means that the author of an artistic work has the right to be identified whenever the work is *inter alia* published commercially, sold or exhibited in public. The right to object to derogatory treatment of a work arises where the treatment amounts to distortion or mutilation of the work or is otherwise prejudicial to the honour or reputation of the author or director, and in the case of an artistic work the right is infringed by a person who *inter alia* exhibits in public a derogatory treatment of the work. The right not to have a work falsely attributed to a person as author would *inter alia* be infringed if a person were to exhibit in public, or issue copies to the public of, an artistic work on which there is a false attribution. It can also be infringed by dealing with an altered artistic work as if it were unaltered.[33]

4.2 IMPLICATIONS OF MORAL RIGHTS

Clearly it is possible for the owner of a work of art to fall foul of the author's moral rights. In particular if reproductions of the works are made it is sensible to identify the artist on such reproductions. Also, when acquiring works of art thought must be given to whether the artist's moral rights have been asserted. The buyer may wish to put appropriate warranties and indemnities in the sale contract (likewise, generally, for copyright[34]). It may even be possible for restorers and those involved in conserving works to fall foul of moral rights.[35] Moral rights also particularly pose challenges for the Internet, as discussed in Chapter 5. Finally, difficult questions arise in connection with what may be derogatory treatment. There are very few reported cases dealing with moral rights in the UK. These all deal with what may be considered "derogatory treatment" within section 80(2) of the CDPA.

(2nd edn.) at 1009—they see this provision as enabling the assignee or licensee fully to exploit the work without any curtailment due to moral rights).

[33]   S.84(6) is similar to the corresponding provision in s.7 of the Fine Art Copyright Act 1862 under which there were several cases dealing with this area: *Carlton Illustrators* v. *Coleman* [1911] KB 771; *Preston* v. *Raphael Tuck* [1926] Ch. 667; see also *Crocker* v. *Papunya Tula Artists Pty Ltd* (1983–1985) 5 IPR 426 (see Laddie (2nd edn.) at 1024–5).

[34]   See also Chap. 7.

[35]   Peter Karlen refers to Californian moral rights legislation as holding restorers and conservators liable for grossly negligent injury to a work, (see P. Karlen, "Moral Rights and Collectors", *Art Law*, January 2000 at www.artcellarexchange.com/moral.html and see also www.publishinglaw.net).

Morrison Leahy Music and Another v. *Lightbond Limited and Others* (1991)[36]

The defendants had produced a sound recording which was a medley or "megamix" of words and music from five compositions of which the second plaintiff (the singer and composer George Michael) was author and the first plaintiff copyright owner. These were interspersed with fill-in music composed by others. The defendants claimed they were permitted to do this pursuant to a copyright clearance they had obtained from the Mechanical Copyright Protection Society of which the first plaintiff was a member. The plaintiffs denied that any clearance applied to the defendants' actions and, as well as suing for infringement of copyright, they claimed that the defendants' actions infringed their moral rights under section 80(2) of the CDPA.

Morritt J held that what the defendants had done clearly amounted to treatment within the meaning of section 80(2)(a) of the CDPA; it was also arguable that such treatment amounted to distortion or mutilation within section 80(2)(b). However this was an interlocutory decision for an injunction pending full trial so the matter as to whether there was in fact derogatory treatment was left by the judge as a question of fact at trial.

Tidy v. *The Trustees of the Natural History Museum & Another*[37]

In this case, an application for summary judgment rather than a full trial, Bill Tidy, the well-known cartoonist, had drawn some cartoons of dinosaurs to be displayed at the Natural History Museum. In May 1993 a book was published. It reproduced Tidy's drawings in smaller dimensions (from 420mm by 297mm to 67mm by 42mm). Tidy made an application for summary judgment on the ground that the reduced size amounted to a distortion (as opposed to a mutilation) of the drawings or was in any event prejudicial to his honour or reputation, i.e. it was derogatory treatment under section 80 of the CDPA. The plaintiff contended that the reduction in size detracted from the visual impact of the cartoons; it would also lead people to believe he could not be bothered to re-draw the cartoons for the book, especially since he was given credit in the book for the drawings.

---

[36] [1993] EMLR 144.
[37] Ch. D, Rattee J, 29 March 1995 [1996] 3 EIPR D–81.

In fact the judge (Rattee J) was not prepared to grant summary judgment in Tidy's favour in the absence of evidence on whether the public considered the reproduction as affecting Tidy's reputation. Nor was it clear beyond argument that the reduction in size was distortion of the original drawings.

Counsel for Tidy had referred to the Canadian Ontario High Court decision *Snow* v. *The Eaton Centre*.[38] In that case legislative language comparable to the CDPA was considered and the judge held that the words "prejudicial to his honour or reputation" involved a "certain subjective element or judgement on the part of the author so long as it is reasonably arrived at". Rattee J held that even if he accepted the Canadian principle he would still have to be satisfied that the view held by the artist was a reasonable one—this inevitably involved applying an objective test of reasonableness. So evidence from members of the public on how the reproduction affected Tidy's reputation in their minds was required.

Pasterfield v. *Denham and Another*[39]

This was an action for infringement of copyright and of moral rights, and passing off, brought by two designers. In 1988 they had been commissioned by Plymouth City Council, the second defendant, to design two leaflets and a brochure to be used to promote the Plymouth Dome, a tourist attraction. They had designed pictures of a satellite, a formation of German bombers, and a detailed cut-away drawing of the interior of the Dome with accompanying text. The leaflets and brochure were used by the second defendant between 1989 and 1993.

In 1994 the second defendant commissioned the first defendant, Mr Denham, to update one of the leaflets used to promote the Dome. This new leaflet still contained copies of the satellite and bomber formation, and a smaller version of the cut-away drawing with a number of alterations. These were the omission of a number of features around the edges of the original drawing and a variation to the colouring of the artwork. Also added alongside the cut-away drawing were the words "Designed and Produced by Denham Design 0752 671787". Around

---

[38] 70 CPR (2d) 105: an injunction was granted to an artist to require the removal of ribbons from a sculpture of 60 geese known as "flight stop". The sculpture was used by the defendants as part of a Christmas display. S. 12(7) of the (Canadian) Copyright Act, RSC 1970, provides that an author has the right to restrain any distortion or modification of his work prejudicial to his honour or reputation.

[39] Plymouth County Court, HH Judge Overend, 9 and 10 March 1998 [1999] FSR 168.

one million copies of this leaflet were produced and distributed by the City Council in 1994 and 1995.

The plaintiffs' claim for copyright infringement failed as the judge held the commission to design the drawings passed equitable title to the City Council, or even if this were not the case there was an implied licence to allow the City Council to use the drawings to promote the dome. Also the passing off claim failed as substantial numbers of the public were unlikely to be confused about the origins of the drawings in the new leaflet produced by Mr Denham.

The plaintiffs' infringement of moral rights claim also failed; the judgment contains a discussion of the law here, citing the Canadian case cited in *Tidy* v. *Trustees of the Natural History Museum* and also *Morrison* v. *Lightbond*. Also cited was the French Supreme Court (Cour de Cassation) case of *Huston* v. *Turner Entertainment*,[40] which held that colourising a black and white John Huston film "Asphalt Jungle" was a breach of the *droit moral*. But *Tidy* was not cited.

The judge held that to find an infringement of the moral right of integrity, the artist must establish that the treatment accorded to his work is either a distortion or a mutilation that prejudices his honour or reputation as an artist. It is not sufficient that the artist is himself aggrieved by what has occurred. Nor is distortion or mutilation alone enough—it must be prejudicial to the artist's honour or reputation.[41] Considering the facts the judge found that the variations in colour did not affect the honour or reputation of the plaintiff, Mr Pasterfield, as an artist; often there are colour variations when artwork is reproduced. In this case they did not come anywhere near what the judge perceived to be the gross difference between a black and white film and a colourised version of the same film. Nor did any of the other differences, omissions and alterations amount to derogatory treatment. Indeed the judge was critical of the plaintiffs' expert considering that his evidence was "seriously flawed".

Also the possibility that other jurisdictions may afford broader or different moral (or indeed economic) rights cannot be overlooked. For example, in the UK there is no exhibition right, i.e. the right to control the public display of a work. But such a right does exist elsewhere, for example in the USA, as discussed in section 3.2.11.

---

[40] 23 IIC 702.

[41] The judge quoted the 2nd edn. of Laddie et al. as authority for this interpretation of s. 80(2) in the absence of a UK decision after full trial on what is meant by "derogatory treatment".

4.2.1 Conclusion—Derogatory Treatment in UK Law

In the absence of a decision on the point in the High Court after full trial, or indeed in the higher courts at all, there remains uncertainty about what may amount to derogatory treatment. Laddie et al. is of the view that "the concept the Act appears to be aiming at is akin to libel but where the harmful act is not the speaking or publishing of untrue words but the derogatory treatment of the author's or director's work".[42] Applying the test in defamation law the question becomes "would right thinking members of the public think less of him?" Certainly *Tidy* and *Pasterfield* stress an objective, rather than a subjective, test. But the scope of derogatory treatment remains uncertain in UK law. For example, it has been argued that the destruction of a work of art is unlikely to infringe the right of integrity under the CDPA.[43] Nor would the siting of a work of art in an unsuitable setting.[44]

If the interpretation of Article 6*bis* of the Berne Convention is also considered, the stress is on derogatory action which would be prejudicial to the artist's honour or reputation. The adjective "derogatory" appears to imply a subjective standard but this is made subject to the more objective criterion of prejudice to honour or reputation.[45] Indeed it has been argued that "honour" and reputation" are more objective concepts, being analogous to the personal interests protected by the law of defamation.[46]

It is possible that at some point in the future the European Commission may propose a directive to harmonise moral rights protection across Europe.[47]

[42] Laddie (2nd edn.) at 1016.

[43] By Laddie (2nd edn.) (at 1016) on the basis that to interpret s.80 in this way would confuse the destruction of the physical embodiment of the work with the destruction of the work itself.

[44] On the ground that this would not be "treatment"—there is no addition to or deletion from the work, hence no treatment of it (see Laddie (2nd edn.) at 1015).

[45] Ricketson at 469.

[46] By Ricketson at 471. Laddie (2nd edn.) considers it likely that a UK court would, where possible, strive to interpret "treatment" in such a way as to give effect to the requirements of the Berne Convention (at 1016).

[47] The need to consider harmonisation in this area in the context of digitisation was recognised by the European Commission's 1995 Green Paper on Copyright and Neighbouring Rights in the Information Society (COM(95)382 final, 16 July 1995). In its 1996 follow-up paper the Commission was of the view that the time was not right for concrete harmonisation initiatives but proposed further to study the development of this area with a view to determining whether existing disparities in national legislation present significant obstacles to exploiting copyright, most notably as regards the integrity of matter protected by copyright (Follow-Up to the Green Paper on Copyright and Related Rights in the Information Society COM(96)568 final, 20 November 1996).

4.3 MORAL RIGHTS IN THE USA

Until 1990 the USA (at least at Federal level) had no express enactment dealing with moral rights, although the US courts had at times offered protection for interests analogous to moral rights through the extension of common law rights or trade mark laws.[48]

Following the Visual Artists Rights Act 1990 (VARA), US copyright law was amended to give authors of certain specified art works the rights of attribution (i.e. to claim authorship and to prevent false attribution to an artist) and integrity (which extends both to *intentional* distortion, mutilation or modification of a work which would be prejudicial to the artist's honour or reputation *and* to any intentional or grossly negligent destruction *of a work of recognised stature*.[49] An explanation of the reasons for the statute was given in its legislative progress in the House Reports:

"An artist's professional and personal identity is embodied in each work created by that artist. Each work is part of his or her reputation. Each work is a form of personal expression (oftentimes painstakingly and earnestly recorded). It is a rebuke to the dignity of the visual artist that our copyright law allows distortion, modification and even outright permanent destruction of such efforts."[50]

VARA does not however meet the minimal protections sought by the Berne Convention[51]: in particular it applies only to works of "visual art" i.e.:

"(1) a painting, drawing, print, or sculpture, existing in a single copy, or a limited edition of 200 copies or fewer that are signed and consecutively numbered by the author, or, in the case of a sculpture, in multiple cast, carved, or fabricated sculptures of 200 or fewer that are consecutively numbered by the author and bear the signature or other identifying mark of the author; or

(2) A still photographic image produced for exhibition purposes only, existing in a single copy that is signed by the author, or in a limited edition of 200 copies or fewer that are signed and consecutively numbered by the author."[52]

[48] Hansmann and Santilli at 97.
[49] See S. 106A, Copyright Act 1976.
[50] HR Rep. No. 101–514, at 15 (1990).
[51] See DuBoff and King at 204.
[52] S. 101, Copyright Act 1976. So, for example, *reproductions* of qualifying works and works destined for commercial purposes (for example, posters, works of applied art) are not covered (see Joyce at 637).

The requirement that to prevent the destruction of a work of visual art the work must be of "recognised stature" has proved controversial and difficult to apply in practice—it goes against a guiding principle of Anglo-American copyright law noted in Chapter 3 that artistic merit is not in general a prerequisite for copyright protection.[53]

Certain US states have also enacted their own legislation to protect the moral right of integrity: California and New York are particularly noted in this regard.[54] For example, the California Art Preservation Act 1979 prohibits intentional "defacement, mutilation, alteration or destruction" of "fine art". "Fine art" is defined as including original paintings, sculpture, drawings etc of "recognised quality".[55]

As at 1997 it was noted that at least 11 US states recognised moral rights in a greater or a lesser degree, notwithstanding VARA.[56]

4.4 ARTIST'S RESALE RIGHT (*DROIT DE SUITE*)[57]

4.4.1 Background

The laws of many European countries have for decades recognised that artists have a right to receive a percentage of the sale price every time one of their works is re-sold. Artists, the argument goes, may have had to sell their works cheaply when young and unknown, and should be able to share in the profits made by art dealers once they achieve fame.

---

[53] See for example *Martin v. City of Indianopolis*, 7th 192 F 3d 608 (US CA, 7th Cir., 1999) and *Carter v. Helmsley-Spear, Inc.*, 861 F Supp. 303 (SDNY 1994) and 71 F 3d 77 (2d Cir., 1995): the view taken by these cases is that "recognised stature" (not defined by VARA) has two elements: (1) merit or intrinsic worth, and (2) a public acknowledgement of that stature by society or the art community.

[54] See DuBoff and King.

[55] This statute has recently been used to protect murals—it has been reported (*Daily Telegraph*, 4 August 2000) that the artist Garth Benton is suing Gordon Getty, son of the art collector J.Paul Getty, because one of his murals in Getty's home was painted over. It was also invoked in a dispute involving the removal of a David Hockney mural in a hotel swimming pool in 1988 (source: Institute of Art and Law, Leicester website, 24 August 2000, www.inst-of-art-and-law.co.uk).

[56] Hansmann and Santilli at 97. According to Peter Karlen, VARA, a Federal statute, "generally preempts much of the various State moral rights statutes, particularly in relation to all those works of art and rights recognised under the Federal statutes. But State statutes still have a role to play in relation to works and rights not covered under [VARA]. Only an individual analysis of each situation will determine whether [VARA] controls or whether state law applies" (Karlen n. 35 *supra*).

[57] This section is based in part on a paper the author presented at the Institute of Art and Law Conference on *Transacting in Art: The Legal Pitfalls*, on 29 October 1996.

In particular the spectre of the artist's wife and children begging in the gutter following the untimely death of the artist was advanced to justify the introduction of *droit de suite* in France—the artists Millet and Degas among others were invoked in this regard.[58] The right, it is argued, would put artists on a par with writers and composers who may continue to earn royalties on the use of their works throughout their term of copyright. Indeed it can be argued that the main source of income for the artist absent *droit de suite* is the first sale, unlike other copyright works where the reproduction right is of greater importance. So *droit de suite* can help to make the artist's exploitation of his or her work more effective and to redress the imbalance with other classes of work.[59]

An American lawyer, Donald Millinger, has put the case for *droit de suite* as follows:

"[T]he fine artist shares none of the gain, if his work is resold for a large profit. The fine artist's economic position thus compares unfavourably with the position of authors or composers who, as their work increases in popularity and value, receive a continuous and increasing source of income from royalty rights. (The American artist's profit, if any, comes on the initial sale. Because the artist's bargaining power is minimal and his sense of business acumen often is less than his buyer's, the work is frequently sold at a low price)."[60]

Others see *droit de suite* as an acknowledgement by society of merits of artistic creativity.[61]

Nevertheless *droit de suite* has its critics. It has been argued that it makes little economic sense in practice. Also it is argued that, absent harmonisation with, for example, New York law, the art market will simply shift from London to countries with no or a weak version of *droit de suite*, such as the US or Switzerland.[62] It has also been stated that once the UK has *droit de suite* there will be an anomaly, in that artists will get no financial benefit when the copyright in a work, as opposed to the work itself, is resold. Yet the value of the copyright in

---

[58] Ricketson at 410–11. For example, the wife of the impressionist Jean-François Millet was left in penury while his paintings sold for millions (see "Artists campaign for EU to drop royalties plan", *Sunday Telegraph*, 26 November 2000).

[59] Ricketson at 412.

[60] He does this in the context of a plea for greater copyright/moral rights protection generally for fine artists in the USA (his article pre-dates VARA): (Millinger at 376).

[61] For example, the European Parliament.

[62] The British Art Market Federation frequently make this point.

such works is often rising steeply, given the increased opportunities for exploitation based on the Internet and character merchandising.[63]

A number of artists also oppose it because they believe it damages the art trade in general, and hence the market for their work. They also argue that it acts as a restraint on what happens to their works on their deaths. Indeed it could be argued that successful artists achieve fame and fortune much quicker now than in the nineteenth century. The artists Georg Baselitz, Jorg Immendorff and Markus Lupertz are among leading German opponents of a harmonised *droit de suite* in Europe.[64] Certainly statistics from Germany and France suggest that only a limited number of artists benefit from the right, and the majority receive only modest sums.[65]

History

The right of resale was first introduced in France in 1920, and for this reason it is often referred to as *droit de suite* (literally "right of following").

Droit de suite is dealt with in Article 14*ter* of the Berne Convention:

"(1) The author, or after his death the persons or institutions authorized by national legislation, shall, with respect to original works of art and original manuscripts of writers and composers, enjoy the inalienable right to an interest in any sale of the work subsequent to the first transfer by the author of the work.

(2) The protection provided by the preceding paragraph may be claimed in a country of the Union only if legislation in the country to which the author belongs so permits, and to the extent permitted by the country where this protection is claimed.

(3) The procedure for collection and the amounts shall be matters for determination by national legislation."

As can be seen from the Berne Convention, *droit de suite* can be claimed only in those countries whose legislation provides for it and only on the basis of reciprocity.

---

[63] See J.N. Adams, "The United Kingdom's *Droit de Suite*" in Dr I.A. Stamatoudi and P.L.C. Torremans (eds.), *Copyright in the New Digital Environment* (Sweet & Maxwell, London, 2000, vol. 8 in the Perspectives on Intellectual Property series) ("Stamatoudi and Torremans"), at 117.

[64] "Fifteen-year reprieve for the UK", *The Art Newspaper,* April 2000, at 1.

[65] See *The Art Newspaper*, n.64 above: "[i]n France, between 1993 and 1995, of the 2,000 artists and their heirs who benefited from *droit de suite*, a mere 2–3% (which includes, for example, the heir of Picasso) received 43% of the sum collected. The remainder got an average of FFr3,000 (£300; $470), from which had to be deducted the 20% levy of the collecting agency".

Austria, the Netherlands, Ireland and the UK are the only Member States of the European Union which do not recognise this right, although, in practice, it is not enforced by all of the others. In contrast, in the USA only California has a right akin to *droit de suite*.[66]

On 25 April 1996, the European Commission presented the European Council with a proposal for a European Parliament and Council Directive to harmonise national laws relating to artists' resale rights.[67]

The Commission's argument for harmonisation was that the differing provisions for artists' resale rights between the various Member States give rise to anomalies which distort sales in the Internal Market. For example, if an English artist were to sell his work in, say, Germany, he would have the right to claim 5 per cent of the sale price as a royalty.[68] On the contrary, if a German artist sold his work in London, no such royalty was payable to him.[69] Also, the legislation of the eleven Member States which do recognise artists' resale rights has marked differences as regards the works covered, the people entitled to receive payment, the rate applied and the basis of assessment.

The aim of the 1996 proposal was to harmonise the legislation of all Members States. But the legislative progress of the proposal to date been complex.

Following the presentation of the initial proposal in April 1996, the Economic and Social Committee delivered a favourable opinion on the proposal.[70] At the first reading by the European Parliament[71] (consulted under the so-called co-decision procedure which gives the Parliament considerable power in the EU legislative process), the Commission's proposal was accepted subject to certain amendments.

---

[66] DuBoff and King at 218–21.

[67] Proposal for a European Parliament and Council Directive on the resale right for the benefit of the author of an original work of art (presented by the Commission), COM(96)97 final.

[68] This derives from the principle of non-discrimination: a Member State cannot treat nationals of other Member States less favourably than its own nationals (see Joined Cases C–92/92 and C–326/92, *Phil Collins and Others* [1993] ECR I–5145).

[69] In a German case a few years ago, three works by the late contemporary artist Joseph Beuys were sold in London. Even though buyer and seller were both German, Joseph Beuys' heirs did not receive any royalties (see BGH, judgment of 16 June 1991— I ZR 24/92 [1994] GRUR 798). The European Commission's calculations show that, out of a sale price of £462,000 (DM1,418,340), art dealers saved about DM71,000. See [1995] 4 EIPR D–94.

[70] The meeting was held on 19 December 1996.

[71] 9 April 1997.

The Commission accepted some of these amendments, and on 12 March 1998 it presented an amended proposal to the Council ("Amended Proposal"[72]). A committee of the Council, the Council's Working Group, then examined this amended proposal in detail. However, it encountered considerable political problems associated with the text of the amended proposal, and gave the text to the Committee of Permanent Representatives in Brussels for consideration. This committee then held a series of meetings in an attempt to settle the key political questions arising. The European Parliament also proposed a number of amendments. The majority of these were accepted in the Council's Common Position of 19 June 2000,[73] adopted following political agreement on the proposed Directive (the Commission reserving its position) on 15 March 2000.[74] The Common Position was then forwarded to the European Parliament for its second reading under the co-decision procedure (see below).

The political agreement was based on a Presidency compromise whereby Member States could not apply the resale right to sales worth less than EURO 4000; there was also a ceiling on the total amount payable set at EURO 12,500. Controversially (as far as the European Commission were concerned), Member States where the right is not currently applied were given the right to opt to apply the resale right only to sales of works by living (not dead) artists for a 10-year transitional period additional to the five-year period for transposition into national law. The Commission opposed the 15-year transitional period on the basis that such a period is too long to achieve a fully functioning single market. Nevertheless the unusually long transitional period was welcomed by the UK, which was strongly opposed to the Directive. Indeed the hope was that the 15-year period would enable an agreement with the USA to be put in place to harmonise the tax at an international level, so as not to put London at a disadvantage to New York. Britain controls approximately 70 per cent of the EU trade in art with an annual turnover of £2.5 billion in one estimate.[75]

---

[72] COM(1998)78 final—96/0085(COD) [1998] OJ C125.

[73] [2000] OJ C300.

[74] See Commission Press Release of April 2000, "Proposed Directive on artists' resale rights—latest developments". 13 of the 15 EU states voted for the compromise deal: Austria and Belgium abstained (see *The Art Newspaper,* April 2000, at 1).

[75] See "Artists must wait for share of resale cash", Deborah Hargreaves, *Financial Times,* 16 March 2000, and "London art market welcomes resale deal", Deborah Hargreaves and Antony Thornycroft, *Financial Times* 17 March 2000.

Having said this, the Commission continues to oppose the Common Position, in particular because of the unusually long transitional period and also the requirement of a threshold and ceiling applying to the payment of *droit de suite*. It is hoping to find a better solution with the institutions concerned to the issue of the application periods for the Directive.[76]

The 2000 Common Position is considered in detail below.

4.4.2 Common Position adopted by the Council on 19 June 2000 "with a view to adopting [a] Directive . . . on the resale right for the benefit of the author of an original work of art"[77]

The Common Position reflects some, but not all, of the principles in the Amended Proposal. For example, it provides that the resale right is to be inalienable, like moral rights, but unlike moral rights under UK law will not be capable of waiver (even in advance). It will apply only to a resale of an "original work of art" which is subsequent to the first transfer of the work by the artist. The resale in question is any act of resale "involving as sellers, buyers or intermediaries art-market professionals, such as salesrooms, art galleries and, in general, any dealers in works of art".[78] However Member States may provide that the right shall not apply to acts of resale where the seller has acquired the work directly from the author less than three years before that resale, and where the resale price does not exceed EURO 10,000. The royalty will be payable by the seller,[79] although Member States may provide that those art-market professionals involved in the resale other than the seller shall alone be liable or shall share liability with the seller to pay the royalty.

[76] Commission Assessment of Common Position of 15/9/00 (CE SEC(2000) 1516). See also section 4.4.3 below.

[77] [2000] OJ C300.

[78] Recital 17 clarifies that "[t]he scope of the resale right should be extended to all acts of resale, *with the exception of those effected directly between persons acting in their private capacity without the participation of an art market professional.*" [emphasis added] The Recital goes on further to clarify that the right is not intended to extend to acts of resale by persons acting in their private capacity to museums which are not for profit and which are open to the public. Furthermore, with regard to art galleries which acquire works directly from the author, Member States are to be allowed the option of exempting from the resale right acts of resale which occur within three years of that acquisition (Recital 17).

[79] Recital 24 states that "[t]he seller is the person or undertaking on whose behalf the sale is concluded".

The Directive, for the avoidance of any doubt, expressly applies to works created before the date of transposition of the Directive in those Member States not yet applying the resale right.[80]

"Original works of art", for the purposes of the Directive, mean "works of graphic or plastic art such as pictures, collages, paintings, drawings, engravings, prints, lithographs, sculptures, tapestries, ceramics, glassware[81] and photographs, provided they are made by the artist himself or are copies considered to be original works of art".[82] The Directive further clarifies that "[c]opies of works of art covered by the Directive, which have been made in limited numbers by the artist himself or under his authority, shall be considered to be original works of art for the purposes of this Directive. Such copies will normally have been numbered, signed or otherwise duly authorised by the artist".

Member States are entitled to set a minimum sale price from which the resale right will apply. This threshold cannot exceed EURO 4,000.[83] Where the royalty is payable it will be set as follows (all sale prices are net of tax):

(a) 4 per cent for the portion of the sale price up to EURO 50,000[84];
(b) 3 per cent for the portion of the sale price from EURO 50,000.01 to 200,000;
(c) 1 per cent for the portion of the sale price from EURO 200,000.01 to 350,0000;
(d) 0.5 per cent for the portion of the sale price from EURO 350,000.01 to 500,000;
(e) 0.25 per cent for the portion of the sale price exceeding EURO 500,000;

---

[80] Art. 10.

[81] This stems from a European Parliament proposal to include "glass" as a work of art to which the right applies. In general, the definition of works to which the resale right applies is substantially the same as the Amended Proposal.

[82] Recital 18 is clear that original manuscripts of writers and composers are excluded from the resale right—this is despite the fact that such works do fall within Art. 14*ter* of the Berne Convention. The Council leaves it to Member States' own laws to decide whether to include such works.

[83] Recital 21 states that the reason for allowing a lower threshold is to promote the interests of new artists.

[84] By way of derogation Member States can set this rate at 5% rather than 4% if they wish.

provided always that the total amount of the royalty cannot exceed EURO 12,500.[85] Also if the minimum sale price is set lower than EURO 4,000, the Member State in question must determine the rate applicable to the portion of the sale price up to EURO 4,000—this rate cannot be lower than 4 per cent.

The royalty is payable to the "author" of the work and (subject to any permitted derogation) after his death to those entitled under him.[86] Member States may provide for compulsory or optional collective management of the royalty.

The term of the right shall be the same as the copyright term of the work (as is the case for moral rights in the UK, generally[87]). But Member States which do not currently apply the resale right will not be required to apply the resale right for a period of up to (effectively) 15 years from the date of adoption of the Directive in respect of artists who have died.[88] This derogation is also subject to any progress made in harmonising *droit de suite* at an international level.[89] Unusually a Recital in the Directive requires negotiations to be entered into at Community level with a view to making Article 14*ter* of the Berne Convention (set out above) compulsory.

The reason for the derogation is given in Recital 16 to the Directive: it is in order to "allow the legal systems of Member States which do not, at the time of adoption of the Directive, apply a resale right for the benefit of artists to incorporate this right into their respective legal systems and, moreover, to enable the economic operators in those Member States to adapt gradually to the aforementioned right whilst maintaining their economic viability, the Member States concerned should be allowed a

---

[85] An earlier proposal by the European Parliament to replace the basis for calculating royalties (the entire sale price) by the difference between the price obtained on resale and the purchase price paid by the seller was rejected. For one thing this would be incompatible with Art. 14*ter* of the Berne Convention. Also this basis is not currently applied in the Community.

[86] Recital 26 helpfully adds: "[t]he persons entitled to receive royalties must be specified, due regard being had to the principle of subsidiarity. It is not appropriate to take action through this Directive in relation to Member States' laws of succession [an attempt by the Parliament to stipulate that after his death the royalty should be payable to the artist's "legal heirs" was rejected on the basis that inheritance law is the exclusive prerogative of Member States and the Directive should not interfere with the author's freedom to choose who should inherit this right]. However, those entitled under the author must be able to benfit fully from the resale right after his death, at least following the expiry of the transitional period referred to above".

[87] See Copyright Term Harmonisation Directive 93/98/EEC [1993] OJ L290 at 9, Art. 1.

[88] Art. 8(1), i.e. only living artists are entitled to benefit.

[89] Art. 8(3) of the Common Position.

limited transitional period during which they may chose not to apply the resale right for the benefit of those entitled under the artist after his death."

To enable artists to collect the royalty, Member States must provide that, for the period expiring three years after the year of the sale, the persons entitled to the resale right are themselves entitled to require any dealer and commercial agent, sales director or organiser of public sales to furnish any information that may be necessary in order to secure payment of royalties in respect of the sale.[90]

It is important to note that authors who are nationals of third countries are to enjoy the resale right only if the legislation in the country of their nationality also permits resale right protection for authors from Member States.[91]

Subject to the derogation referred to above (where the Member State does not already possess a resale right), the Directive must be brought into force within five years from the beginning of the year following that in which the Directive is adopted.

It is important also to note the stated purpose of the resale right as expressed in the Recitals to the Common Position[92]:

> "The resale right is intended to ensure that authors of graphic and plastic works of art share in the economic success of their original works of art. It helps to redress the balance between the economic situation of authors of graphic and plastic works of art and that of other creators who benefit from successive exploitation of their works."

4.4.3 Second Reading of the Council's Common Position

On 12 December 2000 the Council's Common Position received its second reading in the European Parliament. This followed on from the Parliament's Legal Affairs and Internal Market Committee's ("Committee") recommendation for second reading (codecision procedure) of 28 November 2000, which broadly approved the Common Position subject to a few amendments.[93] In particular the Committee

---

[90] Art. 9.

[91] Art. 7. Note however that although enjoyment of the right is effectively to be restricted to Community nationals as well as to foreign authors whose countries afford such protection to authors who are nationals of Member States, a Member State is to have the option to extend enjoyment of the right to foreign authors who have their habitual residence in that Member State (see Recital 28 and Art. 7(3)).

[92] Recital 8(3).

[93] A5–0370/2000 FINAL, dated 29 December 2000.

suggested there should be a uniform minimum price of EUR 1,000 from which the resale right would apply to ensure full harmonisation. Also there should be no ceiling on royalty levels achieved by the artist on the ground that successful artists should not be penalised. The lowest royalty rate should also be set at 1 per cent (for the proportion of the sale price above EUR 200,000.01). Finally, and most controversially, the Committee proposed a transition period of 24 months to implement the Directive, rather than five years. Also Member States such as the UK which do not already have *droit de suite* would only be given an additional 24 months beyond the date for implementation to prepare for the right (as opposed to the additional 10 years contemplated by the Council's Common Position).

Following the second reading, in which the Parliament introduced its amendment proposals, there will be a period of conciliation between the Parliament and the Council, which is now not expected to be resolved until July 2001 at the earliest.[94]

4.4.4 Implications of the Artist's Resale Right/*Droit de Suite* Directive

The UK Government and the British Art Market Federation have continued to be against the introduction of such an artist's resale right.[95] For example, they see London as having a prosperous and valuable art market, which employs more than 40,000 people directly, has a turnover in excess of £2.2 billion (other estimates put this at £2.5 billion—see above), generates valuable tax revenue[96] and is a major attraction for foreign visitors.[97] They would prefer to see the abolition of the right across Europe to create a level playing field, for example with Switzerland and the USA. However, the Directive must be adopted following the so-called co-decision procedure[98]; a qualified majority reached between the Member States will suffice for the adoption. Accordingly, opposition to it by the UK Government alone cannot bar adoption of this Directive if the other Member States want to

---

[94] See "Strasbourg blow over *droit de suite*", *Antiques Trade Gazette*, 23 & 30 December 2000, at 1. See also European Parliament website "Legislative Observatory."

[95] On the ground, *inter alia*, that it will have a harmful effect on the art trade in the UK. See, for example, the discussion in 4.4.1 above.

[96] In 1996 the art market raised an estimated £470 million for the Government.

[97] From an article in the *London Evening Standard*, 19 January 1999.

[98] Art. 251 (ex Art. 189b) of the Treaty of Rome.

see it introduced. Hence the UK Government had to accept the political agreement on the Directive reached on 15 March 2000 (as reflected in the June 2000 Common Position) as the best compromise that could be achieved in order to protect the UK's interests.

The Commission however has always taken a different view. It has been at pains to counteract concerns expressed by art dealers that the introduction of the right would cause the art market to move from those Member States where the right does not at present exist (such as the UK) to countries such as Switzerland or the United States. It has produced tables in support of the Directive showing that the cost of exporting a painting to be auctioned in Switzerland and the cost of auctioning the same painting in France, where the rate is presently 3 per cent of the total sale price (i.e. the rate is higher than the proposed community rate), are about the same.

If implemented, the proposed Directive will have an effect on the UK art trade over time, and some predict job losses as a result. Also, dealers and auction houses will have an extra administrative burden under the Directive, although, as discussed earlier, Member States can introduce collective management of sums paid in respect of the right.

5

Art and the Internet: Copyright, Related Rights and Digitisation

THE MODERN LAW of copyright is frequently considered to represent a balance between conflicting interests: the author's economic/monopoly rights and the need in a liberal society for access to information. Digital technology poses challenges to this balance. This chapter explores some of the issues of special relevance to art.[1]

5.1 COPYRIGHT IN DIGITISED WORKS

Is it the case that a separate copyright can subsist in a digitised work, distinct from the copyright in the original work, just as there can be a separate copyright in a photograph of a painting, distinct from the copyright in the painting itself?[2]

It is submitted that if the digitised image is taken using a digital camera then the skill and labour used by the photographer would appear to qualify the digital image as an "original"[3] photograph for copyright purposes, and therefore it ought to qualify for copyright protection—this is clearly no different from using an ordinary camera—the only difference is in the technology of reproduction.[4]

---

[1] For a recent discussion of the impact of digitisation on copyright law see Stamatoudi and Torremans. For a discussion of art and digitisation see S. Stokes, "Art, Digitisation and Copyright: Some Current Issues", [1998] ARTL 361 and S. Stokes, "The Internet and Copying" Electronic Business Law June 1999, upon which part of this chapter is based.

[2] Graves' Case (1869) LR 4 QB 715 at 723 (see discussion of photographs as artistic works protected by copyright in Chaps. 3 and 6).

[3] As discussed in Chap. 3, the term "original" does not mean new or novel; it refers to the fact that the work must originate from its author. Originality requires an element of independent skill, labour or judgement to produce the copy.

[4] To recap, s.4(2), CDPA defines a "photograph" as "a recording of light or other radiation on any medium on which an image is produced or from which an image may by any means be produced, and which is not part of a film".

However, if the digitised image is simply made by scanning a photograph using a digital scanner it is hard to see how the image can itself benefit from copyright protection—no originality at all is expended in creating the scanned image—it is analogous to a Xerox copy.[5] However, if the scanned image were then to be digitally enhanced or manipulated this could well qualify the digitised image for separate copyright protection.

An issue here will be whether the enhancement was carried out by a person using, for example, a mouse button and relevant software—in this case, provided that person used sufficient originality, the copyright in the enhanced image should vest in that person, i.e. we are talking here about a computer-aided work rather than a computer-generated work. Alternatively, the digital image may have been created automatically without manual intervention and is therefore a computer-generated work.

5.2 COPYRIGHT AND COMPUTER-GENERATED WORKS

Interesting questions arise in the context of computer-generated art works. It is important, first, to distinguish between "computer-generated" and "computer-aided" works. Computer-aided works do not receive special treatment under the CDPA. This is the case where the work is largely generated by a human author, although a computer is used incidentally in order to facilitate the task. An example is a book written on a word processor. The computer is a labour-saving tool. Section 178 of the CDPA defines a computer-generated work as one generated by a computer in circumstances such that there is no human author of it. Provided it is original and satisfies the other relevant criteria for copyright protection discussed earlier, a computer-generated work can benefit from copyright protection. However, the interesting question is who the author of the work for copyright purposes is—section 9(3) of the CDPA provides that in the case of a computer-generated work, the author shall be taken to be "the person by whom the arrangements necessary for the creation of the work are undertaken". It is a point of debate as to what precisely is meant by the ambiguous words "the person by whom the arrangements necessary for the creation of the work are undertaken".

---

[5] See *The Reject Shop* v. *Manners* [1995] FSR 870.

It is certainly not clear how conflicting claims between several programmers, data providers and systems operators can be resolved. In a
decision under the predecessor to the 1988 Act, *Express Newspapers
plc* v. *Liverpool Daily Post & Echo plc*,[6] the court ruled that the author
of grids of letters produced with the aid of a computer for use in prize
draws was the programmer who wrote the relevant software. Contrary
arguments were rejected by Whitford J who said:

> "The computer was no more than a tool. It is as unrealistic (to suggest that
> the programmer was not the author) as it would be to suggest that, if you
> write your work with a pen, it is the pen which is the author of the work
> rather than the person who drives the pen."

In *Express Newspapers* the nexus between one person and the finished work was close, as the programmer was also the person who ran
the program and checked the results. If the nexus is less close disputes
are likely to arise where a number of competing individuals claim to
have "made arrangements necessary for the creation of the work".

5.3 TRANSITORY COPYING AND THE INTERNET

When a copyright work, let us say a photograph of a painting
("Work"), is scanned into computer memory using a digital scanner the
Work will be copied, and if the Work is in copyright, this will amount
to an infringement.[7] Once in electronic form numerous further copies
of the Work can be made, for example on to floppy disk, hard disk—
they will also infringe copyright under the CDPA. Also, transitory
copies of the work will be made—for example, if the work is viewed
on-screen a copy of the work will be made in computer RAM memory—this copy but *not necessarily* the on-screen "copy" will infringe
copyright.[8] Furthermore if the electronic copy of the Work is loaded
onto a computer server (itself an act of copying) which is then accessible on the world wide web, a person browsing the web will, through

---

[6] [1985] 1 WLR 1089.

[7] S.16, CDPA. Again, to recap, to infringe a copyright work by copying it one must,
without licence of the copyright owner, reproduce at least a substantial part of it in any
material form. See also section 6.1 below.

[8] A copy is made by reproducing the whole, or any substantial part of the work in any
material form. It is a point of debate whether the display of a stored work on a computer's VDU screen will constitute reproduction in a material form. It is clear, however,
that the act of calling work up onto a screen will normally involve reproduction in the
memory of the computer which will amount to copying.

instructions sent by that person's computer, download a copy of the work into RAM in his machine—again an act of copying. Indeed, as one author has succinctly put it, "the Internet works by copying".[9]

The Internet is a global computer network which allows computers worldwide to talk to each other. The viewer's ("browser's") computer transmits a request to the server computer holding the website which is being browsed to forward a copy of some particular material that it is storing. This material is not passed directly to the browser's computer. It is broken into packets, each with an address, and sent across the Internet. It is then passed from one computer on the Internet to another, all of which could be said to make a copy, until all the packets are received at the browser's computer.

Thus the exploitation of works in digital form is likely to involve the generation of a number of potentially infringing copies. Copying may also take place in several countries, for example, if the server in question is located in Country Y and the person browsing in Country X then if the copyright laws of X and Y differ this may lead to a different degree of protection between countries.

In practice, however, provided the digital copy of the work is lawfully made available for browsing then those browsing ought to benefit from an implied licence, i.e. the law will imply a licence from the circumstances. But query the scope of this licence.[10]

Other issues which arise in connection with the Internet include:

Caching

A cache is a computer (generally a server) which holds copies of information (for example, the most popular pages on the world wide web), so that users do not have to return to the original server. In general terms cached material can be stored:

(a)   at a geographically closer site, or
(b)   on a more powerful computer, or
(c)   on a computer with a less congested path to the user.

Typically internet service providers (ISPs) store ("cache") frequently-accessed web pages onto their own servers to speed up users' connection times.

---

[9] C. Gringras, *The Laws of the Internet* (Butterworths, London, 1997) at 163 ("Gringras").

[10] See Chap. 6 and nn. 66–7 therein for a fuller discussion of this issue.

A cache is also created by web browsers (such as Microsoft's Internet Explorer software), which can create a cache on the hard disk of the user's computer in addition to the transient RAM copies created whilst browsing. This means that users have easier and quicker access to particular websites. Thus caching can occur both on the user's computer and at server level (so-called "proxy caching").

Caching clearly involves copying a substantial part of a copyright work and (assuming the work is protected by copyright) appears to require a licence from the copyright owner to avoid a claim of infringement. Although convenient for users caching is by no means necessary, and therefore it can be argued that no licence will be implied from the circumstances.

Regardless of its legal status, caching facilitates the copying of entire websites, throwing up obvious copyright issues. The cache site may not be updated as frequently as the original site. Therefore infringing information may have been removed from the original site but not the cache, rendering the website owner and/or the person operating the cache still potentially liable for any infringement actions.

Linking and Framing

Hyper-text links enable a website browser to jump from one website to another, facilitating the accessing of related information.[11] Viewers are often unaware that, having clicked onto a particular word or phrase (usually highlighted and underlined), they have accessed another website. Recent cases have highlighted that when providing hyper-text links care must be taken to prevent the copying of protected materials from another's website without a licence.

[11] "Hyper-link" means a connection between two items of hypertext (the language used to build websites and converted into readable English by browser software). The hyper-link appears on a page of information displayed when browsing a website as an underlined keyword, which if clicked on takes you to another document or website. Whether hyper-linking amounts to copyright infringement was considered in *Shetland Times Ltd* v. *Wills* [1997] FSR 604 (Scottish Court of Session, 24 October 1996). This case (albeit only an interim decision—the case settled before full trial) indicated that copyright did exist in a link to a site. *Shetland News* is a website which provides readers with access to other websites by including links to those pages. *Shetland News* had included in its website headlines that featured in the *Shetland Times*. By selecting a headline a viewer would be connected, via the Internet, to that headline in the *Shetland Times'* website. In this instance Lord Hamilton surprisingly held there was copyright in the headline, although a headline would not be protected as a rule, since alone it would not be regarded as a sufficiently substantial part to justify prevention of copying. The issue is whether a hyper-link is a substantial part of the copyright work of which it is a part.

There is still much debate about the extent to which the use of hyper-text links requires the consent of the person whose site is being linked and/or of the copyright owner, especially where such linking is misleading (for example, by "framing" someone else's content so that it appears on-screen as your own, although in fact it is from a hyper-text linked site with no connection to your site), defamatory or harmful to that person's reputation, or facilitates copying in circumstances such that a licence permitting such copying cannot be implied from the copyright owner.

Liability of ISPs and Others

Internet service providers may charge subscribers for the right to access the Internet, for the use of their bulletin boards and/or for the rental of pages on their server on which they host content on behalf of third parties: they are intermediaries in the sense that they do not themselves determine what appears on the websites they host. A much debated question is whether an ISP can be held liable for copyright infringement occurring on its site, and if so what (if any) knowledge of or participation in the infringement must the ISP have to be liable.

So far UK courts have not given detailed consideration to an ISP's liability for copyright infringement, although the recent defamation case of *Godfrey* v. *Demon Internet Ltd*[12] provides food for thought here. Whilst defamation law is clearly different from copyright, once Demon Internet knew of the defamatory posting on a news group Demon Internet carried, it could not avail itself of a defence that it was innocently hosting defamatory content.[13] It certainly seems unfair that an ISP could be liable for copyright infringement without knowledge that the content it was hosting was infringing (whether actual knowledge or "constructive" knowledge, i.e. implied from the circumstances).

Various other intermediaries are involved in facilitating the transmission of content over the Internet: telecommunications operators may provide the backbone/pipe (in this case they may be said to be acting as a "mere conduit") and may (or others may) provide the intermediate servers and proxy caches. It is debatable to what extent such activities may infringe copyright.

---

[12] [1999] 4 All ER 342.
[13] S. 1, Defamation Act 1996.

ISPs and other intermediaries are concerned that their activities may be held to infringe copyright, and such persons (including the Internet Service Providers' Association in the UK) have been vociferous in seeking to ensure that copyright law does not impose liability on them unfairly.

5.4 TRANSMISSION RIGHT

A major current issue regarding the Internet is to what extent "transmissions" via the Internet are protected by copyright. When a person browses a website, as discussed above, instructions sent from the browser's computer will arrive at the computer (server) which is the physical location of the website and will set in motion the transmission of the relevant text or image in digitised packets over the Internet—these packets are received by the browser's computer and are then converted into on-screen images.

Such "on-demand", interactive, access to copyright material is considered by some to represent a challenge to existing copyright laws. In the UK, at least, for the act of transmission potentially to infringe copyright the transmission will have to amount to either a broadcast (which it clearly is not) or a cable programme service. However, the interactive nature of the Internet appears to rule out cable programme protection.[14]

International concerns about the level of protection for on-line transmissions were addressed in the 1996 WIPO Copyright Treaty[15] and in the proposed Digital Copyright Directive of 10 December 1997. The WIPO Treaty provides for a new right of communication to the public for authors of literary and artistic works. Such persons shall:

> "enjoy the exclusive right of authorising any communication to the public of their works, by wire or wireless means, including the making available to the public of their works in such a way that members of the public may access these works from a place and at a time individually chosen by them."[16]

Once implemented this "communication to the public right" will give artists (and other right holders) clear control over the use made of digitised images of their works over the Internet. Museums and others

---

[14] See Gringras, at 170–1.
[15] Adopted by Diplomatic Conference on 20 December 1996.
[16] Art. 8 (Right of Communication to the Public).

which wish to make use of the Internet will need to bear this right in mind when exploiting images of art works in their collections.

5.5 PUBLICATION RIGHT

Publication right[17] applies just as much to the electronic publication of a work (for example, by putting a copy on a CD-ROM issued to the public or by making it available by means of an electronic retrieval system, for example by putting a digitised copy on a website) as it does to more traditional publishing. Furthermore it can be infringed in an analogous manner to copyright, and this includes making electronic copies. This right cannot therefore be ignored in the digital environment.

5.6 DATABASE RIGHT

As discussed in Chapter 3, a further right analogous to copyright is the new database right introduced on 1 January 1998 by the Copyright and Rights in Databases Regulations 1997 ("Regulations").[18] The Regulations also attempt to harmonise the copyright protection that applies to "databases" following an earlier EC Directive. A database is defined to mean "a collection of independent works, data or other materials which: (a) are arranged in a systematic or methodical way, and (b) are individually accessible by electronic or other means".

The Regulations provide that a database can be protected regardless of whether the individual contents (text, images, moving pictures, etc.) are themselves protected by copyright. This is an issue in particular for collections of pure data (whether or not in electronic form) which are not selected or arranged in an original manner (a telephone directory is an example of this). Given the definition of "database" the Regulations can also apply to CD-ROMs, digital video disks (DVDs), and other collections of text, images, etc. They therefore strengthen the protection afforded to those who produce and compile CD-ROMs, DVDs etc. as opposed to those (such as artists, museums or galleries) who may own rights in their content.[19]

---

[17] See Chap. 3.
[18] SI 1997 No. 3032.
[19] There is some debate about how well copyright protects CD-ROMs: see P. Wienand, "Museums as International Copyright Owners: Use and Abuse of Images;

5.7 IMPLICATIONS OF MORAL RIGHTS FOR THE DIGITAL ENVIRONMENT[20]

The moral rights of paternity and integrity do not apply to computer programs or computer-generated works although surprisingly the right to object to false attribution could theoretically apply to computer programs or computer-generated works. However moral rights can still be relevant to the Internet; it is clear that making digital copies of a work of art ("Work") available on a server for public access over the Internet does amount to "publication".[21] Also it is submitted that showing a copy of the Work on a website is tantamount to exhibiting the copy of the Work in public. Thus moral rights could be infringed by making a digitised copy of the Work available for browsing on a server over the Internet, as the following examples illustrate:

(a) A digitised copy of a Work in which the right of paternity has been asserted is put on a server available for browsing over the Internet. The artist is not identified in relation to the image made available over the Internet. *Prima facie* this would be an infringement of the artist's right of paternity. Also, as discussed earlier, there would be an issue regarding copyright infringement as well.

(b) The digitised copy referred to in (a) is manipulated electronically, for example, the colour tones are altered. This may amount to derogatory treatment.[22] Indeed in the context of

Multimedia Problems; the Internet" (1997) 2 *ARTL* 35. See also I. Stamatoudi, "To What Extent are Multimedia Products Databases?" in Stamatoudi and Torremans, for a discussion of how well database rights can protect multimedia works—she suggests tailor-made legislation is needed to protect multimedia works as database rights protect only primitive forms of multimedia works well, in her view (at 41). In the author's view the Regulations clearly do increase the legal protection available for CD-ROMs, DVDs, etc.

[20] For discussions of the issues from both authors' rights and common law perspectives see A. Françon, "Protection of Artists' Moral Rights on the Internet" and G. Lea, "Moral Rights and the Internet: Some Thoughts from a Common Law Perspective" in Poullaud-Dulian. There is a discussion in *droit d'auteur* jurisdictions about whether the mere act of digitisation *per se* can infringe the right of integrity. The better view appears to be that it does not.

[21] S.175(1)(b) of the CDPA makes clear that publication includes making a work "available to the public by means of an electronic retrieval system". The Internet is one enormous electronic retrieval system. It has also been argued that putting a copy of the Work on a website can also amount to commercial publication (see Gringras at 193).

[22] There is a dearth of case law in this area; as discussed earlier, a treatment is derogatory if it amounts to distortion or mutilation of the work or is otherwise prejudicial to the honour or reputation of the author. However, cases from other jurisdictions dealing

authors' rights systems of moral rights protection it has been discussed whether simply digitising a work could infringe the "right of respect" under French law.[23]

(c) A derogatory hyper-text link is placed on one website linking to an image of an artistic work on another website. Could this be derogatory treatment?[24]

As is clear from Chapter 4, moral rights laws vary substantially in scope from state to state, in particular as regards who possesses such rights and their scope. This has led to arguments that the global nature of the Internet requires a harmonisation of moral rights laws.[25]

But it has also been argued that the very notion of moral rights is under threat from digitisation. The possibility of both perfect and distorted copies seems to fly in the face of the "Romantic" "eighteenth century idea of a work as a perfect, static and self-contained unit, linked to the author as a projection of his personality".[26] On the other hand, the "strong" inalienable nature of moral rights (especially in authors' rights systems) means that an aggressive assertion of moral rights could stifle the exploitation of artistic and other copyright works on the Internet. This has led to calls for a more flexible moral rights system internationally together with collective schemes for moral rights management.[27]

5.8 COPYRIGHT LEGISLATION AND THE DIGITAL FUTURE

Legislative activity in this area has tended to address two issues:

(a) the implementation of the World Intellectual Property Organisation (WIPO) Treaties of 1996 dealing with the challenges of

with the colourisation of films may also be relevant here—see, for example, the well-known French case *Huston* (Civil court,1, 28 May 1991, [1991] JCP II. 21731 (note by Françon).

[23] By Françon in the context of a case involving the *scanning* of the famous photograph of Che Guevara onto T-shirts (Françon n. 20 *supra* at 78–9). Françon also sees the interactivity of the Internet as a challenge to the right of respect (the right of respect is akin to the right of integrity in the Berne Convention).

[24] Or perhaps infringement of other laws which in the past have served on occasion to function as "moral rights", for example, the law of passing off or defamation: Lea n.20 *supra* discusses this example at 98–9.

[25] See, for example, P. Torremans, "Moral Rights in the Digital Age" in Stamatoudi and Torremans.

[26] Lea n. 20 *supra*, at 97.

[27] By Lea n. 20 *supra*. For example in the copyright sphere there are a number of such collective schemes and bodies, e.g. for example, DACS.

copyright and digitisation generally—does existing copyright law adequately protect authors and others involved in exploiting copyright works over the internet?

(b) clarifying the liability of ISPs and other intermediaries.

In Europe two main pieces of recently adopted legislation are particularly relevant:

(a) the E-Commerce Directive[28], dealing among other things with the liability of intermediaries; and

(b) the Digital Copyright Directive[29], which implements the WIPO Treaties and deals with certain other matters, in particular following on from the 1995 EU Copyright Green Paper.

The USA is already ahead of Europe in this area with the enactment in 1998 of the Digital Millennium Copyright Act which deals with the implementation of the WIPO Treaties and other matters, including the liability of intermediaries.

Digital Copyright Directive

The main copyright issues addressed by the Digital Copyright Directive (the "Copyright and Related Rights in the Information Society Directive") are:

(a) clarification of the extent to which the reproduction and distribution rights apply in the digital environment including the scope of fair use/fair dealing exceptions.[30] The reproduction right (subject to limited exceptions) is that authors shall have the exclusive right to authorise or prohibit *direct or indirect, temporary or permanent reproduction by any means and in any form in whole or in part of their works.*[31] In particular, temporary acts of reproduction integral and essential to a technological process but without economic significance of their own are expressly excepted from copyright protection (thus the activities of internet intermediaries may not necessarily infringe copyright).[32]

---

[28] 2000/31/EC, [2000] OJ L178/1.

[29] Adopted on 9 April 2001. See below.

[30] Arts. 5 and 6(4) of the Common Position of 28 September 2000 (see [2000] OJ C344/1).

[31] Art. 2 of the Common Position.

[32] Art. 5(1) of the Common Position: "[t]emporary acts of reproduction . . . which are transient or incidental, which are an integral and essential part of a technological process whose sole purpose is to enable: (a) a transmission in a network between third parties by an intermediary or (b) lawful use of a work or other subject-matter to be made, and

(b) A new right of communication to the public (as part of an on-demand service such as the Internet) to be added to the rights of authors—reflecting the discussion above about the need for a "transmission right" for the Internet: "Member States shall provide authors with the exclusive right to authorise or prohibit any communication to the public of their works, by wire or wireless means, including the making available to the public of their works in such a way that members of the public may access them from a place and at a time individually chosen by them".[33]

(c) Legal protection of anti-copying and rights management systems.[34]

The recent history of the Directive is that the European Parliament held a plenary session to discuss the Directive on 11 February 1999. The Parliament amended the Directive to the advantage of authors and artists. The European Commission did not accept a number of the European Parliament's amendments and on 21 May 1999 presented an Amended Proposal for the Directive.[35] Following the first reading of the proposal by the European Parliament on 27 October 1999, in May 2000 the Council had an in-depth debate on the proposal. While progress was made on a number of major issues, it was generally agreed that further work was necessary before the Council could adopt a common position.[36] Finally, on 28 September 2000, a Common Position was adopted by the Council.[37]

The Directive therefore remained controversial.[38] However on 14 February 2001 the European Parliament voted to accept the Common Position with nine relatively minor compromise amendments. The European Commission fully endorsed these amendments

which have no independent economic significance, shall be exempted from the reproduction right . . .".

[33] Art. 3 of the Common Position.
[34] Chap. III of the Common Position.
[35] [1999] OJ C180.
[36] See Commission Press Release of 25 May 2000.
[37] [2000] OJ C344/1.
[38] See, for example, B. Hugenholz, "Why the Copyright Directive is Unimportant, and Possibly Invalid" [2000] *EIPR* 499. Hugenholz argues *inter alia* that the Directive does little for authors at all. It is geared towards protecting the rights of the commercial sector (producers, broadcasters, etc.) and not the rights of content creators: for example, it fails to prohibit standard-form "buy-out" ("all rights") contracts between publishers and writers/illustrators which are "a deadful practice rapidly becoming routine in the world of multimedia" (at 501). See also T. Vinje, "Should We Begin Digging Copyright's Grave?" [2000] 12 *EIPR* 551("Vinje")—he sees the Directive as *inter alia* failing to achieve copyright harmonisation and to threaten effectively to replace copyright law with technological monopolies. This area is discussed further in Chap. 9.

and the EU's Council of Ministers had no trouble in adopting the Directive in its amended form on 9 April 2001. Once published in the Official Journal, Member States will have 18 months to implement the Directive into national law.

Electronic Commerce Directive[39]

Among other things this Directive clarifies that an intermediary such as an ISP will not be liable for:

(a) acting as a "mere conduit";
(b) "caching"; or
(c) "hosting";
(d) nor is it under a general obligation to monitor information it transmits or stores.

---

[39] 2000/31 [2000] OJ L178/1.

6

Some Current Issues

IN THIS CHAPTER a number of current issues exploring the relationship between copyright and art are examined:

(a) Copyright in photographs;
(b) The use of Internet visual search engines;
(c) Modern art and copyright; and
(d) Aboriginal art and copyright.

6.1 COPYRIGHT IN PHOTOGRAPHS[1]

A matter of considerable debate in UK copyright law is the standard of originality required for photographs to benefit from copyright protection. In particular to what extent should photographs which are simply reproductions in two dimensions of three- or two-dimensional artistic works be protected? This question is of special importance to picture libraries, museums and galleries which exploit photographs of artistic works for commercial gain or fund-raising purposes, and publishers. There is surprisingly little authority on this issue—the leading case, *Graves' Case*,[2] dates back to 1869. Recently a US District Court reconsidered *Graves' Case* in a surprising series of decisions in *The Bridgeman Art Library, Ltd* v. *Corel Corporation*,[3] and the High Court also considered the matter in the context of photographs of (three-dimensional) antiques in July 2000.[4]

---

[1] See S. Stokes, "Copyright in Photographs of Works of Art: The Bridgeman Litigation" (2000) 5 *ARTL* 47, and also "Graves' case revisited in the USA—the Bridgeman Art Library, Ltd v Corel Corporation" [2000] 5 *Ent LR* 104, upon which part of this section is based.

[2] (1869) LR 4 QB 715.

[3] 26 February 1999; Lewis A. Kaplan J, 97 Cir. (LAK) 6232 (US Dist. Ct., SDNY). (The case is reported in the *New York Law Journal*, 24 February 1999 and see also http://www.nylj.com/decisions/99/02/022699ba.htm for a full transcript of the judgment.)

[4] Although *Graves' Case* was not referred to: *Antiquesportfolio.com plc* v. *Rodney Fitch and Co Ltd*, *The Times*, 21 July, 2000 (Ch. D; Neuberger J).

6.1.1 Background

Before looking at the *Bridgeman* case it is worth recapping what was in issue in *Graves' Case*. *Graves' Case* was a case under the Fine Art Copyright Act 1862. This Act was the first to accord photographs copyright protection in English law. Section 1 of the Act afforded to the author (being a British subject or resident within the dominions of the Crown) of every original painting, drawing and photograph *inter alia* the sole and exclusive right of copying, engraving, reproducing and multiplying such painting or drawing, and the design thereof, or such photograph, and negative thereof, by any means and of any size. In this case one J.B. Walker was charged with infringing Henry Graves' copyright in a number of paintings and three photographs. Of particular relevance were the photographs—these were taken from three engravings made for Graves, the copyright in the engravings belonged exclusively to Graves, and they were the first and only photographs of these subjects. One of the points at issue in the case was whether the photographs were protected by copyright.

Counsel in support of Graves argued that there was copyright—a photograph from an engraving of a picture is an original photograph, hence by implication protected by the Act. In opposition it was stated that these photographs were not original photographs, as they were taken from a work of art. They were mere copies of the engraving, and not original in the sense intended in section 1 of the Act.

The relevant part of Blackburn J's judgment (with which the other two judges agreed) is as follows:

> "It has been argued that the word 'original' is to be taken as applying to a photograph. The distinction between an original painting and its copy is well understood, but it is difficult to say what can be meant by an original photograph. All photographs are copies of some object, such as a painting or a statue. And it seems to me that a photograph taken from a picture is an original photograph, in so far as to copy it is an infringement of this statute."[5]

Indeed Blackburn J's judgment hits on the central issue—all photographs are a copy of something. In this sense they are different from other artistic works. So what is the standard of originality required by English law? The prevailing view is that expressed in Copinger[6]:

---

[5] At 723.

[6] At 3–104. This was cited with approval by Neuberger J in *Antiquesportfolio.com plc* v. *Rodney Fitch and Co Ltd*, *The Times*, 21 July 2000.

"Provided that the author can demonstrate that he expended some small degree of time, skill and labour in producing the photograph, (which may be demonstrated by the exercise of judgement as to such matters as the angle from which to take the photograph, the lighting, the correct film speed, what filter to use, etc.) the photograph ought to be entitled to copyright protection, irrespective of its subject matter."[7]

This view had gained general acceptance by those exploiting photographic libraries and using photographs, although the application of *Graves' Case* as authority for establishing the standard of originality to be used today was questioned in the 1995 (second) edition of Laddie[8]. So it was with considerable surprise that at the end of 1998 the Bridgeman Art Library found that a US District Court denied copyright protection to its picture library images when it attempted to sue Corel for copyright infringement, the court citing English law as authority for its decision. This case is worthy of careful review.

6.1.2 The *Bridgeman* Case

Facts

The plaintiff is a leading British art library founded by Lady Bridgeman. It has a large collection of photographs (both as transparencies and digital image files) taken of works of art which are themselves out of copyright (i.e. in the public domain) but to which Bridgeman claims copyright in the photographs. Corel is a leading Canadian software house and had recently started to market a CD-ROM collection of reproductions of paintings of European masters in the USA, the UK and Canada. This was called "Professional Photos CD

---

[7] It is also worth noting a case predating *Graves*, *Newton* v. *Cowie and Another* [1827] 4 Bing. 234, 130 ER 759, which concerned the piracy of nine engraved copies of drawings—another case involving the reproduction by mechanical means of another artistic work. What copyright in an engraving protected, according to Best CJ, was not the picture from which the engraving was taken—another engraver could equally well copy that; rather the labour of the engraver was protected (at 246): "the engraver, although a copyist, produces the resemblance by means very different from the painter or draftsman from whom he copies;—means which require great labour and talent . . . The . . . engraver does not claim the monopoly of the use of the picture from which the engraving is made; he says, take the trouble of going to the picture yourself, but do not avail yourself of my labour, who have been to the picture, and have executed the engraving" (at 245–6).

[8] At 3.56—see discussion below.

Rom masters". The images were bought from "Off the Wall Images"—a company which no longer exists. Bridgeman claimed that Corel had infringed 120 of its images of paintings in the public domain by including these images on its CD-ROM. It was claimed that Corel's digital images must have been copied from the Bridgeman reproductions because no other authorised reproductions of those works exist. Bridgeman sued in the New York federal court, alleging copyright infringement and other claims. Both parties moved for summary judgment.

Held (Judge Kaplan)

On 13 November 1998, the Southern District Court of New York granted the defendant's motion for summary judgment dismissing the plaintiff's copyright infringement claim on the alternative grounds that the allegedly infringed works—colour transparencies of paintings which themselves are in the public domain—were not original and therefore not permissible subjects of valid copyright and, in any case, were not infringed.[9] The court applied UK law in determining whether the plaintiff's transparencies were protected by copyright and applied US law to determine whether there was infringement. The Court noted, however, that it would have reached the same result under US law. Additionally, the Court held that even if the photographs were protected by copyright they could not be infringed by Corel's photographs as the only similarity between them was that "both are exact reproductions of public domain works of art". Under well-settled US law, where the only similarity between two works relates to uncopyrightable elements, there can be no infringement as a matter of law.[10]

Following the entry of final judgment, the court, in the words of the judge, "was bombarded with additional submissions". On 23 November 1998, the plaintiff moved for re-argument and reconsideration, arguing that the court had erred on the issue of originality. It asserted that the court had ignored the US Register of Copyright's issue of a certificate of registration for one of the plaintiff's transparencies ("The Laughing Cavalier"), which it took as establishing the subsistence of copyright, and that the court had misconstrued British copyright law in that it failed to follow *Graves' Case*. At about

---

[9] *The Bridgeman Art Library, Ltd.* v. *Corel Corp.*, 25 F Supp. 2d 421 (SDNY 1998).

[10] For a discussion of the first decision see the case note in [1999] *Ent. LR* N–32 by Robert W. Clarida.

the same time, the court received an unsolicited letter from Professor William Patry, author of a copyright law treatise, which argued that it had erred in applying the law of the United Kingdom to the issue of copyright protection. The plaintiff then moved for an order permitting the filing of an *amicus* brief by one of its associates, The Wallace Collection, to address the UK law issue. The court granted leave for the submission of the *amicus* brief and invited the parties to respond to Professor Patry's letter. Accordingly the case was re-argued and reconsidered and judgement was given by Judge Kaplan on 26 February 1999.

At the outset of his second judgment, Judge Kaplan made clear that:

> "it is worth noting that the post-judgement flurry was occasioned chiefly by the fact that the plaintiff failed competently to address most of the issues raised by this interesting case prior to the entry of final judgement. In particular, while plaintiff urged the application of UK law, it made no serious effort to address the choice of law issue and no effort at all (apart from citing the British copyright act) to bring pertinent UK authority to the Court's attention before plaintiff lost the case. Indeed, it did not even cite Graves' case, the supposedly controlling authority that the Court is said to have overlooked".

Nevertheless as the judge felt the issues were significant beyond the immediate interests of the parties he was prepared to allow a re-argument and reconsideration of the case.

Choice of Law

The judge considered Professor Patry's arguments and US law generally, especially in relation to the Copyright Clause of the Constitution[11] (which permits Congress to enact legislation protecting only original works, with originality determined in accordance with the meaning of the Copyright Clause) and the Copyright Clause's relation to the Berne Convention, the Universal Copyright Convention and the US Berne Convention Implementation Act of 1988 (the "BCIA"). After a technical review of the law relating to treaties such as the Berne Convention and their effect on the protection of foreign copyrights in the USA, the judge considered it was quite clear that whilst US copyright law (the Copyright Act 1976, as amended by the BCIA) extended certain copyright protection to the holders of copyright in Berne Convention works, the Copyright Act was the exclusive source of that protection.

[11] US Const. Art. I, §8, Cl.8.

Accordingly in the case of the photographs in issue the subsistence of copyright in them was properly a question of US law which limits such copyright protection to "original works of authorship . . .".[12]

Originality and Copyright

(a) United States Law

The court's previous opinion was that the plaintiff's exact photographic copies of public domain works of art would not be protected by copyright under US law because they were not original. In view of the court's conclusion here that US law governed on this issue, the judge considered it appropriate to give a somewhat fuller statement of the court's reasoning.

According to the judge it is clear US law that photographs are "writings" within the meaning of the Copyright Clause of the US Constitution.[13] In short in US law, according to the judge, "there is broad scope for copyright in photographs because 'a very modest expression of personality will constitute sufficient originality' ".[14]

The judge cited a leading US copyright text (Nimmer) to the effect that there "appear to be at least two situations in which a photograph should be denied copyright for lack of originality", one of which the judge considered directly relevant here: "where a photograph of a photograph or other printed matter is made that amounts to nothing more than slavish copying".[15] Nimmer thus concluded, according to the judge, that a slavish photographic copy of a painting would lack originality.

Also the judge was of the view that there was little doubt that many photographs, probably the overwhelming majority, reflected at least the modest amount of originality required for copyright protection. This could include posing the subjects, lighting, angle, selection of film and camera, evoking the desired expression, and almost any other variant involved.[16] But "slavish copying", although doubtless requiring technical skill and effort, does not qualify.[17] He also referred to the

---

[12] Copyright Act 1976 (s.102(a)).

[13] He cited in particular *Burrow-Giles Lithographic Co* v. *Sarony* 111 US 53 (1884).

[14] See M.B. Nimmer & D. Nimmer, *Nimmer on Copyright* (M Bender, New York, 1998)) §2.08[E][1], at 2–130 (cited as "Nimmer")).

[15] *Ibid.*, 208[E][1]at 2–131.

[16] He cited *Rogers* v. *Koons*, 960 F 2d 301, 307 (2d Cir.), 506 US 934 (1992), and *Leibovitz* v. *Paramount Pictures Corp.*, 137 F 3d 109, 116 (2d Cir. 1998).

[17] He cited *Hearn* v. *Meyer*, 664 F Supp. 832 (SDNY 1987), where, according to Judge Kaplan, Judge Leisure held that "slavish copies" of public domain reproductions

Supreme Court in *Feist*, where "sweat of the brow" alone was not the "creative spark" which is the *sine qua non* of originality.[18] The judge found that in this case the plaintiff by its own admission had laboured to create "slavish copies" of public domain works of art. Thus he had no difficulty in finding that "while it may be assumed that this required both skill and effort, there was no spark of originality—indeed, the point of the exercise was to reproduce the underlying works with absolute fidelity". He therefore found that the works were not original and not protected by copyright.

The judge also discussed the plaintiff's technical defence that, as the US Register of Copyright issued a certificate of registration for one of the plaintiff's transparencies ("The Laughing Cavalier"), this demonstrated that its photographs were protected by copyright under US law. The judge considered this argument misguided: while the certificate was *prima facie* evidence of the validity of the copyright,[19] including the originality of the work, the presumption was not irrebuttable.[20] Here, the judge was of the view that the facts pertinent to the issue of originality were undisputed. The court held as a matter of law that the plaintiff's works were not original under either United Kingdom or United States law and therefore not entitled to copyright protection.

(b) United Kingdom Law

It is somewhat surprising that the judge, although he concluded that his decision on the law governing the subsistence of copyright rendered the point moot, nevertheless felt able to state that the plaintiff's copyright

of public domain original works of art were not protected by copyright despite the great skill and effort involved in the copying process, and minor but unintentional variations between the copies and the works copied.

[18] 499 US 340. In light of this he also commented that it was not entirely surprising that an attorney for the Museum of Modern Art, ("an entity with interests comparable to plaintiffs and its clients"), not long ago presented a paper acknowledging that a photograph of a two-dimensional public domain work of art "might not have enough originality to be eligible for its own copyright" (Judge Kaplan cited B. Wolff, *Copyright*, in ALI–ABA Course of Study, Legal Problems of Museum Administration, C989 ALI-ABA 27 at 48, and also L.A. Greenburg, "The Art of Appropriation: Puppies, Piracy ,and Post-Modernism", (1992) 11 *Cardozo Arts & Ent. LJ* 1, 20–1 (photographic copies of original art photographs taken by the famous photographer, Edward Weston, which were made to "deconstruct the myth of the masterpiece" were not copyrightable)).

[19] S.410(c), Copyright Act 1976.

[20] For example, *Lakedreax* v. *Taylor*, 932 F 2d 1103, 1108 (5th Cir. 1991). Indeed, the Copyright Act leaves the "evidentiary weight to be accorded the certificate . . . [to] the discretion of the court." (s.410(c)).

claim would fail even if the governing law were that of the United Kingdom, as opposed to the United States.

According to the judge, the plaintiff's attack on the court's previous conclusion that its colour transparencies were not original and therefore not protected by copyright under UK law depended primarily on its claim that the court failed to apply *Graves' Case*, the supposedly controlling authority that the plaintiff did not even cite in its opposition to defendant's motion for summary judgment. In particular the judgment of Blackburn J quoted above was cited. The plaintiff and the *amicus* in its brief argued that the plaintiff's photographs of public domain paintings are protected by copyright under UK law on the clear authority of *Graves' Case*.

The judge however was of the view that the antiquity of *Graves' Case* was overlooked, as well as the subsequent development of the law of originality in the United Kingdom. In particular one of the leading UK copyright texts, the second edition of Laddie, was cited in detail by the judge to the effect that originality presupposes the exercise of substantial independent skill, labour, judgement and so forth. According to Laddie there is room for originality in a photograph in three respects. First, there can be originality which does not depend on the creation of the scene or object to be photographed—this includes the angle of shot, light and shade, exposure, effects achieved by means of filters, developing techniques, etc: "in such manner does one photograph of Westminster Abbey differ from another at least potentially".[21] Secondly, there may be creation of the scene or subject to be photographed, such as the arrangement or posing of a group. Thirdly, a person may create a worthwhile photograph by being at the right place in the right time and capturing and recording a scene unlikely to recur.

The judge then discussed Laddie's questioning of the continued authority of *Graves' Case* under the above analysis. Laddie stated:

> "It is submitted that *Graves' Case* . . . does not decide the contrary, since there may have been special skill or labour in setting up the equipment to get a good photograph, especially with the rather primitive materials available in those days. Although the judgments do not discuss this aspect it may have been self-evident to any contemporary so as not to require any discussion. If this is wrong it is submitted that *Graves' Case* is no longer good law and in that case is to be explained as a decision made before the subject of originality had been fully developed by the courts."[22]

---

[21] At 3.56 (Laddie et al. 2nd edn.).
[22] Laddie et al. (2nd edn.), 239 n.3.

This analysis according to the judge, was quite pertinent in this case. Most photographs according to the judge, are "original" in one, if not more, of the three respects set out in Laddie and therefore are protected by copyright. But the plaintiff's difficulty here is that it is seeking protection "for the exception that proves the rule": photographs of existing two-dimensional articles (in this case works of art), each of which reproduces the article in the photographic medium as precisely as technology permits. "Its transparencies stand in the same relation to the original works of art as a photocopy stands to a page of typescript, a doodle, or a Michelangelo drawing."[23]

Although the plaintiff argued that the photocopier analogy was inapt because taking a photograph requires greater skill than making a photocopy and the transparencies involved a change in medium, according to Judge Kaplan, "the argument is as unpersuasive under British as under U.S. law . . . The allegedly greater skill required to make an exact photographic, as opposed to Xerographic or comparable, copy is immaterial".

The judge then went on to refer to the Privy Council case of *Interlego AG v. Tyco Industries, Inc.*,[24] which held that "[s]kill, labour or judgment merely in the process of copying cannot confer originality. . .".[25] This point, according to the judge, was exactly the same as the lack of protection under US law for a "slavish copy". Nor was the change in medium (i.e. from painting to photograph), standing alone, significant:

> "a copy in a new medium is copyrightable only where, as often but not always is the case, the copier makes some identifiable original contribution. In the words of the Privy Council in *Interlogo AG*: '[t]here must . . . be some element of material alteration or embellishment which suffices to make the totality of the work an original work'."[26]

Indeed, the judge considered that the plaintiff's expert effectively conceded the same point, "noting that copyright 'may' subsist in a photograph of a work of art because "change of medium is likely to amount to a material alteration from the original work, unless the change of medium is so insignificant as not to confer originality."

The judge was of the view, as the court noted in its earlier opinion, that "[i]t is uncontested that Bridgeman's images are substantially

---

[23] The judge noted that the plaintiff conceded that a photocopy was not original and hence not copyrightable.
[24] [1988] 3 All ER 949, 970 (appeal taken from Hong Kong).
[25] *Ibid.*, at 971, *per* Lord Oliver.
[26] *Ibid.*, at 972, *per* Lord Oliver.

exact reproductions of public domain works, albeit in a different medium".[27] There was no suggestion that they varied significantly from the underlying works. In consequence, the change of medium was immaterial, according to the judge.

6.1.3 Comment

The seriousness of the issues raised in *Bridgeman* caused the UK Museums Copyright Group, which assists museums with copyright matters, both to commission an in-depth report on the case and seek a written opinion from the leading copyright barrister, Jonathan Rayner James Q.C. (one of the authors of Copinger). According to the Group, Mr Rayner James had no doubt that UK copyright law protected photographs of works of art, citing him as follows:

> "[A]s a matter of principle, a photograph of an artistic work can qualify for copyright protection in English law, and that is irrespective of whether . . . the subject of the photographs is more obviously a three dimensional work, such as a sculpture, or is perceived as a two dimensional artistic work, such as a drawing or a painting . . ."[28]

Bridgeman is not of course binding on UK courts. Also it can be argued that the picture library images in question, by virtue of the careful photography and lighting involved in order to show artistic works to best effect (better probably than a gallery visitor would see), in no way compare to a mere photocopy or slavish copy. Nevertheless Judge Kaplan's careful review of the English authorities in his second decision, in particular the important Privy Council case of *Interlego* v. *Tyco* is of considerable interest. It is at least arguable that the antiquity of *Graves' Case* and the particular facts in issue (the owner of the copyright in the photographs and the engravings was the same person and they were the first and only photographs of these subjects) mean that this case is now less than persuasive especially in the light of the Privy Council in *Interlego* v. *Tyco*. The following comments of Lord Oliver in *Interlego* v. *Tyco* (cited in part by Judge Kaplan) about what the test of originality should be seem particulary relevant:

---

[27] 25 F Supp. 2d at 426. The judge noted that Lady Bridgeman, the plaintiff's principal, testified that the goal of the transparencies was to be as true to the original work as possible (*Bridgeman*, Dep. 15).

[28] See the Museums Copyright Group Press Release of December 1999. The author is grateful to Emma Williams of the Museums Copyright Group for this information.

"Originality in the context of literary copyright has been said in several well known cases to depend on the degree of skill, labour and judgement involved in preparing a compilation . . . the amount of skill, judgement or labour is likely to be decisive in the case of compilations. To apply that, however, as a universal test of originality in all copyright cases is not only unwarranted by the context in which the observations were made but palpably erroneous. Take the simplest case of artistic copyright, a painting or a photograph. It takes great skill, judgement and labour to produce a good copy by painting or to produce an enlarged photograph from a positive print, but no on would reasonably contend that the copy painting or enlargement was an 'original' artistic work in which the copier is entitled to claim copyright. Skill, labour or judgement merely in the process of copying cannot confer originality."[29]

It is therefore submitted that following *Bridgeman* there is some doubt about the copyright protection of photographs which are themselves simply copies of other artistic works. *Graves' Case* may no longer be good law. Having said that, there are contrary arguments: these and a recent case in a similar area are considered below before reaching a final conclusion.

Bridgeman has recently been criticised by another leading copyright barrister, Kevin Garnett Q.C.[30] He sees the reasoning in the case as flawed. In particular he views Lord Oliver's speech in *Interlego* as clearly *obiter*, as not addressing the specific issue and furthermore as not taking into account *Graves' Case* or the House of Lords in the later case of *Walter v. Lane*.[31] In particular, it is clear that photographs are protected by copyright irrespective of their artistic quality and the skill of the photographer is often faithfully to reproduce what is in front of the camera—in many ways, according to Garnett, such a skill is analogous to the reporter who faithfully reproduces the spoken words of a speaker, as in *Walter v. Lane*. Mere photocopies are also different in kind from the photographs in *Bridgeman*: photocopying is a wholly mechanical process. Also although it is a copy of a painting, such a

---

[29] At 971.

[30] K. Garnett (also an author of Copinger), "Copyright in Photographs" [2000] *EIPR* 229.

[31] [1900] AC 539. This case concerned literary copyright: the House of Lords held that an independent reporter's copyright subsisted in the verbatim report of a public speech. The status of this case was, according to Garnett, recently confirmed by Browne-Wilkinson V-C in *Express Newspapers plc v. News (UK) Ltd* [1990] 1 WLR 1320: "[a]s a result of [*Walter v. Lane*] it was established that the mere reporting of the words of another gives rise to a reporter's copyright so long as skill and judgment have been employed in the composition of the report" (at 1325).

photograph is nevertheless different in character and quality from the painting and therefore is sufficiently different to secure copyright protection, although the photograph is derived from the painting.

Certainly a consideration of other authorities and the context of *Interlego* can be used to challenge *Bridgeman*—another case helpful to Garnett, which he does not cite, is *Martin* v. *Polyplas*[32] which afforded copyright protection to a coin engraved in three dimensions from a drawing.[33]

Finally a case similar to, but by no means the same as, *Bridgeman, Antiquesportfolio* v. *Fitch*,[34] was recently heard by the High Court in London in an application for summary judgment. This case concerned *inter alia* whether copyright could subsist in photographs of antiques (i.e. of three-dimensional items as opposed to the photographs of paintings considered in *Bridgeman*). The authorities discussed earlier (namely *Bridgeman,* Copinger, and Laddie (second edition) as well as the US text, *Nimmer on Copyright*,[35] but not *Graves' Case*) were all considered by Neuberger J. He was of the view that the positioning of the three-dimensional object in question (unless it was a sphere), the angle at which it was taken, the lighting and focus, and similar matters could all be matters of aesthetic or even commercial judgement, albeit at a very basic level. In particular in this case the photographs appeared to have been taken with a view to showing particular aspects and features of the items such as their colour, the glaze (in the case of pottery) and other details. He also thought a relevant factor might be that the photographer had chosen particular items as either typical or especially fine examples of the artefact in question. Taking all these factors together he held that the photographs were protected by copyright.

Nevertheless the judge expressly did *not* decide whether copyright could consist in photographs of paintings—this was not a matter he needed to decide. However he did observe that, as was suggested in *Nimmer on Copyright,* such photographs could well be protected by copyright if the photographer could show he had used some degree of skill and care in taking the photograph—this would be sufficient to make them "original" for copyright purposes.

[32] [1969] NZLR 1046.
[33] See Cornish at 388. See also *Newton* v. *Cowie and Another* (1827) 4 Bing. 234, 130 ER 759, discussed above at n. 7 *supra*, which predates *Graves' Case*.
[34] *Antiquesportfolio.com plc* v. *Rodney Fitch and Co Ltd, The Times*, 21 July 2000.
[35] At 2.130.

In light of *Antiquesportfolio* it is submitted that in the UK the *Bridgeman* photographs would still be likely to benefit from copyright protection despite the uncertainties surrounding the application of *Graves' Case*. It is hard to see how in most cases a court could reasonably make a distinction between photographs of two- and three-dimensional items: the labour and skill in aspects of selection, focus, angle, shutter speed, lighting, etc. are common to both sorts of photograph. There may be more choice in how to photograph a three dimensional object in terms of aspect, positioning and background, but arguably sufficient skill and labour will be involved in photographing a picture as well.[36]

6.2 COPYRIGHT AND VISUAL SEARCH ENGINES: FAIR USE AND FAIR DEALING IN THE ON-LINE ENVIRONMENT[37]

In December 1999 a US District Court caused considerable surprise by holding that the use by an Internet "visual search engine" of others' copyright images was *prima facie* copyright infringement but was justified under the "fair use" doctrine. If upheld on appeal to the United States Court of Appeals for the Ninth Circuit it is argued that the case

[36] It is also interesting to note what Neuberger J said in the context of what copyright in a photograph *protects* (where there is infringement). In *Antiquesportfolio*, the infringing photographs (taken from *Millers Antiques Encyclopaedia* in which Reed Books claimed copyright), as well as being reproduced in various sizes on the claimant's website prepared by the defendants (which Neuberger J held to be copyright infringement), were also traced by the defendants to create logos, watermarks and business cards for the claimant. In the latter case Neuberger J considered Copinger (at 7–86) as representing the law on determining copyright infringement of photographs. In particular what copyright serves to protect is the author's work of origination: so a photograph can be infringed both by literal copying and where the defendant recreates the feeling and artistic character of the photograph where a substantial part of the photograph is thereby taken. The judge held that tracing the photographs did not amount to copyright infringement: neither were the feeling and artistic character of the photographs taken nor was there any substantial taking of the photographer's skill and labour: the focusing, camera angle, lighting etc. were not appropriated, the logos were not very detailed in any event and their shape was determined by the shape of the object in the photograph in question. However, whether a detailed drawing of a photograph of a nineteenth-century bureau used on a brochure cover infringed was left to trial, although the judge suspected it did infringe.

[37] See *Leslie A. Kelly v. Arriba Soft Corp* (United States District Court, Central District of Southern California, Southern Division, Case No. SA CV 99–560 GLT [JW]; Judge Gary L. Taylor, 15 December 1999). This section is a revised and expanded version of S. Stokes, "*Leslie A Kelly v. Arriba Soft Corp*: A View from the United Kingdom" [2000] 12 *EIPR* 599.

will raise significant issues for artists, photographers and others who allow their images to be used on the Internet.[38]

It is worth analysing the case and what the English courts may make of such an action.

6.2.1 Facts

Arriba (now known as ditto.com Inc ("Ditto")) operates a "visual search engine" on the Internet. Unlike other Internet search engines it retrieves images instead of text, and produces a list of reduced "thumbnail" pictures related to the search query.

During the period relevant to the case the search engine in question was known as the "Arriba Vista Image Searcher". By clicking on the desired "thumbnail" picture, the Arriba Vista user was able to view an "image attributes" window displaying the full-size version of the image displayed by opening a link to the originating website[39] (without any other part of the originating website being seen), a description of its dimensions and an address for the website from where it originated. By clicking on the address the user could link to the originating website for the image.[40]

The search engine operates by maintaining an indexed database of approximately two million thumbnail images. These thumbnails are obtained by the operation of Ditto's "crawler", a computer program that travels the web in search of images to be converted into thumbnails and added to the index. Ditto's employees then screen and rank the images and eliminate any which are inappropriate.

[38] On 24 July 2000 The American Society of Media Photographers, Inc., The Authors Guild, Inc., and the North American Nature Photography Association filed an *amicus curiae* brief in support of the plaintiff-appellant Kelly on the basis *inter alia* that the District Court's fair use analysis, if accepted, would seriously harm the legitimate copyright interests of freelance photographers and other authors of copyright works. It appears that other *amicus* briefs have also been filed and the case is to be heard by the Ninth Circuit Court of Appeals in 2001 (see netcopyrightlaw.com for updates on the position and Leslie A. Kelly's comments on the case).

[39] In other words the full-size image was not technically located on the defendant's website. According to the decision, it appears that images of the plaintiff's photographs were stored briefly in full on the defendant's computer (server) until the thumbnail is made—they are then deleted.

[40] Apparently as at December 1999 (the time of the decision) Ditto had modified its search engine so that when a ditto.com user clicks on a thumbnail, two windows open simultaneously. One window contains the full-size image; the other contains the originating web page in full.

The plaintiff was a photographer specialising in photographs of the California gold rush country and also in photographs related to the works of Laura Ingalls Wilder (of *Little House on the Prairie* fame). He publishes his photographs in books and on two websites, one of which provides a virtual tour of California's gold rush country and promotes his book on the subject, and the other markets corporate retreats in that area.

In January 1999 around 35 of the plaintiff's images were indexed by the Ditto crawler and put in the defendant's image database. As a result these images were made available in thumbnail form to users of the defendant's visual search engine.

The plaintiff objected and Ditto removed the images from its database, although due to some technical difficulties some reappeared on occasion. In the meantime the plaintiff sued the defendant for copyright infringement and also violation of the Digital Millennium Copyright Act (DMCA) by removing or altering the copyright management information associated with the plaintiff's images.

The hearing was one for summary judgment.

6.2.2 Decision

The judge had no difficulty in finding a *prima facie* case of copyright infringement: the defendant did not dispute the validity of the plaintiff's copyright or his ownership. Nor did it dispute it had reproduced and displayed the plaintiff's images in thumbnail form without authorisation.

So the issue was whether the infringement was justified on the basis of "fair use" under US copyright law. According to the judge:

> " 'Fair use' is a limitation on copyright owners' exclusive right 'to reproduce the copyrighted work in copies.' 17 U.S.C. § 106(1). It is codified at 17 U.S.C. § 107, which provides:
>
> Notwithstanding the provisions of sections 106 and 106A, the fair use of a copyrighted work, including such use by reproduction in copies or phonorecords or by any other means specified by that section, for purposes such as criticism, comment, news reporting, teaching (including multiple copies for classroom use), scholarship, or research, is not an infringement of copyright. In determining whether the use made of a work in any particular case is a fair use the factors to be considered shall include:

    (1) the purpose and character of the use, including whether such use is of a commercial nature or is for nonprofit educational purposes;

    (2) the nature of the copyrighted work;

    (3) the amount and substantiality of the portion used in relation to the copyrighted work as a whole; and

    (4) the effect of the use upon the potential market for or value of the copyrighted work.

The fact that a work is unpublished shall not itself bar a finding of fair use if such finding is made upon consideration of all the above factors.

Fair use is an affirmative defense, and defendants carry the burden of proof on the issue."[41]

The judge then went on to consider the four factors and reached a conclusion on each of the four factors as follows:

Purpose and Character of the Use

The court found the "transformative" nature of the use of the plaintiff's images very significant—the court cited the US Supreme Court decision in *Campbell* v. *Acuff-Rose Music*[42] which concerned an alleged parody of the song "Oh Pretty Woman": "the more transfomative the new work, the less will be the significance of other factors, like commercialism, that may weigh against a finding of fair use". The judge considered the defendant's use of the images was very different from the use for which the images were originally created. The plaintiff's works are artistic works used for illustrative purposes. The defendant's visual search engine and related thumbnail images are for a functional not an artistic, aesthetic purpose: to catalogue and improve access to images on the Internet.

Also although the use was commercial it was "somewhat more incidental and less exploitative than more traditional types of commercial use".[43]

So overall, despite the fact that the defendant's old (and then current) search engine allowed users to view and potentially download full-size images without necessarily viewing the rest of the originating web page detracted from this argument to an extent, the court found that the purpose and character of the defendant's use were on the whole significantly transformative and therefore the first factor weighed in favour of fair use.

[41] At 2–3.
[42] 510 US 569, 579 (1994).
[43] At 3.

Nature of the Copyright Work

The judge cited *Campbell* to the effect "that some works are closer to the core of intended copyright protection than others, with the consequence that fair use is more difficult to establish when the former works are copied'.[44] In the view of the court artistic works like the plaintiff's photographs are part of that core. The court therefore found the second factor weighed against fair use.

Amount and Substantiality of the Portion Used

According to the judge the analysis of this factor on the basis of *Campbell* focuses on "the persuasiveness of a [copier's] justification for the particular copying done, and the enquiry will harken back to the first of the statutory factors, for . . . the extent of permissible copying varies with the purpose and character of the use".[45]

In the view of the court, if only the thumbnail index were at issue, the defendant's copying would be likely to be reasonable in the light of its purposes—the judge seemed to accept the defendant's arguments that for a visual search engine to work such reduced size and resolution, thumbnail, images were necessary: it was noted that the thumbnail images could not be enlarged into useful images. The image attributes page (displaying the full-size image separated from its originating web page), however, was more problematic as it was in the court's view remotely related to the purposes of the search engine.

The court therefore found the third factor weighed slightly against fair use.

Effect of the Use on the Potential Market or Value of the Copyrighted Work

According to the judge the fourth factor inquiry, following *Campbell* again, "examines the direct impact of the Defendant's use and also considers 'whether unrestricted and widespread conduct of the sort engaged in by the defendant . . . would result in a substantially adverse impact on the potential market for the original' ".[46]

---

[44] At 586.
[45] At 586–7.
[46] *Campbell* n. 42 *supra* at 590.

The relevant market according to the judge was the plaintiff's websites as a whole. The photographs were used to promote the products sold by the plaintiff's websites (including the plaintiff's books and corporate tour packages) and to draw users to view the additional advertisements posted on those websites. According to the judge "the fourth factor addresses not just the potential market for a particular photo, but also its 'value'. The value of Plaintiff's photographs to Plaintiff could potentially be adversely affected if their promotional purposes are undermined."[47]

The defendant argued that there was no likely negative impact as its search engine did not compete with the plaintiff's websites and in fact would actually *increase* the number of users finding their way to those sites.

The plaintiff argued that the market for his various products had been harmed. The plaintiff argued that the defendant's conduct allowed users improperly to copy and use the plaintiff's images from the defendant's site. The search engine also enabled users to "deep link" directly to the pages containing retrieved images, and thereby bypass the "front page" of the originating website. Thus users would be less likely to view all of the advertisements on the websites or view the website's entire promotional message. But the judge found the plaintiff had shown no evidence of any harm or adverse impact.

So in the absence of any evidence about traffic to the plaintiff's websites or effect on the plaintiff's businesses, the court could not find any market harm to the plaintiff. The court found that the defendant met its burden of proof by offering evidence tending to show a lack of market harm, and the plaintiff had not been able to refute that evidence. The court therefore found the fourth factor weighed in favour of fair use.

Conclusion

Fair Use

The court therefore found two of the four factors weighed in favour of fair use, and two weighed against it.

Decisive here was the first factor. The defendant never held the plaintiff's work out as its own, or even engaged in conduct specifically directed at the plaintiff's work. According to the judge "[the] Plaintiff's

---

[47] *Leslie A Kelly* v. *Arriba Soft Corp.* at 5.

images were swept up along with two million others available on the Internet, as part of [the] Defendant's efforts to provide its users with a better way to find images on the Internet. [The] Defendant's purposes were and are inherently transformative, even if its realisation of those purposes was at times imperfect.[48] Where, as here, a new use and new technology are evolving, the broad transformative purpose of the use weighs more heavily than the inevitable flaws in its early stages of development."[49]

Having weighed all of the fair use factors together the court found that the defendant's conduct constituted fair use of the plaintiff's images.

The Digital Millennium Copyright Act

The plaintiff raised an interesting argument that the defendant had violated section 1202(b) of this Act[50] by displaying thumbnails of the plaintiff's images without displaying the corresponding copyright management information consisting of a standard copyright notice in the surrounding text. This argument was given short shrift by the judge and appears not to be the subject of the appeal.

6.2.3 Comment

This case raises a whole host of issues about the protection of copyright on the Internet and exemplifies the thorny issues courts worldwide are now tackling. On the one hand it seems desirable that visual search engines can be used, to the benefit of all Internet users. Although a US case, it highlights the current debate in Europe over the so-called Digital Copyright Directive[51] about the balance struck between the

---

[48] For example, the ability to display full images of the Plaintiff's photographs without the other aspects of the originating website.

[49] *Leslie A Kelly* v. *Arriba Soft Corp.* at 5.

[50] S. 1202(b) states:
No person shall, without the authority of the copyright owner or the law:
(1) intentionally remove or alter any copyright management information,
. . .
(3) distribute . . . copies of works . . . knowing that copyright management information has been removed or altered without authority of the copyright owner or the law, knowing, or, with respect to civil remedies under section 1203, having reasonable grounds to know, that it will induce, enable, facilitate, or conceal an infringement of any right under [federal copyright law].

[51] Directive on Copyright and Related Rights in the Information Society—see Chaps. 5 and 9

rights of copyright owners and others in the context of the effective functioning of the Internet. Certainly the case highlights the current US approach to "fair use" which focuses on the transformative character, if any, of the defendant's work.[52]

But of course the extension of the fair use doctrine in this case clearly raises issues for artists, photographers, etc. The appeal is awaited with much interest. In the closing words of the *amicus curiae* brief:

> "This court's decision . . . will affect copyright rights for generations to come. The guise of fair use must not be used to permit the taking of millions of entire copyrighted works (not just portions of them) for commercial purposes in competition with the owners of those works, just because technology makes it easy and convenient to do so. Such an approach conflicts with the fundamental purposes of copyright and the creative incentives it seeks to foster."[53]

6.2.4 A View from the UK

It is interesting to speculate what the outcome might have been if the case had involved infringement in the UK of photographs by a living British photographer. The analysis that follows focuses on copyright and moral rights protection for the photographer; database rights aspects (of primary relevance to the person constructing a search engine database or a web site hosting the images) are not therefore considered.

Would there be Prima Facie *Infringement of Copyright?*

On the facts clearly yes: copying of all or any substantial part of a copyright work is "primary" infringement of copyright in the work[54] and copying includes for these purposes both "storing the work in any medium by electronic means"[55] and also making copies "which are transient or are incidental to some other use of the work".[56]

---

[52] For a review of recent US fair use cases see Sterling at 364–9.
[53] Conclusion, at 20.
[54] S.16, CDPA. See also the recent *Antiquesportfolio* case discussed in section 6.1 above: the judge in that case was clearly of the view that even small-scale reproduction by digital means of entire photographs on a website was copyright infringement.
[55] S.17(2), CDPA.
[56] S.17(6), CDPA.

Would there be a Defence Analogous to that of "Fair Use"?

It appears not. The fair dealing defences in English law are much more narrowly drawn than the US "fair use" doctrine and include only fair dealing in the context of research and private study,[57] and for criticism, review and news reporting.[58] These do not appear particularly relevant here.[59] Nor does it appear that an English court would be swayed by any argument that the public interest in this case would demand that the copying be permitted: this appears ruled out following the recent Court of Appeal decision in *Hyde Park Residence* v. *David Yelland*.[60]

Moral Rights Aspects

Under UK law, as discussed in Chapter 4 "authors" such as photographers benefit from moral rights protection in addition to copyright. An English court in these circumstances would therefore also have to entertain any claim by the photographer that his "moral rights" had been infringed, if, for example, (having asserted this right) he was not identified in connection with the commercial publication of his works (which ought to include web publishing[61]). Of more interest in this case is whether the production of the thumbnail image could be said to infringe the photographer's moral right not to have his work subjected to derogatory treatment.[62] Treatment includes any alteration or adaptation of the work, and such treatment is derogatory "if it amounts to distortion or mutilation of the work or is otherwise prejudicial to the honour or reputation of the author".[63] It might therefore be argued

---

[57] S.29, CDPA—see section 3.2.10 of Chap. 3 above.

[58] S.30, CDPA.

[59] The only such defence potentially relevant seems that of fair dealing for purposes of research or private study—it is submitted that what is being carried out here is not "research or private study" within their ordinary meanings: of course the defendant may argue that the whole purpose behind its activities is to permit research (i.e. web searching). But even if accepted this argument appears to probably fall foul of s.29(3)(b), CDPA ("copying by a person other than the researcher . . . is not fair dealing if . . . The person doing the copying knows or has reason to believe that it will result in copies of substantially the same material being provided to more than one person at substantially the same time and for substantially the same purpose.") Also the pre CDPA cases of *Stillitoe* v. *McGraw-Hill Book Co.* [1983] FSR 545 and *University of London Press Ltd* v. *University Tutorial Press Ltd* [1916] 2 Ch. 601 held that facilitating private study or research *for others* did not fall within the similar exemptions in the earlier copyright Acts.

[60] [2000] *Ent LR* N–77, [1999] RPC 655, [2000] 3 WLR 215.

[61] S.77, CDPA

[62] S.80, CDPA.

[63] S.80(2)(b), CDPA.

that a thumbnail image is a clear distortion of the work, although this may be difficult to sustain in the light of the limited case law in this area.[64]

However the defendant might in any event seek to raise the defence that moral rights do not apply as the database and search results produced by the search engine are "a collective work of reference".[65] This however appears to stretch such a definition beyond its context in the CDPA of "encyclopaedia, dictionary, yearbook or other collective work of reference".

Implied Licence

As discussed in Chapter 5, it can be argued that both express and implied copyright licences are central to the effective functioning of the Internet. Could it therefore be argued under UK law that, by making their images available on the Internet, photographers and other creators of images have granted implied licenses to enable the copying and cataloguing of their works where necessary to search the Internet?

There is a debate about the circumstances in which such a copyright licence will be implied. The classic approach, based on contract cases dealing with the implication of terms into contracts, is to be cautious about the existence and scope of any such licence.[66] In particular as there is unlikely to be a contract between the photographer and search engine operator and the photographer will probably have included an on-screen licence on his website restricting copying without his consent in any event, it is perhaps difficult to see why such a licence would be

---

[64] As discussed in Chap. 4. For example, in *Tidy* v. *Trustees of the Natural History Museum* (1995) 39 IPR 501 the scaling down of the plaintiff's cartoons of dinosaurs was held to be a "treatment" of the work but the matter of whether this was "derogatory" was left until full trial. See also *Pasterfield* v. *Denham and another* [1999] FSR 168: "what the plaintiff must establish is that the treatment accorded to his work is either a distortion or mutilation that prejudices his honour or reputation as an artist. It is not sufficient that the author is aggrieved by what has occurred" (*per* HH Judge Overend).

[65] S.79(5) and 81(4) of the CDPA.

[66] So, for example, a term will be implied if it is necessary to give business efficacy to the contract or it satisfies the "officious bystander" test (in practice these may well be the same tests—see *per* Steyn LJ in *Watts* v. *Lord Aldington* [1999] LTR 578 at 596–7), and not merely because it is reasonable; also the term to be implied must be the minimum necessary in the circumstances and the term must be clear (see in the context of copyright *Ray* v. *Classic FM plc* [1998] FSR 622, *Antiquesportfolio.com plc* v. *Rodney Fitch and Co Ltd*, *The Times*, 21 July 2000, and generally Copinger 5–208 to 5–216). It is also possible for a licence to be implied from conduct, trade practice or custom, and by estoppel and acquiescence.

implied from the circumstances. Nevertheless it has been argued that the operation of search engines may fall within either a public interest defence to copyright infringement or the more general legal doctrine of "non-derogation from grant".[67] But this must be doubted, given the Court of Appeal's rejection of a broad public-interest defence in *Hyde Park Residence Ltd* v. *Yelland*[68] and the very limited scope of the "non-derogation from grant" principle.[69] So, absent any further judicial clarification of the matter, the existence and scope of any implied licence in such circumstances remain unclear.

European Developments

The recently adopted Electronic Commerce Directive[70] contains no exceptions to copyright infringement that appear relevant in this case: the "mere conduit", "caching" and "hosting" exceptions from liability do not appear to be relevant.[71] Nor does the so-called Digital Copyright Directive[72] provide any clear guidance on this area.[73] So an English court, it is submitted, would be likely to decide *Arriba* rather differently.

6.3 MODERN ART AND COPYRIGHT[74]

The copyright protection afforded to a variety of modern and contemporary art is a matter of some debate. Often such works either strain to fall within any category of "artistic work" under the CDPA or, even if

---

[67] By Prof. H.L MacQueen, "Copyright and the Internet" in Edwards and Waelde chap. 9 at 208–10. He cites the first instance formulation of the public interest defence by Jacob J in *Hyde Park Residence* v. *Yelland* [1999] RPC 655 and in *Mars UK Ltd* v. *Teknowledge Ltd* [2000] FSR 138; he also cites the non-derogation from grant argument acknowledged by Jacob J in *Mars* and deriving from *British Leyland* v. *Armstrong* [1986] AC 577 and the later more restrictive Privy Council case *Canon Kabushiki Kaisha* v. *Green Cartridge Co (Hong Kong) Ltd* [1997] AC 728.

[68] [1999] RPC 655.

[69] In *Canon* Lord Hoffmann referred to the doctrine as "exceptional", and any extension of the doctrine beyond the facts in *British Leyland* should be treated with some caution—it is in reality a defence based on "public policy" (at 737–40).

[70] Directive 2000/31 on legal aspects of electronic commerce [2000] OJ L178/1.

[71] See Arts. 12–15 [2000] OJ L178/1.

[72] See Chap. 5.

[73] See Chaps. 5 and 9.

[74] For a discussion of the position internationally see Bently and Sherman at 248–9 and 254–7.

they appear to fall within a specific category, their protection is uncertain as they may not be "original".

It is worth considering what copyright protection UK law might give various twentieth-century art forms, assuming that the artist is either alive or died less than 70 years ago.

6.3.1 Ready-mades, *Objets Trouvés* and *Assemblage*[75]

In this art form the artist elevates ordinary objects to the status of art, challenging accepted ideas about what art is. Marcel Duchamp's exhibition of a bicycle wheel attached to a stool and signed by the artist, which was exhibited as art in a gallery in 1913, represents the first so-called "ready-made". The everyday, "found object" or "*objet trouvé*", used as the ready-made may also be used as part of an *assemblage* (see below).

Ready-mades would have to fall within the definition of "sculpture" under the CDPA in order to be protected by copyright as "artistic works". As discussed in Chapter 3, UK law defines sculpture very broadly. But even if considered to be "sculpture", are such works original? Here the originality consists in taking the found object out of its usual setting and exhibiting it in an artistic context. Bently and Sherman consider that under UK law if the object was created with an artistic purpose in mind then the courts are more likely to protect the work.[76]

In *Creation Records Ltd. and others* v. *News Group Newspapers Ltd.*[77] it was argued by counsel for the plaintiffs that, along with other contemporary art works, Carl Andre's famous brick "sculpture"[78] ought to benefit from copyright protection. Whilst this point was not developed further by the judge, the "permanence" of such works was distinguished from the transitory assembly of found objects the subject

---

[75] The definitions of these terms are derived from the Glossary in *The 20th-Century Art Book* (Phaidon Press, London, 1996).

[76] Bently & Sherman at 267; as discussed in Chap. 3, whilst UK law protects sculptures irrespective of artistic quality, it may also be that the courts would be minded in such circumstances to follow the test for artistic quality in the context of works of artistic craftsmanship when considering ready mades: the intention of the artist/craftsman is crucial (see *Merlet* v. *Mothercare* [1986] RPC 129).

[77] 16 Tr. L 544, *The Times*, 29 April 1997, discussed in Chap. 3.

[78] *Equivalent VIII* (1966), controversially acquired and displayed by the Tate Gallery.

matter of this case—the latter did not qualify for protection either as a sculpture or as a collage. In any event recent cases discussed in Chapter 3 (in particular *Metix* v. *Maughan*) suggest the courts are more willing to look at the intention and status (as "artist") of the creator when deciding to class a work as a "sculpture".

Where a number of found objects are brought together to form a work on canvas, such as Arman's "Crusaders", in which stacks of paint brushes are assembled and stuck together to form the work, then an *"assemblage"* is created. It is suggested that where the *assemblage* consists of items affixed to canvas then, following the definition of collage put forward by Lloyd J in *Creation Records*, "[i]n my view a collage does indeed involve as an essential element the sticking of two or more things together" such works are likely to be protected as collages under UK law.

6.3.2 Appropriation Art[79]

Here the artist expressly sets out to "borrow" images from other sources and include or assimilate them into his or her own work. Whilst this practice can be traced to Dadaism, Surrealism and Pop Art,[80] "appropriation art" is rooted in postmodernism.[81] It can therefore be debated whether appropriation art is sufficiently original, as here the

---

[79] See B. Sherman, "Appropriating the Postmodern: Copyright and the Challenge of the New" (1995) 4 *Social & Legal Studies* 31 for a discussion of this area and how real the perceived challenges of appropriation art to copyright law actually are. For example L.A. Greenberg, in her discussion of, among other things, *Rogers* v. *Koons* ("The Art of Appropriation: Puppies, Piracy and Postmodernism" (1992) 11 *Cardozo Arts and Entertainment Law Journal* 1), considers appropriation art represents "the most radical challenge to copyright laws to date" (at 33). Sherman lists examples of appropriation art as including Mike Bildo's full-size copies of paintings by Cézanne, Matisse, Pollock, Lichtenstein and Picasso (to which Bildo attaches his signature and renames them) and Marcel Duchamp's addition of a moustache to a copy of the Mona Lisa (at 32). Koons' appropriation of the "String of Puppies" photograph, the subject of *Rogers* v. *Koons*, discussed below, is another example.

[80] Sherman n. 79 *supra* at 32 (citing A. Bonnett, "Art, Ideology and Everyday Space: Subversive Tendencies from Dada to Postmodernism" (1992) 10 *Society and Space* 69).

[81] "Reappropriating existing representations that are effective precisely because they are loaded with pre-existing meaning and putting them into new and ironic contexts is a typical form of postmodern . . . critique" (Linda Hutcheon, commenting on postmodern photography including the work of Cindy Sherman, Sherrie Levine and Martha Rosler, in her *The Politics of Postmodernism* (Routledge, London 1989) at 44). See also Sherman n. 79 *supra*: "[b]y placing a well-known object such as the American flag, a painting by Picasso or an advertising logo in a new context, the appropriation artist aims to denaturalize it and thus to provide the borrowed object with a new meaning or vocabulary" (at 32).

expressive form (as opposed to merely the idea) of the original work is copied. So issues arise similar to those already considered in the discussion of the *Bridgeman* case earlier in this chapter. In addition the appropriation artist can herself be open to a complaint of plagiarism, of copyright infringement, even if a defence of "parody" is raised. This is considered further below.

It is worthwhile citing the Privy Council in *Interlego* v. *Tyco* again for what is necessary to afford copyright protection to a copy of a work: "[t]here must in addition be some element of material alteration or embellishment which suffices to make the totality of the work an original work".[82] In the context of artistic works such alteration or embellishment must be "visually significant".[83] It is not enough that what is done is to convey "information"[84]—so although in the process of appropriation the meaning of the work is changed by placing it in a new context, its visual significance may well not be. Hence it may not benefit from copyright protection.[85]

6.3.3 Minimalist Art

"Minimalist art is [art] pared down to its essentials."[86] Do such works embody sufficient effort to be protected by copyright? UK law has afforded copyright protection to a variety of simple drawings, including a hand for a voting card,[87] as discussed in Chapter 3, so it is submitted that copyright protection ought not to be a problem for most minimalist paintings and drawings. However the scope of protection will be very limited.

Indeed in a recent decision, Rimer J, when considering the copyright protection in engineering manufacturing drawings for a mobile blast-cleaning machine, concluded that an argument that the skill and effort in producing the drawing in question were too trivial to justify a claim of

---

[82] *Per* Lord Oliver in *Interlego AG* v. *Tyco Industries Inc and others* [1988] 3 All ER 949 at 972.

[83] See Chap. 3.

[84] This is properly the subject of literary works in copyright law (see *Exxon* v. *Exxon Insurance* [1982] RPC 69). See Sherman n. 79 *supra*, at 49 n.22.

[85] See *ibid.*, 38–40. See also *per* Lord Oliver in *Interlego AG* v. *Tyco Industries Inc and others* [1988] 3 All ER 949: "essentially artistic copyright is concerned with the visual image" (at 972).

[86] *20th-Century Art Book*, Glossary (see n.75 *supra*).

[87] *Kenrick* v. *Lawrence* (1890) 25 QBD 93.

originality was one easy to advance but which he was not willing to accept. The judge quoted from the essay entitled "Prose and Dr Tillotson" by Somerset Maugham, in which Maugham talked about an unforgettable and haunting picture by Mondrian consisting of some black lines and a red one on a white background and suggested that any viewer might think he could easily produce the work himself as it looked so simple. Maugham ended his essay by challenging the reader to try.[88]

Certainly the UK position is to be distinguished from that in the USA where, for example, the Register of Copyright refused to register a logo for "New York Arrows" comprising four angled lines forming an arrow and the word arrow in cursive script.[89]

6.3.4 Modern Art and Advertising—Gillian Wearing, Mehdi Norowzian and Beyond

Some of the most creative British artists of recent times have abandoned or radically modified the use of traditional artistic media. Gillian Wearing, winner of the 1997 Turner Prize, is one of the best known of the so-called YBAs (Young British Artists). A number of her works have also provided inspiration for advertising campaigns. For example, "Signs" (1993), a photographic work, where people on the street were asked by the artist to write down what they were feeling at the time on a sign they would then hold up in front of the camera (a well-known one being of a young businessman with a sign reading "I'm Desperate") apparently inspired a car advertisement. The advertisement showed a security guard, a harassed mother and others holding up signs that stated what they were supposed to be feeling ("Sensitive" in the case of the security guard, "Sex Chocolate Sex Chocolate" in the case of the mother). "2 into 1", where the voices of mother and sons were transposed, was emulated in a computer game advertisement.

The artist protested about the taking of her ideas, considering it to be "theft", especially as there was no reference to her work.[90] But no court proceedings ensued (or at least have been reported).

---

[88] *SPE International Ltd* v. *Professional Preparation Contractors (UK) Ltd* [2000] EIPR N–19; transcript at page 20.

[89] *John Mullere & Co* v. *New York Arrows Soccer Team* 802 F 2d 989 (8th Cir 1986), discussed in Bently & Sherman at 257.

[90] For background on Gillian Wearing and the works of art discussed see "Daring Wearing" by Miranda Sawyer (an interview with the artist), *The Observer Magazine*, 3 September 2000.

A recent copyright case, *Norowzian* v. *Arks Limited & others (No.2)*[91] which went as far as the Court of Appeal, has expressly considered the copyright protection afforded to contemporary artistic works. This is reviewed below.

Facts in *Norowzian* v. *Arks*

The plaintiff, Mr Norowzian, was a film director and also a successful director of advertising films. In 1992 he directed a short film, *Joy*, which was made to demonstrate his creativity to potential advertising clients, rather than being an express piece of advertising. *Joy* was a very short film with no dialogue, produced on a very low budget and shot on the flat roof-top of a London building. The set was simply a canvas sheet draped over an existing structure on the roof where the filming took place. The cast was one man, casually dressed, who performed a strange dance to music.

According to the judge at first instance (Rattee J) the particularly striking feature of the visual impact of the film was the result of the filming and editing techniques employed by Mr Norowzian: the filming was carried out with a camera in a fixed or "locked off" position, and the editing made extensive use of a process called "jump cutting". As defined by Rattee J "jump cutting" "is a film editing process whereby the editor excises pieces of the original film within a sequence of movements by the actor, with the result that on the edited version of the film he appears to have performed successively, without an interval, two movements that could not have immediately succeeded each other".[92] The result was a film containing apparent sudden changes of position by the actor/dancer which could never have been performed as successive movements in reality. In the trial this was referred to as giving the film a "surreal effect".[93]

According to Mr Norowzian *Joy* tells the story of the development of the emotions of the sole character from diffidence to exuberant joy, portrayed by a development of his movements from tentative to increasingly broad and confident. Rattee J was of the view that there was no doubt that it was a striking example of a talented film director's art.

In 1994 a filmed advertisement for Guinness stout was shown in cinemas and on television in Eire and Northern Ireland and later (as a

---

91 [1998] FSR 394, [1999] FSR 79 (Rattee J), [2000] FSR 363 (CA).
92 At 81 (FSR).
93 *Ibid.*

remake authorised by Guinness) in England and Wales. Called *Anticipation*, it portrays a man who waits for his pint of Guinness to settle by carrying out a series of dancing movements to music with no dialogue. There were two characters (drinker and barman), and a similar jump-cutting technique to that used in *Joy* was applied to the film with a similar result: the dancing man appeared to indulge in a series of jerky movements that could not be achieved by a dancer in reality.[94] The makers of *Anticipation* had seen *Joy* (indeed Mr Norowzian was asked to produce a similar commercial for Guinness but declined— Guinness' advertising agents then went off to produce a commercial with an atmosphere broadly similar to that in *Joy* but with a different storyboard), as had the actor who played the drinker.

Following letters before action sent in 1994, 1995 and 1996, in 1997 the plaintiff commenced proceedings for copyright infringement and passing-off against the defendant advertising agency for Guinness (Arks) and its client Guinness Brewing Worldwide Ltd, the second defendant, together with the third defendant, Guinness plc, the holding company of the second defendant. The case was the subject of three judgments.

Interlocutory Judgment (Application to Strike Out Part of the Defence)—before Mr A.G. Steinfeld, QC Sitting as a Deputy Judge of the High Court, 17 December 1997[95]

The plaintiff claimed copyright in the dramatic work recorded by the film, that the making of the film and its subsequent public display were torts committed by the defendants based on passing off, and also that film copyright was infringed by a copy being made of his film. At an early stage in the proceedings there was an application to strike out the claim for copyright infringement of film copyright.

The plaintiff claimed that the defendant's film was purposely made so as to resemble the plaintiff's film and that it reproduced the essential features of the plaintiff's film. Copyright infringement was claimed on the basis that the making of the defendant's film was "copying" of the plaintiff's film within the meaning of sections 16(1)(a) and 17(1) of the CDPA.

The defendants argued that for there to be copyright infringement of the plaintiff's copyright in his film, either an exact copy of the film itself

---

[94] *Ibid.*
[95] [1998] FSR 394.

or of a substantial part of it had to be made, or at any event there had to be incorporated within the allegedly infringing copy at least some material which was an exact copy of the plaintiff's film.

The issue was whether there could be "copying" of a film under section 17(1) of the CDPA without making an exact copy of it or any part of it, but merely by making a close imitation of it. There was no prior English authority on the point, although the judge found support for his reasoning in two Australian cases.[96] He found that there was no "copying" of the plaintiff's film in the sense of infringement of the film copyright for the following reasons.

The CDPA defines a film as "a recording on any medium from which a moving image may by any means be produced".[97] As discussed earlier in this book, "films" are one of the descriptions of "work" in which copyright can subsist under section 1(1)(b) of the CDPA. However the "work" protected in this case is not the ideas or themes or action of the film: in film copyright law, unlike literary, musical, dramatic or artistic copyright, there is no underlying work protected—all that is protected is the film *per se*, i.e. the *recording*. So although the CDPA restricts the copying of films, what is restricted is the copying of the actual recording—i.e. frames from the plaintiff's film have to be mechanically copied, for example, by a photographic process or copying onto compact disc or video, etc.

This is in distinction, say, from literary copyright, where what is protected is the work in question—so copying a book which embodies a work can infringe copyright in the work whether the book is mechanically copied (for example, photocopied) or dictated or producing a colourable imitation of it.

In short, the judge was firmly of the view that there cannot be copyright infringement of the copyright in a film "unless there has been a copying of the whole or a part of the film itself in the sense of a copying of the whole or a part of the particular recording of that film".[98] In this case the film had been remade and no frame of the original film was included in the reshooting.

---

[96] *CBS Records Australia Ltd* v. *Telmark Teleproducts (Aust.) Pty Ltd* (1987) 9 IPR 440 and *Telmak Teleproducts Australia Pty Ltd* v. *Bond International Pty Ltd* (1986) 5 IPR 203 and (1986) 6 IPR 97.

[97] S.5(B)1.

[98] [1998] FSR 394 at 400.

Judgement of Mr Justice Rattee 17 July 1998[99]

At trial the judge considered only whether *Anticipation* infringed the plaintiff's copyright in the dramatic work recorded by his film *Joy*. The claim of passing off was abandoned during the trial. It was common ground at trial that the only description of copyright work relevant to the case was a dramatic work, and that the plaintiff was entitled to no copyright under the CDPA in respect of *Joy* unless it was, or was a recording of, a dramatic work under the CDPA. Section 3(1) of the CDPA provides that a dramatic work includes a work of dance or mime. Furthermore, section 3(2) of the CDPA provides that a dramatic work must be recorded in writing or otherwise for copyright to subsist in it. The plaintiff argued that *Joy* was clearly a work of dance and mime recorded on film.

Rattee J was of the view that what was recorded in *Joy* was not a dramatic work: according to the judge a work of dance or mime had to be, or be capable of being, physically performed. This was not the case here due to the jump-cutting technique used by the plaintiff to make the film.[100] He was also of the opinion that a film *per se* could not be a dramatic work under the CDPA. So the plaintiff's claim was defeated. Nevertheless in case he was wrong, the judge expressed an *obiter* opinion that even if *Joy* had been a dramatic work it would not have been infringed by *anticipation*. Although similar techniques were used to make it derived from the plaintiff's film, there was no reproduction of a substantial part of the subject matter of *Joy*. *Joy* depicted a character growing in self-awarenesss, whilst *Anticipation* showed a man waiting impatiently for his beer to settle.

Interestingly Rattee J dismissed the argument of Mr Norowzian's counsel that the judge's conclusion that *Joy* was not a work entitled to protection under the CDPA would leave a serious lacuna in the protection of works of originality under the CDPA. Surely Mr Norowzian deserves protection for the admitted originality of his film as a manifestation of the film maker's art? A principle behind the CDPA was to protect work of originality from copying. But the judge was reluctant

---

[99] [1999] FSR 79.
[100] The only authority cited by the judge for this was Lord Bridge in *Green* v. *Broadcasting Corporation of New Zealand* [1989] RPC 700 at 702: "it seems to their Lordships that a dramatic work must have sufficient unity to be capable of performance".

to fill the resulting lacuna "by giving a forced construction to the meaning of the term 'dramatic work' as used in the [CDPA]".

Also when performing his assessment of the similarity of the two films in the context of assessing copying the judge was content to rely on his own judgment rather than any expert—"in my judgement, the expenditure of time and money on expert evidence on this sort of question is to be deprecated". The judgment of Rattee J received critical comment at the time. In particular Ian Jeffrey and Dominic Farnsworth argued that the judge's decision was not a satisfactory response to the problems of principle raised. In their view the concept of a dramatic work in UK law should be interpreted or if necessary extended "to give reasonable protection to originally devised and sufficiently developed sequences of events which are capable of conveying narrative meaning to an audience".[101] Indeed they saw an expanded definition of "dramatic work" as giving protection to artists whose works did not easily fall within the category of "artistic works" under the CDPA. One example they cited was Cornelia Parker and in particular her and Tilda Swinton's work, "The Maybe", of 1997 in which the actress Tilda Swinton lay in a glass case in the Serpentine Gallery for hours at a time, apparently sleeping.

In any event the matter was reconsidered in the Court of Appeal.

Court of Appeal Judgment of 4 November 1999[102]

In giving judgment both Nourse LJ and Buxton LJ found that a film could of itself be a dramatic work under the CDPA. This point was not advanced to any extent in the High Court. The expression "dramatic work", according to Nourse LJ as a matter of construction, had to be given its natural and ordinary meaning. According to the judge a dramatic work "is a work of action, with or without words or music, which is capable of being performed before an audience".[103] A film was often, although not always, a work of action and it was capable of being performed before an audience. Hence it could be a "dramatic work". But it need not also be a recording of a dramatic work (which *Joy,* like many cartoon films, was not).

---

[101] "No Joy in Anticipation" [1998] *EIPR* 474 at 477.
[102] *Norowzian* v. *Arks Ltd and Others (No.2)* [2000] FSR 363, Nourse, Brooke and Buxton LJJ.
[103] At 367.

Buxton LJ agreed, relying on Article 14*bis* of the Berne Convention to the effect that "dramatic works" also include not only drama in any traditional or normal sense but also cinematography.

Having found *Joy* to be protected by copyright as a dramatic work, the court then went on to consider whether *Anticipation* copied all or a substantial part of *Joy*. Counsel for Mr Norowzian had argued that *Joy* derived its original dramatic impact from a number of factors including the filming and editing techniques used. These, he argued, were part of the skill, labour and judgement which Mr Norowzian applied to making *Joy* and, combined with the other similarities, their combined effect was to demonstrate that *Anticipation* borrowed much of its dramatic impact from *Joy*. He therefore submitted that *Anticipation* reproduced a substantial part of the dramatic content of *Joy*, and therefore there was copyright infringement.[104]

The court rejected these arguments and held that copyright was not infringed. Nourse LJ's reasoning is particularly relevant to the protection of art works by copyright:

"As [Rattee J] recognised, the highest that can be put in favour of [Mr Norowzian] is that there is a striking similarity between the filming and editing styles and techniques used by the respective directors of the two films. But no copyright subsists in mere style or technique. [Counsel for the defendant Arks Ltd] instanced the technique of pointillism, which was originated by the neo-impressionists Seurat and Signac. That was a telling example. If, on seeing La Baignade, Asnières at the Salon des Artistes Indépendents in 1884, another artist had used precisely the same technique in painting a scene in Provence, Seurat would have been unable, by the canons of English copyright law, to maintain an action against him. Other examples of original artistic styles or techniques whose imitation in the production of an entirely different subject matter would not found such an action might be the 'sprung rhythm' of Gerard Manley Hopkins' verse or the thematic build-up of Sibelius's second symphony. So here, the subject matter of the two films being, as [Rattee J] said, very different one from the other, the similarities of style and technique are insufficient to give [Mr Norowzian] a cause of action against the defendants."

According to Buxton LJ the essence and originality of *Joy* rested in its subject matter: a representation in stylised form of a young man hesitating with tension when coming amongst a group of unknown people

---

[104] As discussed in H. Porter, "A 'Dramatic Work' Includes . . . a Film" [2000] *Ent. LR* 50 at 52. For another view of the CA decision see J. Hughes and M. Parry, "An Unsettling Feeling: a Second View of the *Norowzian* Decision" [2000] *Ent. LR* 56.

but gradually gaining self-confidence. That essence and originality were not reproduced at all in *Anticipation*.[105]

6.3.5 The Limits of Appropriation—"The Loves of Shepherds 2000"[106]

The controversy late in 2000 surrounding Glenn Brown's Turner Prize entry "The Loves of Shepherds 2000" brought into public debate the issue of when does "inspiration" or "appropriation" amount to copyright infringement? As will be apparent from the discussion so far, it is clear that the law can intervene when the act of appropriation amounts to copyright infringement. For example in May 2000 the well known UK artist, Damien Hirst, was reported to have paid an undisclosed sum to charity to settle an allegation that his 20-foot bronze sculpture, "Hymn" (recently sold for £1 million) was a direct copy of toy company Humbrol's "Young Scientist Anatomy Set" (retailing at £14.99).[107]

In the case of "Loves of Shepherds 2000" there appears little doubt that Glenn Brown's alleged "copy" of Anthony Roberts's book jacket illustration for the Robert A. Heinlein novel, *Double Star*, appears to be a clear case of copyright infringement.[108] Indeed following the House of Lords in *Designers Guild* (discussed in Chapter 3) it is difficult to think of a more classic case of copyright infringement.

However a number of art critics were quoted as saying that in "The Loves of Shepherds" Glenn Brown, although obviously (allegedly) "inspired" by the book jacket illustration, had used considerable skill and creativity to produce his work. Indeed Glenn Brown was quoted by *The Times* at the time as saying, "I have radically altered Roberts's work in terms of scale and colour". This highlights the different approaches that can be taken to appropriation and the conflicts that can in UK law arise when artists insist on their legal rights when appropriation has occurred.

---

[105] At 370.

[106] See S. Stokes, "A Touch of Genius", *Legal Week*, 14 December 2000, at 23.

[107] BBC News, 19 May 2000.

[108] This was certainly the view of lawyers who commentated on the case at the time. Mr Roberts is also said to be taking legal action against Mr Brown (BBC's *Front Row* feature on appropriation, Radio 4, 1 January 2001). It is submitted that if *Designers Guild* is applied to "The Loves of Shepherds 2000" there appears a clear case of copyright infringement: comparing this picture *as a whole* with the book jacket as a whole, based on photographs from newspapers at the time, one is clearly a copy of the other, albeit that certain elements (colour, scale, etc.) are different.

6.3.6 The Limits of Appropriation—Parody[109]

Parody is a word with a wide range of meanings, and appropriation may or may not involve parody. Parody may include an element of satire or ridicule, and in more general terms the work parodied is effectively re-used in whole or part to perform a different function from the original work. However, unlike plagiarism, where the intention is to conceal the derivation of the work copied, the parodist needs to rely on the audience's awareness of the target work or genre to be successful—"the complicity of the audience is the *sine qua non* of its enjoyment".[110] A leading author on the subject, Linda Hutcheon, has spoken of parody as "imitation characterised by ironic inversion, not always at the expense of the parodied text".[111] According to Gredley and Maniatis, Hutcheon also sees parody as "one of the major forms of self-reflexivity in twentieth century art forms, marking 'the intersection of creation and re-creation, of invention and critique' ".[112] As well as copyright and moral rights, other intellectual property rights may also protect against parody.[113]

[109] See M. Spence, "Intellectual Property and the Problem of Parody" (1998) 114 *LQR* 594; E. Gredley and S. Maniatis, "Parody: A Fatal Attraction? Part1: The Nature of Parody and its Treatment in Copyright" [1997] 7 *EIPR* 339 ("Gredley and Maniatis"), and W.J. Gordon, "Taming the Certainties of Property and Restitution: A Journey to Copyright and Parody", *Oxford Electronic Journal of Intellectual Property Rights* October 1999, (http://www.oiprc.uk.ac.uk/EJWP1399.html) for a law and economics approach to parody and copyright infringement.

[110] Gredley and Maniatis n.109 *supra*, at 340.

[111] L. Hutcheon, *A Theory of Parody: The Teaching of Twentieth-Century Art Forms* (Methuen, London, 1985) ("Hutcheon") at 6. See also her later work, *The Politics of Postmodernism* (Routledge, London, 1989).

[112] Gredley and Maniatis (n.109), at 339, citing Hutcheon, at 2.

[113] Law of passing off, trade marks and registered designs (Spence n.109 *supra*, at 598–601). The use of trade mark law by corporations in North America to suppress parody or criticism is considered by Coombes. For example in 1972 The Coca-Cola Company prevented the marketing of "ENJOY COCAINE" posters in the same style as the well-known slogan "ENJOY COCA-COLA" (*Coca-Cola Co v. Gemini Rising Inc.,* 346 F Supp.1183, 1193 (EDNY 1972)). According to Coombes US trade mark law will generally protect against parody (especially in a commercial context) on the ground of either confusion or (more likely) the application of the trade mark dilution doctrine in favour of the proprietor of the mark. This doctrine seeks to prevent the tarnishing or erosion of the reputation of a trade mark even if there is no confusion as such. US trade mark law can potentially restrict artists who appropriate trade marks, whether words, signs or images (which may or may not be protected by copyright as well). Coombes (at 73–4) cites the artist Hans Haacke's work "Metromobilitan" which used Mobil Oil's trade marks to criticise Mobil's activities in South Africa and its sponsorship of South African art in the era of apartheid, and in respect of which legal action was threatened. UK trade

The parodist is unlikely to face problems if only the style or genre of other works is made the subject of parody, for there is then unlikely to be copyright infringement. However where the expression, as opposed to the mere idea, of a work is copied for the purposes of parody then there may well be an issue.

UK law, unlike Spanish,[114] Belgian[115] and French[116] law, makes no express exceptions for parody. A parody will constitute an infringement of copyright if the parodist has taken a substantial part of the protected work, although merely "conjuring up" the work being parodied will not normally amount to infringement.[117] Parodists also potentially face liability for infringement of moral rights—that of derogatory treatment and the right to object to false attribution of authorship.[118] It is a matter of some debate when a parody may constitute derogatory treatment.[119] Does the parody have to be offensive to the spirit of the

mark law has only a very limited common law doctrine of dilution (see Kerly at 14.82 and 14.83) and it also has a very limited statutory basis (see s.10(3), Trade Marks Act 1994). An example where an attempt to prevent a commercial parody failed in the law of passing off on the basis that the mark was used on different goods (i.e. there was no common field of activity) was the use of "Schlurppes" as a "joke" (in contrast to "Schweppes") in *Schweppes Ltd v. Wellingtons Ltd* [1984] FSR 210. See also Chap. 8 for a discussion of trade mark law including the law of passing-off (in particular the publication of the satirical secret political diaries of Alan Clark were prevented *inter alia* by the law of passing-off—see *Clark* v. *Associated Newspapers* [1998] RPC 261 discussed in Chap. 8 and below).[114] Real decreto legislativo, 12 abril 1996, Num. 1/1996, Propriedad Intelectual, Art. 39.

[115] Loi de 30 juin 1994 relative au droit d'auteur et aux droits voisins, Art. 22.

[116] Loi de 1 juillet 1992 relative au code de la propriété intellectuelle, Art. 112–5. Note that the Digital Copyright Directive will permit Member States to allow exceptions in their copyright laws to permit "use for the purpose of caricature, parody or pastiche" (Art. 3(k)).

[117] S. 16, CDPA: see for example the music and literary copyright case *Williamson Music Ltd v. Pearson Partnership Ltd* [1987] FSR 97: the test formulated by Judge Paul Baker QC in this case was "whether the parody, on the one hand, conjures up the idea of the original work and no more than the idea or, on the other hand, whether it uses a substantial part of the expression of the original work" (at 107). It is no longer a defence to argue that because a parody is itself an original copyright work there is no copyright infringement (see for example the criticism of this (old) approach by Falconer J in *Schweppes Ltd and Others* v. *Wellingtons Ltd* [1984] FSR 210 approved by Judge Paul Baker QC in *Williamson Music Ltd* (at 106)—if a substantial part is taken then unless a fair dealing defence can be relied upon (for example, for purposes of criticism or review, s. 30(1)) CDPA, there will *prima facie* be infringement; see below).

[118] Under s. 84(1) of the CDPA, which is actionable without proof of damage. See *Alan Kenneth Mackenzie Clark* v. *Associated Newspapers Ltd* [1998] RPC 261—this case involved a spoof diary of the politician Alan Clark by Peter Bradshaw entitled "Alan Clark's Secret Political Diaries"; the plaintiff succeeded under both s. 84(1) and the law of passing-off.

[119] See Spence n. 109 *supra*, at 597–8.

work, or will most parodies not be derogatory treatment in any event? This is because they will not usually be prejudicial to the artist's honour or reputation as they will not be made out to be the work of the artist.[120] Others argue that moral rights should strongly protect against parody.[121]

By way of example of the difficulties the law of copyright and moral rights faces when dealing with artistic parodies, consider the Swedish case *Max Walter Svanberg* v. *Leif Eriksson*.[122] The plaintiff was a well-known artist in Sweden and recognised internationally as a surrealist. The defendant was a well-known satirist and exhibited a reproduction of one of Svanberg's works to which Eriksson had added serigraphically printed comments and printing instructions. The intention was to add to the debate in Sweden about the propriety of selling reproductions of graphic works and to act as a satire on the commercial practices involved in graphic art. The plaintiff sued for infringement of copyright. The case eventually went to the Supreme Court of Sweden. The Supreme Court held that Eriksson's additions, which covered only a minor portion of Svanberg's work, could clearly be distinguished from Svanberg's work and no material alteration to the central elements of Svanberg's work had taken place. So the artistic integrity of Svanberg's work was not compromised and Svanberg's reputation as an artist had not suffered as a result of Eriksson's actions to the reproduction.[123]

It is possible that certain parodies may benefit from one of the "fair dealing" defences under the CDPA, in particular fair dealing for the purposes of criticism or review.[124] However this is only a defence to

---

[120] This is the view taken by Copinger (at para. 11–46): citing *Clark* v. *Associated Newspapers Ltd* [1998] RPC 261 (a case in which derogatory treatment did not arise as there was no "treatment" of the plaintiff's work—the plaintiff's style rather than his actual work was involved): only where the treatment is made out to be the plaintiff's can there be infringement, according to Copinger. Copinger however foresees one case where there may be derogatory treatment as being where those who read, see or hear the plaintiff's work will no longer be able to do so without recalling to mind the parody, to the prejudice of his honour or reputation.

[121] Ricketson at 486.

[122] [1979] *EIPR* D-93.

[123] Indeed the County Court of Appeal in this case stated (and this was not overruled by the Supreme Court) that derived art forms were common in artistic and especially modern art circles: artistic practice in this area should be borne in mind when considering the issue of infringement and artists' rights (at 94).

[124] S. 31: in *Williamson Music* v. *The Pearson Partnership Ltd* Judge Paul Baker Q.C. seemed to accept that fair dealing for the purpose of criticism or review might be successfully relied on in certain circumstances but declined to discuss the matter further in

copyright infringement and not infringement of moral rights. Certainly a parody can fall within the much broader "fair use" doctrine in the USA as a form of criticism—unlike UK and Canadian law, for example, the US fair use doctrine is in general far more flexible as regards parodies.[125] Nevertheless in *Rogers* v. *Koons*[126] the celebrated *kitsch* artist Jeff Koons was unable to rely on this defence when sued for copyright infringement in respect of a sculpture he created. The sculpture was a copy of a well-known black and white photograph, "Puppies", showing a man and a woman on a bench with a string of eight German Shepherd puppies. Koons argued that he had created a parody of modern society. However the court was of the view that the work copied must itself be, at least in part, the object of parody—this was to set some practicable boundaries to this defence.[127] The defendant's "bad faith" and "profit-making motives" were also fatal to his case.[128]

There remains a continuing debate about whether parody should be afforded special treatment under the law. According to Spence four

this case (Copinger at 9–18). But Copinger foresees problems with this defence. There must be "sufficient acknowledgement" of the work parodied, i.e. an acknowledgement identifying the work in question by its title or other description and identifying the author unless (in the case of a published work) it is published anonymously or (in the case of an unpublished work) it is not possible to ascertain the identity of the author by reasonable enquiry (Copinger 9–21). Both Spence (n. 109 *supra*) and Copinger see such a defence as unlikely in many cases, as it appears to run counter to publishing practice and "one of the benchmarks against which a parody can be judged is its success in making a connection with the work being parodied without any form of express reference" (Copinger at 9–18).

[125] See *Campbell* v. *Acuff-Rose Music, Inc.* 510 US 569 (1994). Gordon contrasts the limited fair-dealing defences in Canadian law with the fair use doctrine in the USA, and she cites a Canadian case involving the parodic use of a Michelin logo by a trade union where an argument that *Acuff-Rose* be applied was rejected (*Cie Générale des Etablissements Micheline-Michelin & Cie* v. *C.A.W.-Canada* (1996) 71 CPR 3d 348) (Gordon n. 109 *supra* at 9). According to Gredley and Maniatis, the Supreme Court in *Acuff-Rose* in any event arguably reinforced a narrow, traditional view of parody, placing it firmly in the context of ridiculing distortion or criticism—"[t]o justify a finding of fair use, the parody must—at least in part—recognisably target and comment on or criticise the original work" (at 343). Certainly this was the view taken in *Rogers* v. *Koons* (see below) which was cited by Justice Kennedy in *Acuff-Rose*.

[126] 960 F 2d 301 (2nd Cir.1992).

[127] See DuBoff and King at 186.

[128] See Gredley and Maniatis at 342. Gredley and Maniatis critically discuss at some length the approach of the US courts to parody and in particular the application of the fair use defence as elaborated in *Koons*, the landmark *Campbell* v. *Acuff-Rose Music* case and others. They conclude: "[t]he theoretical and practical difficulties of applying the US fair use doctrine to parody, and of arriving at a consistent and coherent approach which would establish certainty both for parodists and owners of parodied works, has led to calls for the redefinition of parody and its recognition as a separate art-form for copyright purposes" (at 343).

arguments often advanced are[129]: (a) parody should be treated as a distinctive genre as it deserves special treatment; (b) the problem of parody is one of "market failure" as owners of copyright works are unlikely to grant licences to permit the creation of parodies and so the law should intervene to allow new creative works such as parodies to come into existence[130]; (c) parody involves the "transformative" use of a copyright work, i.e. a new creative work arises which is not a market substitute for the earlier work notwithstanding its dependence on it[131]; and (d) the parodist's right to free speech should be protected.[132]

In conclusion Spence considers that parody by itself does not require special legislation in the UK—existing statutes and laws potentially give judges the scope to balance the rights of intellectual property holders and the free speech rights of parodists.[133]

---

[129] See Spence (n .109 *supra*)at 601–15.

[130] See Gordon n.109 *supra*.

[131] It is argued that allowing transformative uses encourages the production and dissemination of texts and that it is also necessary for the preservation of certain types of artistic discourse (see Spence n.109 *supra*, at 605 citing the German case *Alcolix* [1994] GRUR 206 at 208 (BGH)). According to Spence (at 607) the argument in this case was that artists must be able to use existing works if they are to communicate effectively, to speak freely about and through the artistic tradition in which they work, although as Spence rightly points out this seems to be a variant of the argument that parody should fall within the right to free speech. As discussed above UK law once recognised this idea (which stems from *Glyn* v. *Weston Feature Film Company* [1916] 1 Ch. 261 at 268: "no infringement of the plaintiff's rights takes place where the defendant has bestowed such mental labour upon what he has taken and has subjected it to such revision and alteration as to produce an original result" (*per* Younger J)) but this is now no longer the case—see *Williamson Music* (n. 117 *supra*). Nevertheless Laddie opens the door to this idea (for example, "where the parody does not really injure the copyright owner, save in his amour propre" (at 3.142 n.6)—see also the possibility that a form of the fair use doctrine might still apply in the UK (at n. 138 of Chap. 3 of this volume). In any event a number of other jurisdictions do give weight to this idea (for example, Australia (probably), the USA (see *Campbell* v. *Acuff-Rose Music Inc)*, Germany and Italy: Spence n. 109 *supra*, 605–6).

[132] It should not be forgotten that copyright, in the sense of printing privileges, arose as a means of suppressing free speech and more particularly religious heresy.

[133] At 615–20. In particular he refers to cl. 3 of the Human Rights Bill as requiring the courts to interpret existing intellectual property statutes in a manner compatible with the right to free speech and to keep that right in view when fashioning remedies for intellectual property infringement. In fact Art. 10(1) of the European Convention on Human Rights has been raised before the courts in the context of parody by Counsel for the defendants in *Alan Clark* v. *Associated Newspapers Ltd* [1998] RPC 261 at 269–70. Lightman J gave this argument short shrift, describing it as totally misconceived; there was no interference with the defendant's freedom of expression in this case (the right of the defendant to parody the works of the plaintiff was never in question and in any event Art. 10(2) makes clear that the right is subject to the rights of others, in this case the right to object to false attribution of authorship). Kerly also strikes a note of caution, citing *Daniels* v. *Walker* [2000] 1 WLR 1382 to the effect that the courts will need to be

6.3.7 Appropriation and Parody: Some Concluding Thoughts

As Yen has eloquently pointed out,[134] striking a balance between the interests of authors and the public is crucial in setting the limits to which copyright law can be used to prevent appropriation. Yen stresses that authorship in its broadest sense is possible only when future authors are able to borrow from those who went before them. If too much of a work is reserved as private property through the copyright system then would-be authors will find it impossible to create. Hence, as stated earlier in this book a strong public domain is a vital part of any copyright system.

6.4 ABORIGINAL WORKS

Aboriginal or indigenous works of art pose a particular challenge to copyright law. In particular Aboriginal peoples may well wish to have redress should items with a particular religious or cultural significance be copied in inappropriate ways or in breach of tribal secrecy.[135] For example in Australia "the right to create paintings and other artworks depicting creation and dreaming stories, and to use pre-existing designs and well recognised totems of the clan, resides in the traditional owners (or custodians) of the stories or images".[136] These and similar

persuaded that Art. 10 adds anything to how free speech issues are already dealt with by the courts (Kerly at paras. 22–26 to 22–35). See also *Ashdown* v. *Telegraph Group* (Ch D, 11 January 2001).

[134] Yen at 159–61.

[135] If such works are not in the public domain then the law of confidence may be a useful source of protection: see *Foster* v. *Mountford* (1976–1978) 29 FLR 233, where the Supreme Court of the Northern Territory suppressed the publication of an anthropology text which revealed tribal secrets. See also Chap. 8.

[136] *Per* von Doussa J in *Milpurrurru and Others* v. *Indofurn Pty Ltd and Others* (1994) 130 ALR 659, at para. 12. The Judge (at para. 13) also noted that under Aboriginal law it is the responsibility of the traditional owners to take action to preserve the dreaming, and to punish those responsible for the breach (even if they themselves had no control over or knowledge of what occurred). Sanctions can include the removal of the right to participate in ceremonies and to paint stories, to be ostracised, to pay money, and in serious cases the possibility of physical violence, such as spearing, being inflicted. It is therefore not surprising that Aboriginal artists have been forced to take action against those infringing their copyright: by vigorously pursuing their rights Aboriginal artists may well be hoping for more lenient treatment by their clans. Linked to this is also the extent to which the common law should recognise traditional or customary law—in the landmark case of *Mabo* v. *Queensland* (1992) 175 CLR 1, the High Court of Australia held that the common law of Australia recognises a form of native (land) title. See generally,

works may fail to be adequately protected by copyright/moral rights because, for example[137]:

(a) it may be difficult to show that they are original works for copyright purposes—often such works are evolutionary and derivative in nature.[138] However this may not necessarily rule out a finding of "originality" in all cases—see for example the Australian case of *Milpurrurru and Others* v. *Indofurn Pty Ltd and Others*[139];

(b) (related to (a)), who the author is may be a difficult question to determine in any event, given that such works are frequently communal in nature—UK copyright law for example does not recognise a "communal author" of a copyright work (although

M. Blakeney, "Protecting Expressions of Australian Aboriginal Folklore under Copyright Law" [1995] 9 *EIPR* 422 ("Blakeney").

[137] See generally E. Evatt, "Enforcing Indigenous Cultural Rights: Australia as a Case-Study" in UNESCO and Institute of Art and Law, *Cultural Rights and Wrongs* (Institute of Art and Law, Leicester, 1998) ("Evatt"). Also for a summary of Australian developments and cases relating to Aboriginal art see C. Golvan, "Aboriginal Art and Copyright: An Overview and Commentary Concerning Recent Developments" [1999] *EIPR* 599 ("Golvan"). He notes that Aboriginal artists have been involved in litigation to protect their copyrights on an almost continual basis since 1988, beginning with the *Bulun Bulun* case. In this 1988 case John Bulun Bulun and other Northern Territory artists brought an action in the Federal Court in Darwin concerning the unauthorised reproduction of their artwork on T-shirts. The case settled before judgment and a sum of $150,000 was paid in settlement.

[138] As discussed in Chap. 3, the "author" is crucial to whether a work is "original" or not: "the work must not be copied from another work . . . it should originate from the author" (*University of London Press* v. *University Tutorial Press* [1916] 2 Ch 601 at 608) (see Sherman at 118–25).

[139] See n.136 *supra*. *Milpurrurru* involved an action brought by three aboriginal artists and the Public Trustee for the Northern Territory in whom the Administration and Probate Act 1988 had vested the real and personal property of five other Aboriginal artists who had died before the proceedings commenced, against the importers into Australia of carpets made in Vietnam which reproduced the artists' designs. In this case, although the artwork followed traditional Aboriginal form and was based on dreaming themes, the judge held that each work of art was one of intricate detail and complexity reflecting great skill and originality, and therefore "original" for copyright purposes (at para. 20). The judge also had no difficulty in finding that those carpets which were not exact reproductions of the works of art nevertheless reproduced a substantial part of the works in question (and hence were infringing), despite the respondents' argument that what was reproduced were designs, symbols and themes common to many Aboriginal works of art (see paras. 69–90). Counsel for the applicant artists, Colin Golvan, has stated that in his view von Doussa J adopted a liberal approach in favour of the artists to the issue of substantial copying, indicating a strong preference on the part of the judge to prohibit the unfair and unauthorised practices of the respondents in the circumstances (see Golvan n.137 at 600).

protection is afforded to "anonymous" works[140]); a work can be one of joint authorship, but then all the authors need to be identified. In any event even if there is an identifiable author this can still cause problems for the community as a whole. The fact that the work in question may have been authorised by traditional custodians will not be enough to give these persons rights in the work as well should, for example, the creator decide to exploit the work outside the parameters permitted by the community. Indeed this was precisely the situation in the Australian case of *Yumbulul* v. *Reserve Bank of Australia*[141]: the Aboriginal artist Terry Yumbulul was criticised by his clan for allowing a reproduction of his work (a *Morning Star* pole produced under the authority of the clan). French J in this case stated, "Australia's copyright law does not provide adequate recognition of Aboriginal community claims to regulate the reproduction and use of works which are essentially communal in origin".[142];

(c) what is copied is the style of the work in question or its subject matter or themes—whilst this may cause offence to the group in question, the copying falls on the idea side of the idea/expression dichotomy and therefore copyright is not infringed. An example is the acrylic dot style used in traditional Aboriginal art in Australia which is not protected[143];

(d) the work in question, such as a body painting, may lack any requirement of "fixation"[144];

(e) moral rights may be unavailable or not properly applicable especially where the harm is communal[145];

(f) the works may be in the public domain as far as copyright law is concerned (even though considered secret by the tribal group or people "owning" the work), having been created more than life plus 70 years from the act of infringement at issue; or

(g) even if the courts find there has been infringement, the remedy awarded will generally be to compensate the artists themselves by way of damages and not to compensate their communities for

[140] S.57, CDPA.

[141] (1991) IPR 481.

[142] At 490.

[143] Evatt at 73. Although note the approach of von Doussa J in *Milpurrurru* (see n.136 *supra*).

[144] As discussed in section 3.2.4 of Chap. 3.

[145] Moral rights are not given express recognition in Australian copyright law, although this is likely to change (see Kenyon (n. 148 *infra*)). In any event moral rights are "personal" as opposed to communal in nature.

inappropriate use of their images.[146] However a recent Australian case, *John Bulun Bulun and Anor* v. *R&T Textiles Pty. Ltd.*[147] has recognised that Australian Aboriginal artists can have a fiduciary duty to their community. While the artist was entitled to pursue the exploitation of the work of art for his own benefit, he was still under a fiduciary duty not to act in a manner likely to harm the communal interests of his clan. Equity would therefore intervene in circumstances where the artist (as the copyright owner at law) failed or was unable to take legal action to protect communal interests.[148]

Nevertheless, despite the encouraging development of this area in Australia, it remains the view of many commentators that copyright law as developed in the Western world, with its emphasis on copyright as a species of private property, is ill-suited to protecting traditional

---

[146] The principles underlying the award of damages in this area have been given detailed consideration by the Australian courts in *Milpurrurru* (see n.136 *supra*) and in *John Bulun Bulun and Anor* v. *R&T Textiles Pty Ltd* (includes corrigendum) [1998] 1082 FCA (3 September 1998). In *Milpurrurru* von Doussa J noted that although the applicants argued that the unauthorised use of their works of art was in effect the pirating of cultural heritage, under copyright law damages could be awarded only in so far as the "pirating" causes a loss to the *copyright owner* (as opposed to his or her community). However von Doussa J nevertheless acknowledged the communal aspects by stating that the anger and distress directed at the artists by their community arising out of the infringement could constitute part of the compensation for "personal suffering" by the artists, a recognised head of damages for copyright infringement in his view (see paras. 144–146). In any event in this case the judge felt able to award substantial additional damages for flagrant infringement of copyright (following the English Court of Appeal in *Williams* v. *Settle* [1960] 1 WLR 1072) in recognition *inter alia* of the harm caused to the living artists in their cultural environment (paras. 158, 160). The judge's approach to damages has also been considered by Blakeney (see n.136)—he sees the recognition of cultural harm in this case as a recognition that customary Aboriginal laws may be taken into account in quantifying the damage suffered (at 443).

[147] See n.146.

[148] See Golvan (n. 149 *infra*) and A.T. Kenyon, "The Artist Fiduciary—Australian Aboriginal Art and Copyright" [1999] 2 *Ent. LR* 42. The case involved a claim of copyright infringement by the Aboriginal artist John Bulun Bulun and (through John Bulun Bulun) his clan in respect of fabric printed in Indonesia and imported into Australia. The fabric was found to infringe John Bulun Bulun's work "Magpie Geese and Water Lillies at the Waterhole", which had a very significant place in the cultural and spiritual life of the artist's indigenous community, the Ganalbingu people. The judge (von Dousa J again) however rejected an argument that, based on customary law and old common law copyright cases, there was collective or communal ownership of the copyright itself: copyright is now solely a creature of statute. In particular s. 35(2) of the (Australian) Copyright Act 1968 effectively precludes any notion of group ownership in an artistic work unless it is of "joint authorship"—here there was no suggestion that the author was anyone other than John Bulun Bulun.

works.[149] The copyright protection afforded to Aboriginal and similar works is part of a wider discussion of how traditional knowledge in its broadest sense is protected by law, including intellectual property law—in other words are indigenous cultural rights adequately protected at law?[150] Should *sui generis* forms of protection for "traditional knowledge", for example, be introduced[151] on the ground that the Anglo-Saxon system is too much centred on a single identifiable author with personal property rights?[152] Or should traditional knowledge simply be viewed as being (and remaining) in the "public domain" on the basis that it should not be "commodified" or made the subject of a property right and the free flow of information thereby impeded?

There are developments in this area at the international level, albeit very slow moving. For example in 1982 the United Nations Educational, Scientific and Cultural Organisation (UNESCO) and the World Intellectual Property Organisation (WIPO) proposed Model

[149] See, for example, M. Blakeney, "The Protection of Traditional Knowledge under Intellectual Property Law" [2000] 6 *EIPR* 251 at 256. See also C. Golvan: "[o]ne of the challenging aspects of the Aboriginal copyright litigation has involved attempts to create meaningful links between the interests of the artists and the culture and practice of the Western legal system" (Golvan, "Aboriginal Art and Copyright—An Overview and Commentary Concerning Recent Developments" (1996) 1 *Media and Arts Law Review* 151).

[150] For a discussion of the Australian experience see Evatt n.137 *supra*.

[151] In Australia, the introduction of specific rights for Aboriginal artists has been criticised as unduly emphasising "traditional" "authentic" Aboriginal art at the expense of urban Aboriginal artists who operate outside their traditional culture: see S. Gray, "Freedom or Fossilisation: Proposed Legislative 'Protection' for the Work of Aboriginal Artists", paper presented at the 50th Anniversary Conference of the Australasian Law Teachers' Association, *Cross Currents: Internationalism, National Identity & Law* 1995. Arguments in favour of collective, community *sui generis* rights protection (rather than the expansion of copyright/IP law itself to deal with some of the current issues) is that such a system (unlike IP law) will not be rooted in the "colonial" Western concept of IP, which is simply incapable of adapting to communal, traditional concepts of property and its exploitation. See WIPO Draft Report on Fact-finding Missions on Intellectual Property and Traditional Knowledge (1998–1999), Draft for Comment, 3 July 2000 ("WIPO Draft Report") (available at http://www.wipo.int). See also n.152 below.

[152] In contrast indigenous customary law emphasises group ownership and community involvement in decision-making: see K. Puri, "Is Traditional or Cultural Knowledge a Form of Intellectual Property?", *Oxford Electronic Journal of Intellectual Property Rights*, January 2000 (http://www.oiprc.ox.ac.uk/EJWP0100.pdf). Prof. Puri takes takes the view that "[the] IP regime is inherently inappropriate or dysfunctional in relation to the needs of indigenous peoples . . . a *sui generis* legislation is the answer". He also argues for the revision of the Agreement on Trade-Related Aspects of Intellectual Property Rights (TRIPS) to include specific rights to protect indigenous peoples' traditional knowledge and IP rights: Arts. 22, 23 and 24, for example, should be amended to provide for the introduction of indigenous collective certifications and geographical indications to protect indigenous arts, cultural expressions and traditional knowledge.

Provisions for National Laws on the Protection of Expressions of Folklore Against Illicit Exploitation and other Prejudicial Actions—these were adopted by WIPO and UNESCO in 1985.[153] In 1989 the UNESCO General Committee adopted a "Recommendation on the Safeguarding of Traditional Culture and Folklore". In 1993 there was also a Draft United Nations Declaration on the Rights of Indigenous Peoples.[154]

Despite these activities an effective international regime for the protection of expressions of "folklore" has not developed. So in 1997 a joint UNESCO/WIPO World Forum on the Protection of Folklore was convened.[155] In 1998 WIPO was given the mandate to undertake exploratory research to identify the issues for the intellectual property system and to assess the needs of stakeholders in the field of traditional knowledge—this took place during 1998–1999. During 2000 and 2001 WIPO will carry out further work in this area and in particular is to organise intellectual property training workshops for traditional knowledge stakeholders and conduct case studies and pilot projects in this area.[156]

---

[153] Several countries have enacted legislation based in part on these Model Provisions, including Nigeria (see Blakeney, n. 149 *supra*). This is really a form of *sui generis* protection—see WIPO Draft Report (n.151).

[154] Art. 12 included the right "to maintain, protect and develop the past, present and future manifestations of their cultures, such as . . . artefacts, designs, ceremonies . . . visual and performing arts . . .". Other rights relating to intellectual property were also formulated and/or recognised—see Blakeney n.149 *supra*, at 258–9.

[155] At the end of the Forum a Plan of Action was adopted which expressed concerns about the adequacy of copyright law and the need for a new international agreement on the *sui generis* protection of folklore: the participants from the UK and USA however expressly disassociated themselves from the Plan of Action (see Blakeney n.149 *supra*, at 260).

[156] See WIPO Draft Report (n.151 *supra*).

7

Some Practical Issues

THIS CHAPTER[1] LOOKS at some practical copyright issues facing museums, galleries, and art publishers.

7.1 COPYRIGHT IN THE CONTEXT OF ART LOANS[2]

In Chapter 3, passing reference was made to some of the issues that can arise in the context of art loans. Can the loaned works be photographed (whether they are on public display or not)? Could the artist exercise their moral rights in the context of the contemplated exhibition? One way these and other issues can be dealt with is to ensure that an art loan agreement is in place that specifically deals with artists' rights. What provisions are finally included in an art loan agreement depends of course upon the respective interests and bargaining power of the parties. However, it is clear that both the lender and borrower will want certain rights and protections under the agreement. An additional dimension is added if the works being loaned are still in copyright.

Set out below and following on from the discussion of copyright and moral rights in Chapter 3 is a non-exhaustive checklist of the sorts of things borrowers and lenders should consider including in their loan agreements.

---

[1] For further practical guidance in the area of art and copyright see for example the 5th edn. of M.F. Flint, N. Fitzpatrick and C.D. Thorne, *A User's Guide to Copyright* (Butterworths, London, 2000) which contains a chapter on "Artists, Photographers, Art Galleries, Art Dealers and Museums" (chap. 28). See also P. Wicnand, A. Booy and R. Fry, *A Guide to Copyright for Museums and Galleries* (Routledge, London, 2000).

[2] Bently & Sherman treat this area at some length. See also S. Stokes in *Art Loans and Exhibitions* (Institute of Art and Law, Leicester, 1996) upon which this section is based.

Lender

A. Publicity/Use of Lender's Name and Reputation

A.1 Ensure the lender's name is properly referred to, used and pub-licised in the borrower's gallery and on publicity materials and elsewhere as appropriate. Reserve the right of approval of the lender for this. Also ensure the control and protection of good-will in the lender's name and any trade marks/logo on mer-chandising, for example, the right to approve quality of merchandising, use of name, marks or logo.[3]

A.2 Oblige the borrower to produce sufficient guides of a high qual-ity to satisfy public demand.

A.3 Require the borrower to seek the approval of, and co-operate with, the lender, over publicity generally (including, for exam-ple, television documentaries, etc.).

B. Copyright/Moral Rights

B.1 If possible, the lender will want to ensure that the borrower assigns back to the lender all copyright in any photographs or other reproductions of the lender's collection that the borrower makes or commissions. This gives the lender the strongest copy-right position and to satisfy the likely needs of the borrower the lender can grant a licence back of this copyright on the follow-ing terms:

B.1.1 restrict use to specified uses: catalogues, posters, post-cards, classes of merchandise and subject to royalty pay-ments if deemed appropriate. Take care to exclude the grant of electronic rights (for example, rights to publish or digitally transmit images on CD-ROM or over the Internet) and the right to film/broadcast unless intended.

B.1.2 ensure consent is required to sub-license or assign granted rights.

---

[3] Whilst not the specific subject of this book, museums and galleries may wish to con-sider trade mark protection for their names and logos, and trade mark protection has even been sought as a means of protecting copyright works once copyright has expired or in anticipation of its expiry—the works of Beatrix Potter and Frederick Warne's use of trade marks to protect them (and in particular the characters in them) are an example of this. See also Chap. 8.

B.1.3 restrict the conditions under which flash photography etc. may be used.

B.1.4 ensure the lender is acknowledged as the copyright owner on all reproductions, including the use of ©.

B.1.5 restrict who may be allowed to copy the collection (for example, make it an obligation that no photography be allowed—this is particularly important for loans of sculpture and works of artistic craftsmanship) and ensure any photographers, etc. who do copy it assign their rights to the lender.

B.1.6 set out the rights of academic users regarding fair dealing, etc.

B.1.7 the copyright licence should spell out the territory and duration of the licence and whether it is exclusive or non-exclusive.[4]

B.2 Provide a limited right to use transparencies and publicity materials, etc., of the lender to aid the borrower to create its own exhibition guides, etc.

B.3 If the work is in copyright, ensure that it is the responsibility of the borrower to seek the permission of the relevant copyright owners and to comply with moral rights legislation as appropriate for the borrower's activities under the loan agreement.

B.4 Ensure that the loan of works is not to be construed as authorising the borrower (or others) to make copies of the lender's works which are in copyright.

B.5 Indemnify the lender in the event that the borrower infringes the intellectual property rights of the artist or other copyright owners. Also ensure general indemnity from the borrower for breach of the loan agreement and especially copyright/publicity provisions.

Borrower

The borrower will want similar provisions regarding publicity and rights to reproduce as may be offered by lender, but will need to make sure that any rights granted are broad enough and sufficient for its likely requirements, based on its current copyright policy. The borrower will also want to ensure that it has the right to continue to sell reproductions, merchandise, and as appropriate otherwise to use the lender's copyright material following the end of the loan.

[4] An exclusive copyright licence should always be in writing (see s.92, CDPA).

Also the borrower should consider asking for the following:

(a) a warranty and indemnity from the lender that the works are not in copyright; if the works are in copyright the lender should be obliged to provide details of the copyright owner and to provide the copyright owner's written consent to the loan (if appropriate).

(b) an indemnity from the lender in respect of intellectual property infringement claims in respect of negatives, transparencies, publications, etc., supplied by the lender for the borrower's use.

(c) If the borrower has a commercial subsidiary or other associated entity which is involved in merchandising ensure that any copyright or trade mark/name licences granted by the artist or lender will allow such an entity to carry out appropriate reproduction or merchandising.

7.2 COPYRIGHT AND SETTING UP A WEBSITE: ACQUIRING AND USING IMAGE RIGHTS

By way of a practical illustration of how copyright applies to the Internet and some of the issues in acquiring and using image rights, the legal issues faced by a gallery which has decided to make images of certain items in its collection available for a "virtual tour" on the Internet are considered.[5]

Having decided which works will be put on "virtual" display, the gallery will need to ensure that, by putting digital copies on its server accessible over the Internet, it will not be infringing someone else's copyright. To this end, it will need to ensure that where any of the works of art in question are still in copyright, appropriate consents are obtained from the artist or the artist's estate or other right-holder.

[5] WIPO is exploring assisting museums to go on-line by way of a museums project to assist museums in developing countries in particular. In its *Primer on Electronic Commerce and Intellectual Property Issues* (WIPO, Geneva, May 2000—available at http://ecommerce.wipo.int) ("WIPO") it sees the Internet as offering museums a "unique opportunity, largely unexplored to date, to make their cultural riches available to any person in the general community with access to a computer network" (at para. 279) but also notes that "[o]nce in digital form, concerns about protection of intellectual property rights have come to the fore. These concerns have sometimes paralyzed those who would otherwise embrace enthusiastically the new technologies. Without any security system, the image of a museum artifact, for example, can be copied, altered and disseminated without authorisation on a world-wide basis quickly, cheaply and without detection" (at para. 280).

Furthermore, where existing photographs are being digitised in order to create the tour, the copyright position regarding the photographs will also have to be explored. The gallery must either own the copyright in the photographs or ensure that the licences it has from the photographers are sufficiently broad to allow electronic exploitation of the images.[6]

Having satisfied itself that it does have the necessary rights to publish the works over the Internet, the gallery then needs to give some thought to protecting its rights. A website and its contents are capable of protection by copyright and database rights, and therefore appropriate copyright notices should be used in connection with the website. Furthermore, attention should be paid to any moral rights issues as discussed elsewhere in this book as appropriate.

Further to protect the gallery's position, it would be sensible to require persons accessing the site expressly to agree to be bound by an electronic copyright licence, i.e. in order for them to view the site they need to click on a button agreeing to be bound by on-screen licence terms and conditions. These terms and conditions could be very short, simply to the effect that images on the site are available only for viewing on screen for personal use and may not be printed out, downloaded on to floppy disk or other permanent form or hyper-linked to other websites without the prior consent of the gallery. Such an on-screen licence should be effective under English law.[7]

Practical protection against copying can also be incorporated, for example, by limiting the resolution of the works of art viewed on screen so that they are useful only for browsing and cannot be reproduced to a high enough quality for commercial purposes. Furthermore, for particularly important images, one could consider using some sort of digital watermark technology which would enable the source of any copies to be identified.[8]

---

[6] For a general discussion of the issues involved in determining the scope of any on-line rights which may have been granted (from a US perspective) see M.F. Radcliffe, "On-Line Rights: How to Interpret Pre-Existing Agreements" [1996] 9 *EIPR* 494. For a UK view see Copinger 5–222.

[7] See A.D. Murray, "Entering into Contracts Electronically: The Real W.W.W." in Edwards and Waelde, Chap. 2.

[8] For a discussion of the various technologies available here, as well as steps being taken to help manage and clear rights in the on-line environment such as Electronic Copyright Management Systems, see L. Jones, "An Artist's Entry into Cyberspace: Intellectual Property on the Internet" [2000] 2 *EIPR* 79, 88–90; M. Schippan, "Purchase and Licensing of Digital Rights: The VERDI Project and the Clearing of Multimedia Rights in Europe" [2000] 1 *EIPR* 24, and WIPO (see n. 5 *supra*). The Hermitage Museum of St Petersburg makes its digital collection available free of charge for personal use only

Of course, if at some point a gallery or picture library decides to market images from its collection commercially over the Internet the need for clear licence terms and conditions must be stressed. Also it would be prudent to consider some sort of subscription mechanism whereby only those who have supplied verified credit card details, for example, ("subscribers") are allowed to download relevant images, and furthermore these images can be supplied in encrypted form so that only subscribers (who will have access to the relevant encryption technology) can view them and utilise the images.

7.3 THE USE OF IMAGES IN ART BOOKS: THE LIMITS OF FAIR DEALING

The production of glossy art books full of high quality reproductions of works of art and devoted to particular artists or schools remains a significant publishing activity world-wide. Originally the preserve of commercial publishers, the larger museums and galleries are now publishers themselves.

It is a question of considerable importance to artists to what extent their work can be reproduced in such works without their consent on the ground that reproductions of their pictures are being used for the purposes of fair dealing, i.e. for the purposes of criticism or review.

This question was recently the subject of litigation in the UK which centred on the reproduction of a number of Matisse's works in a number of well-known books published by Phaidon Press including *The 20th Century Art Book*, *The Art Book* and *Minimum*. The beneficiaries of the Matisse estate, Les Heritiers Matisse, brought a copyright infringement action against Phaidon Press Ltd. The claim was supported by the Design & Artists Copyright Society (DACS) which acts as agent for the Matisse family in respect of UK copyright matters. The case was originally brought in 1992 but was reactivated in 1998 following several years of inactivity during the completion of various probate matters relating to the estate. The case settled before trial on terms favourable to the Matisse estate, but fortunately the solicitors acting for the plaintiffs[9] have commented on the case in some detail, although the precise terms of the settlement no doubt remain confidential.[10]

and incorporates a system of invisible watermarks to ensure that the digital use of its images can be monitored (WIPO n. 5 *supra*, at para. 282).

[9] Suzanne Garben and Ruth Hoy of Denton Hall (now Denton Wilde Sapte).

[10] S. Garben and R. Hoy, "Coffee Table Art Books—Unfair Dealing" [2000] *Ent. LR* 19.

According to the plaintiffs' solicitors, it was claimed that Phaidon had breached *inter alia* section 16 of the CDPA (copying the works) and section 17 (issuing copies of the works to the public). Phaidon did not deny copying of certain of Matisse's paintings but relied on two defences:

(a) that the pictures had been included in its books for the purpose of criticism and/or review of the works (i.e. the section 30(1), CDPA fair dealing defence); and

(b) in any case Phaidon had the benefit of a prior licence.

Concentrating on the first defence, "fair dealing for the purpose of criticism and review" is a two stage test:

(a) is the work "criticism" or "review" of either the copyright work or another work?; and

(b) is the use that has been made of the copyright work "fair"?

7.3.1 Criticism or Review

According to the plaintiffs' solicitors, when considering whether an act is for "criticism" or "review" "judges have consistently had regard to the dictionary definitions of those terms. It is accepted that 'criticism' is the act of passing judgement on the quality of a particular work, whilst 'review' is the resulting critical article or report",[11] although it might also be added that these words are of wide and indefinite scope which should be interpreted liberally. As has been said, "any attempt to plot their precise boundaries is doomed to failure".[12] Certainly criticism of a work includes criticism of style as well as of the ideas found in the work and its social or moral implications. Indeed even unbalanced and strongly expressed criticism falls within the fair dealing defence.[13]

When looking at one of the books in issue, *The 20th Century Art Book*, which reproduces "The Dance" by Matisse, 80–90 per cent of the

[11] *Ibid.*, 19

[12] *Pro Sieben Media AG v. Carlton UK Television Ltd and Another, The Times,* 7 January 1999; [1999] FSR 610, *per* Robert Walker LJ at 620–1.

[13] Robert Walker LJ in *Pro Sieben* at 621, citing *Time Warner Entertainments Co v. Channel Four Television plc* [1994] EMLR 1 (an interlocutory appeal concerning the discharge of an injunction against the showing of a television programme criticising the withdrawal of "A Clockwork Orange" in the UK), and at 619.

page is taken up by the image with a brief description of the work and its context at the top of the page. The Matisse estate argued that this text was not "criticism or review" for a number of reasons including that:

(a) the text was small and incidental, and the use of the image was there to attract the reader to buy a "glossy coffee table book": it was hardly criticism or review of the work;
(b) the text itself could in any event not be described as "criticism" as it was merely descriptive of the work;
(c) furthermore the text was very general—explaining "Fauvism" in the main, rather than criticising the work.[14]

Having set out various arguments as to why the use of the Matisse works was not criticism or review, the plaintiffs' solicitors then argued that in any event, even if the use was for these purposes, it was not "fair dealing".

7.3.2 Fair Dealing

Following *Pro Sieben*, the plaintiffs' solicitors point out that "the test of fairness was an objective test, in that the views of the person making the copy, whilst important, should not be decisive of the issue".[15] They also cite the important fair dealing case *Hubbard* v. *Vosper*[16] in which Lord Denning stated that three factors need to be considered in determining "fairness":

(a) the number and extent of the reproductions;
(b) the use made of them
(c) the proportion of the work consisting of the reproductions compared to the proportion of the work containing comment and analysis.

The Matisse estate argued that on the basis of these factors there was no fair dealing, especially in the light of the small amount and lack of prominence of the "purported criticism".

The plaintiffs' solicitors state that, because as part of the settlement Phaidon Press paid a fair licence fee for the use of the works, this

---

[14] Garben and Hoy n. 10 *supra*, at 20.
[15] *Ibid.*
[16] [1972] 2 QB 84.

suggests that they did not believe they had a good section 30(1) defence, but there is no indication in the article by Garben and Hoy of what arguments were used by Phaidon Press in its defence.

7.3.3 Comment

It can certainly be argued, as the plaintiffs did, that what Phaidon was doing was not criticism or review in the dictionary definition of these terms. However, following the dicta of Robert Walker LJ in *Pro Sieben* about the breadth of these words, one could see Phaidon arguing that there was legitimate criticism and review taking place: setting Matisse in the context of other twentieth-century artists and commenting on his work.[17]

Perhaps the strongest argument in favour of the estate was that the dealing was not "fair". In addition to the factors set out by Lord Denning in *Hubbard* v. *Vosper*, as cited by Garben and Hoy in their article and set out above, a number of other factors strongly go against a fair-dealing argument. Certainly fairness is to be judged by an objective standard—whether a fair-minded and honest person would have dealt with the copyright work in the manner in which the defendant did for the purpose in question.[18]

It is also well established that the degree to which the alleged infringer's use of the work competes with the exploitation of copyright by the owner is a very important consideration: "it is not fair dealing for a rival in trade to take copyright material and use it for his own benefit".[19] In this case the plaintiffs (through DACS) were presumably prepared to license the use of their images in return for a royalty. The defendant's activities were for commercial gain and deprived the owners, the plaintiffs, of royalty income. In such circumstances unless, following Chadwick LJ's recent exposition of fair dealing in *The Newspaper Licensing Agency Ltd* v. *Marks and Spencer plc*,[20] there is some overriding element of public advantage which justifies the

---

[17] The publication of comment as well as criticism appears to fall within the scope of criticism and review—see Chadwick LJ in *The Newspaper Licensing Agency Ltd* v. *Marks and Spencer PLC* [2000] 3 WLR 1256 at 1277C–F (CA).

[18] *Per* Peter Gibson LJ in *ibid.*, at 1269E, citing Aldous LJ in *Hyde Park Residence Ltd* v. *Yelland* [2000] 3 WLR 215 at 227G.

[19] *Per* Lord Denning in *Hubbard* v. *Vosper* [1972] 2 QB 84 at 93.

[20] [2000] 4 All ER 239.

subordination of the rights of the copyright owner, then there will not be "fair dealing". It is difficult to see any such public advantage here.

7.4 COPYRIGHT IN COMMISSIONED ART WORKS[21]

The copyright position in commissioned portraits and other artistic works is potentially complex. The CDPA makes clear that, with effect from 1 August 1989, the copyright in any new commissioned works will, absent special circumstances,[22] remain vested in the artist or photographer as "author".[23] However in respect of pre-CDPA commissioned works the copyright will in general remain with the person commissioning a portrait and certain other artistic works.[24]

Setting aside the issues which apply to pre-CDPA works, it is still possible for there to be an equitable transfer of title from the artist to the commissioner in certain circumstances.[25] A recent case illustrating this was *Durand* v. *Molino*.[26] The claimant was a well-known artist of the Royal Family, especially the late Princess Diana. The first respondent was a restaurateur with a business in London called "Da Mario", run by the second respondent Mario & Peppe Limited. The claimant sued the respondents for infringement of copyright in three pictures:

1. "Four Seasons"—commissioned by the first respondent in 1992 in consideration of £15,000 worth of credit for meals at "Da Mario" and including a portrait of Mr Molino. It was agreed that the painting would hang at "Da Mario" and that it could be

---

[21] See S. Stokes, "Copyright in Commissioned Paintings" [2000] 5 *ARTL* 77, upon which this section is based.

[22] For example the work is created in the course of employment (s.11(2), CDPA).

[23] This is the result of s.11, CDPA (the author of a work is the first owner of the copyright in it) and also because an assignment of copyright is not effective unless it is in writing signed by the assignor (s.90(3), CDPA).

[24] See for example Copyright Act 1956, s.4(3). The date of creation of the work is crucial to determine whether the applicable rules are those under the 1956 or 1911 Copyright Act or under earlier law (see Copinger 5–29 to 5–40 for a comprehensive discussion of this area).

[25] For example, in equity due to some express or implied contract term or given all the circumstances (see for example *Massine* v. *de Basil* [1936–45] Mac. CC 223; also see *Warner* v. *Gestetner Ltd* (unreported but cited for example in *Saphena Computing Ltd* v. *Allied Collection Agencies Ltd* [1995] FSR 616 at 634) (copyright to be owned by commissioner where the work was made specifically for the commissioner's business and at his expense and neither party can have contemplated that the maker of the work would have any genuine use for it himself)—see generally Copinger 5–166 to 5–185).

[26] *Andrew Durand* v. *Mario Molino & Anor* [2000] ECDR 320.

reproduced on menu covers. However Mr Durand claimed that the reproduction of the painting on postcards, business cards, greetings cards and match books infringed his copyright, for which he had given no such licence. Mr Molino accepted that Mr Durand (as author) was the legal owner of the copyright, but he argued that he was either beneficially entitled to the copyright, or at the very least he had an implied exclusive licence to use the work for commercial purposes in his restaurant.

2. "Pizza Diana 1996"—depicting Mr Molino presenting a pizza to Diana, Princess of Wales, a customer of "Da Mario". The consideration was £12,000 of which £4,000 was paid in cash and £8,000 was credit for meals. It was agreed that Mr Durand would retain the copyright but that Mr Molino could reproduce the painting on special menus and invitations, and on greetings cards. Mr Durand also designed a postcard reproducing the picture. Other reproductions required the claimant's prior written consent, not to be unreasonably withheld. At the grand launch of the picture it was photographed by a freelance press photographer and published nationally and locally. Mr Durand claimed that the respondents had infringed copyright in "Pizza Diana 1996" by authorising the photograph, and by distributing or making available to the public greeting cards and postcards of the picture that had been overprinted, which, it was asserted, was in breach of his publication right by reason of an implied term that Mr Durand had to approve all reproductions, and by the respondents continuing to distribute the overprinted reproductions after 1 October 1997.

3. "Pizza Diana 1997". Mr Durand and Mr Molino agreed that following the Princess of Wales' death "Pizza Diana 1996" had to be changed or not used. Mr Durand agreed to alter "Pizza Diana 1996" and on 30 September 1997 purported to withdraw his copyright licence for "Pizza Diana 1996". The altered (overpainted) painting, called "Pizza Diana 1997" was substantially changed and returned to the artist on 29 October 1997. Mr Durand tried to negotiate new terms for reproducing "Pizza Diana 1997" but none had been agreed before the painting was returned. Mr Molino then commissioned the printing of business cards, bill cards, greetings cards, and postcards reproducing "Pizza Diana 1997", and Mr Durand then alleged breach of copyright of "Pizza Diana 1997".

It was held, taking each painting in turn:

1. "Four Seasons". Applying the decision of Lightman J in *Robin Ray* v. *Classic FM plc*[27], which, according to Pumfrey J, articulated principles of law which were "well understood and have been applied for many years", he found that by implication, based on the facts of the case, Mr Molino was beneficially entitled to the copyright in "Four Seasons" which must be transferred to him from the artist, Mr Durand. Crucial to this decision was that the painting was commissioned in a commercial context with a view to reproduction, which at the very least meant that Mr Molino should have a perpetual exclusive licence—he needed to be able to exclude others from reproducing the work. But in addition, as the common purpose of the parties was that the painting should be hung in Mr Molino's restaurant and Mr Molino was the *subject* of the painting, then according to the judge *prima facie* Mr Molino should have complete control of the work. Therefore it was right to imply beneficial ownership to Mr Molino in this case and not just an exclusive licence. The judge also considered that the artist was in any event protected in relation to Mr Molino's exploitation of the work by the moral rights provisions in the CDPA.

2. "Pizza Diana 1996". The judge found that, based upon the agreement between the parties, Mr Durand retained the copyright. The reproductions in issue were licensed—overprinting did not convert the original licensed reproductions into unlicensed ones. Nor could an attempt by Mr Durand to revoke his copyright licence succeed. Furthermore, as far as Mr Molino's "authorisation" of the press photographer's copying of the painting was concerned, it was clear law (following *CBS Songs Ltd* v. *Amstrad Consumer Electronces plc*[28]) that authorisation required more than standing by whilst infringement took place—certainly Mr Molino did not encourage or approve the photography.

3. "Pizza Diana 1997". On the facts Mr Molino had a licence to reproduce this painting on the same terms as for Pizza Diana 1996. As no consent for the reproductions in question had been obtained, there was infringement.

It is submitted that this case is useful in providing a further example of the circumstances in which the courts will imply beneficial ownership

[27] [1998] FSR 622.
[28] [1988] AC 1013.

of copyright to the person commissioning a work, where there is no express written assignment from the author. The discussion of what is required to constitute "authorisation" is also useful and will give comfort to art galleries where visitors take unauthorised photographs of copyright works in their collections.[29] The utility of moral rights protection for artists was also expressly recognised by the judge.

[29] See Chap. 3 at n. 111.

8

Art and Intellectual Property Rights Other Than Copyright

STRICTLY SPEAKING INTELLECTUAL property rights other than copyright, such as the law of trade marks and passing off and breach of confidence, are outside the scope of this book. However there will be circumstances where the interests of an author/artist or owner of a copyright work are damaged by activities which fall outside the scope of copyright (including moral rights) protection. For example the activity may involve no substantial reproduction of the protected work or the work copied may not qualify for copyright protection. It is therefore worth bearing in mind the possibility of other remedies or forms of protection. What follows is a brief discussion of some relevant areas. For more information the reader is referred elsewhere. [1]

8.1 BREACH OF CONFIDENCE

Under UK law this is purely a creation of the common law. An action for breach of confidence may be available in addition to copyright

[1] Practitioner texts in the area of trade marks and brand protection include D. Kitchin, D. Llewelyn, J. Mellor, R. Meade and T. Moody-Stuart, *Kerly's Law of Trade Marks and Trade Names* (13th edn., Sweet & Maxwell, London, 2001) ("Kerly"); C. Morcom, A. Roughton and J. Graham, *The Modern Law of Trademarks* (Butterworths, London, 1999) ("Morcom"); and Isaac. See also J. Drysdale and M. Silverleaf, *Passing Off Law and Practice* (Butterworths, London, 1995) and C. Wadlow, *The Law of Passing Off* (Sweet & Maxwell, London, 1995). See also generally Copinger, chap. 21. For breach of confidence see F. Gurry, *Breach of Confidence* (Clarendon Press, Oxford, 1984) ("Gurry") and Copinger, chap. 20. For domain names see Edwards and Waelde. For a detailed consideration of "brand stretching" and merchandising see Isaac, chap. 5.

infringement for unpublished works.[2] Indeed the leading early case on the subject, *Prince Albert* v. *Strange*,[3] concerned the publication of etchings by Prince Albert and Queen Victoria which had been created for their own use and not for publication. The defendants had acquired some impressions of the etchings in breach of confidence from a printer who had access to the etchings. The court granted an injunction restraining the defendants from publishing not just the copies of the etchings but also a catalogue describing the etchings. Hence a breach of confidence action can go beyond copyright law in protecting "ideas" (in this case the catalogue which would not itself infringe any copyright in the etchings although derived from them), as well as their expression (the etchings).[4] It can also be used in circumstances where the work disclosed to the public in breach of confidence is not itself protected by copyright, as in the case of the assembly of objects for the Oasis album cover in *Creation Records* v. *News Group Newspapers*,[5] discussed in Chapter 3. Also a recent conceptual work of art by Anna Livia Lowendahl-Atomic uses the law of confidence as an intrinsic element of the work.[6]

It should be noted that the "fair dealing" defences do not apply in the case of breach of confidence. Different persons may also own the copyright from those entitled to bring an action for breach of confidence.

---

[2] For there to be an actionable breach of confidence three requirements must be satisfied: (a) the information imparted must be "confidential" (i.e. not something which is public property and public knowledge); (b) the information must be imparted in circumstances where an obligation of confidence is imposed, and (c) there must be a breach of the obligation of confidence (for example, see the dictum of Megarry J in *Coco* v. *A.N. Clark (Engineers) Ltd* [1969] RPC 41 at 47). There is also a possible "public interest" defence to breach of confidence (see Copinger at 20–02). Note also *Douglas and Others* v. *Hello! Ltd*, *The Times*, 16 January 2001, which is authority for an actionable right of privacy in English law grounded in the equitable doctrine of breach of confidence and which concerned the use of photographs—see A.Melville Brown, "For Our Eyes Only", *Law Society Gazette*, 25 January 2001, at 30.

[3] 2 De Gex & Sm. 652, 64 ER 293, (on appeal) (1849) 1 Mac. & G 25, 41 ER 1171.

[4] See Gurry n. 1 *supra*, 20–1.

[5] [1997] EMLR 444; *The Times*, 29 April 1997 (Ch. D): this was an interlocutory application where an arguable case was found that the taking of a photograph of the *assemblage* and its publication were in breach of confidence. See also *Shelley Films Ltd* v. *Rex Features Ltd* [1994] EMLR 134 (the physical appearance of a closed film set also protected by the law of confidence) and *Fraser* v. *Thames Television* [1984] QB 44 (a plot or developed idea is protected by the law of confidence even if not protected by copyright). Note, however, that merely vague ideas (such as that for a new nightclub in *De Maudsley* v. *Palumbo* [1996] FSR 447) which are not sufficiently developed to be capable of producing a result will not be protected (see Copinger at 20–11).

[6] The work consists of a series of 60 secrets that are for sale under the terms of a contractual confidentiality agreement (see H. Lydiate, "Mum's the Word", *Art Monthly*, December 2000/January 2001, at 61).

8.2 PASSING OFF

In the UK the law of passing off may aid an artist who finds that another is passing off his or her work as the other's.[7] This is in addition to any moral right claim, for example for false attribution of authorship or a claim of copyright infringement, and extends beyond the artist to successor owners of their copyright or their publisher. Central to liability in passing off is the need for a misrepresentation.[8] For example in the "Alan Clark Diaries" case referred to earlier in the context of parody, the issue was whether a substantial (or large) number of readers of the *Evening Standard* (in which the "parodied" articles appeared) had been misled or were likely to be misled about the authorship of the articles, although that deception had to be more than momentary and inconsequential.[9]

It is also possible to commit passing off by representing a work which *is* the plaintiff's as being the work of someone else (so-called "reverse passing-off"[10]). This clearly overlaps with the moral right of paternity. The exploitation of a work as the author's which has been altered or revised without the author's consent can also be passing off,[11] as may also be the case if old material of an author is published as new work.[12]

It will be a clear-cut case of passing off if an artist with an established reputation in their name finds another trader using their name in the course of trade to pass off their designs as those of the artist. However it is much more difficult to establish that the imitation of an artist's

---

[7] The "classical trinity" of requirements for passing off are: (a) a reputation or goodwill acquired by the plaintiff for his goods, name or mark; (b) a misrepresentation by the defendant leading to confusion (or deception), causing (c) damage to the plaintiff (see *Consorzio del Prosciutto di Parma* v. *Marks & Spencer plc* [1991] RPC 351 at 368, *per* Lord Oliver in *Reckitt & Coleman Products Inc* v. *Borden Inc* [1990] 1 WLR 491 at 499, and Copinger at 21–02).

[8] *Erven Warnink* v. *Townend* [1980] RPC 31 at 93, *per* Lord Diplock.

[9] *Alan Clark* v. *Associated Newspapers Ltd* [1998] RPC 261. Here the reputation of Alan Clark as an author was protected by the law of passing off—his reputation and goodwill as an author were placed at risk, as were the prospective sales of his published works and the market value of his rights to exploit his works.

[10] See for example *Bristol Conservatories Ltd* v. *Conservatories Custom Built Ltd* [1989] RPC 455 (CA). US cases where this has happened include *Sanchez* v. *Stein* No. 80CV1208 (1980) (the defendant was alleged to have sold works of the plaintiff as the defendant's own creation, the "Winged Wolves" case (see DuBoff and King at 210) and *Smith* v. *Montoro* 648 F 2d 602 (9th Cir. 1981) (film credits) (DuBoff and King at 211).

[11] Copinger 21–13.

[12] Copinger 21–14.

style can be passing off.[13] The difficulty of course is that in most cases even if the artistic styles in question are similar it will be clear that the works in question emanate from different artists, hence there is no actionable misrepresentation. In any event the authors of Copinger take the view that passing off is unlikely, except where a particular style or characteristic has become associated with an artist and another has so nearly copied it so as to lead to confusion.[14] Copinger cites *Gordon Fraser Gallery Ltd* v. *Tatt*[15] in support, a case which concerned rival greetings card manufacturers: the defendants offered for sale cards which bore a distinct resemblance to the plaintiff's, which had a distinctive individual style. In an application for an interlocutory injunction it was held that mere imitation of an artistic style by itself would be unlikely to amount to passing off[16]—there would need to be a sufficient misrepresentation so that a person buying the defendant's cards would be under the impression that they were published by the plaintiffs—this was not the case here.[17]

Despite the difficulties in sustaining a passing off action in respect of artistic styles or designs, often claims in copyright infringement and passing off are pleaded together, especially where the copyright claim is weak. So for example, in the leading case on works of artistic crafts-manship, *George Hensher Ltd* v. *Restawhile Upholstery (Lancs) Ltd*, as well as claiming breach of copyright in their furniture designs the plain-

---

[13] Copinger 21–18.

[14] See for example *Marengo* v. *Daily Sketch and Daily Graphic Limited* [1992] FSR 1 (CA): "[n]o one is entitled to protection against confusion as such. Confusion may result from the collision of two independent rights or liberties and where that is the case neither party can complain; they must put up with the results of the confusion as one of the misfortunes which occur in life. The protection to which a man is entitled is protection against passing off which is quite a different thing from mere confusion. . . . If all that a trader is doing is to carry on trade in his own name and [in] disposing of or advertising his goods does no more than make the perfectly true statement that the goods are his goods, no other trader is entitled to complain" (*per* Lord Greene, MR at 2).

[15] [1966] RPC 505.

[16] In this case the judge was of the view that "a similarity of artistic style, or even a similarity of content and design, which does not, or may not, amount to a breach of copyright, would be too indefinite a feature to rely upon as the basis of granting relief in respect of passing off" (*per* Buckley J at 509).

[17] "[I]t seems to me that the artist . . . would have some difficulty in saying that [he] had a monopoly in producing works in [his style]. I am not concerned here with any question of copyright, but only with questions of passing off; and merely effecting the style, or imitating or adopting the style, [of] an artist, would it seems to me to be a difficult ground on which to base a claim for passing off if that was the only basis for the claim" (*per* Buckley J at 508).

tiff also claimed in passing off.[18] In *Norowzian* v. *Arks,* discussed in Chapter 6, a claim in passing off was abandoned during the trial.[19] In *Merchandising Corp. of America* v. *Harpbond*[20] (a case concerning Adam Ant's facial make-up: see Chapter 3), a claim in passing off that by reproducing pictures of the plaintiff Adam Ant in their magazines (which included a picture of Adam Ant altered by the defendants to replicate his facial make-up) the defendants were holding themselves out as licensees of the plaintiffs failed.[21]

In the USA, however, an artist's style was held to be a protectable trade dress in *Romm Art Creations Ltd* v. *Simcha International Ltd.*[22] However a number of other similar US actions have failed, so perhaps *Romm* should be doubted.[23]

In conclusion, it is also worth noting that UK law grants very little protection to an artist's name and personality as such.[24]

---

[18] The passing off claim failed at first instance before Graham J and was not the subject of the appeal ([1975] RPC 31)—it failed as the plaintiffs did not have a sufficient reputation in the shape of their goods to found a passing off action.

[19] See [1999] EMLR 67 at 76.

[20] [1983] FSR 32.

[21] Lawton LJ was of the view that there was no evidence that the defendants were doing this, and even if they were what they did was not damaging to Adam Ant's reputation (at 47).

[22] 786 F Supp. 1126 (EDNY 1992). Trade dress is the overall appearance or "look" of a product or service—to succeed confusion about the source of the goods or services concerned is likely, among other things (see DuBoff and King at 200–2). *Romm* concerned the style of the Israeli artist Itzchak Tarkay's posters and limited editions. The defendant distributed posters and limited editions strikingly similar to the plaintiff's. In this case the court held that Tarkay's images served no purpose other than to identify their source and there was a likelihood of confusion as to source in this case (see DuBoff and King at 201). So there was trade dress infringement even though no copyright infringement.

[23] See *Leigh* v. *Warner Bros.* 10 F Supp.2d 1371 (SDGa. 1998); *Hughes* v. *Design Look, Inc.* 693 F Supp. 1500 (SDNY 1988) (concerned paintings by Andy Warhol); and *Galerie Furstenberg* v. *Caffaro* 697 F Supp. 1282 (SDNY 1988) (Salvador Dali's style was not a trade mark—a counterfeiting case), all are discussed in DuBoff and King (at 40–1 and at 201–2). See also W.M. Borchard, *Trademarks & the Arts* (2nd edn., Kernochan Center for Law, Media and the Arts, Columbia Law School, New York, 1999) at 45 and 77–8.

[24] See Copinger 21–45 to 21–48. In particular it is debatable to what extent the unauthorised use of an artist's name or image to endorse someone else's product is actionable in passing off. See for example *Lord Brabourne* v. *Hough* [1981] FSR 79 and *Kaye* v. *Robertson* [1991] FSR 62 (the plaintiff, the actor Gorden Kaye, was photographed and interviewed by the defendants whilst in hospital following an accident—the defendants announced they were going to publish an article on this on the basis that Mr Kaye had consented: it was held that Mr Kaye was not a trader in relation to his interest in his story and his accident, so there was no passing off. See also P. Jones, "Manipulating the Law Against Misleading Imagery: Photo-montage and Appropriation of Well-known Personality" [1999] 1 *EIPR* 28 and see generally the discussion below about trade mark protection for an artist's name.

8.3 TRADE MARKS

In the USA the name "Picasso" has been held to be a trade mark in the context of Picasso and his heirs licensing various goods (including art reproductions, eyewear and scarves). The court recognised that the name "Picasso" and his famous signature had acquired a secondary meaning and his heirs had a right to profit from the use of his name and reputation.[25] A similar view was taken in a dispute relating to the domain name "samfrancis.com" between the administrator of the expressionist artist Sam Francis' estate and a commercial art gallery which had registered the domain name.[26]

In the UK, trade mark law (as opposed to passing off) protects *registered* trade marks and the main element in UK trade mark infringement actions is confusion (as opposed to misrepresentation in passing off). Also a registered trade mark is a property right in its own right[27]; passing off however protects the right in the goodwill of the trader or business concerned as opposed to any property in the mark (or name or get up) itself.[28]

To secure a trade mark registration in the UK, the mark applied for must be a "sign capable of being represented graphically which is capable of distinguishing goods or services of one undertaking from those of other undertakings. A trade mark may, in particular, consist of words (including personal names), designs, letters, numerals or the shape of goods or their packaging".[29] So it is possible for artistic works

---

[25] *Visual Arts and Galleries Ass'n* v. *Various John Does* , discussed in DuBoff and King at 192–3. This appears to be a case in US law (s. 43(a) of the Lanham Act 1946 which prohibits "a false description of origin, or any false description or representation" in connection with any goods or services which are introduced into commerce (DuBoff and King at 191–2)) giving protection to an unregistered trade mark; in UK law such an action needs to be brought in passing off if the mark is not registered. DuBoff and King also make the point that under US law only a well-known artist such as Picasso would be able to argue that their own name had a secondary meaning (i.e. an established customer association between the name and the artist's work) and hence could be protected as a trade mark.

[26] *Frederick M. Nicholas, Administrator, The Sam Francis Estate* v. *Magdison Fine Art, Inc.* (2000)—see section 8.4 below.

[27] S. 2, Trade Marks Act 1994 ("TMA"). The monopoly granted by a trade mark is in respect of the classes of goods and services for which it is registered.

[28] What is protected in passing off is "the property in the business or goodwill likely to be injured by the misrepresentation" (*per* Lord Parker in *A G Spalding & Brothers* v. *A W Gamage Ltd* (1915) 32 RPC 273 (HL)).

[29] S.1, TMA.

as well as an artist's name (or pseudonym) or signature[30] to be registered as a trade mark provided there are no grounds for refusing the trade mark application.[31]

There may, however, be difficulties in securing a trade mark registration for an artist's name in all cases.[32] Names can be registered as trade marks, provided there are no grounds for refusal. However in light of the Court of Appeal's decision in *Re Elvis Presley Trade Marks*,[33] the applicant may have some difficulty. This is because trade marks serve to function as "badges of origin" for the goods or services in respect of which the mark is applied for. Clearly if the mark is applied for in respect of, say, posters or engravings produced by the artist then the mark can function as a badge of origin: it can serve as an indication that the goods/services are supplied *by or under the control of* the person whose name it is. However if the mark is simply used for unrelated merchandising or souvenir purposes by a well-known artist then the matter may well be different.[34] Ironically the more well-known the name of the artist the less likely it is that their name can

[30] The more distinctive the signature is the more likely it is to be registered as a trade mark: signatures are *prima facie* distinctive for trade mark purposes, but not inevitably so (see Laddie J in *Re Elvis Presley Trade Marks* [1997] RPC 567 at 558). See also the further discussion of *Elvis* below.

[31] The grounds can be absolute (for example, the mark fails to satisfy the requirements of s. 1(1), it is devoid of any distinctive character, etc. (s.3, TMA)), or relative (for example, it is identical or confusingly similar to an earlier trade mark (s.5, TMA)) or it is a protected emblem such as a national flag (s.5, TMA)).

[32] It should also be added that there is no copyright in a name: *Du Boulay v. Du Boulay* (1869) LR 2 PC 430.

[33] [1999] RPC 567 upholding Laddie J [1997] RPC 543. The decision was under the old Trade Marks Act 1938 and was to the effect that the marks applied for, "Elvis", "Elvis Presley" and a signature of Elvis Presley, were neither distinctive of, nor capable of distinguishing, the applicant's goods (cosmetics and other goods in Class 3). See generally Morcom n. 1 *supra*, 5.50–5.51. For a case under the current Act (TMA) see *Jane Austen Trade Mark* [2000] RPC 879: the applicant, a toiletry business, sought to register "JANE AUSTEN" in respect of various toiletries. Its application was refused under s.3(1)(b) of the TMA on the basis that it was devoid of any distinctive character. The application was opposed by the trustees of the Jane Austen Memorial Trust who owned Jane Austen's house and museum in Hampshire and who had developed a trade in related souvenirs. It was held that unless educated through use to see the name differently, the public would not regard "Jane Austen" as a badge of origin. However it should be noted that Kerly advises caution in relying too heavily on *Elvis* when considering similar "personality-based" trade mark applications, as the 1994 Act regime is more permissive than the previous 1938 Act (Kerly at 22–49 to 22–54).

[34] Simon Brown LJ in *Elvis* made clear that in this case there was absolutely no connection between the class of products in question (toiletries) and the things for which Elvis Presley was famous (at 597). He went on to state: "there should be no a priori assumption that only a celebrity or his successors may ever market (or licence the marketing of) his own character. Monopolies should not be so readily created" (at 598).

function as a badge of origin for trade mark purposes—the name is at risk of merely being indicative of the content or character of the goods (i.e. it refers back to the artist concerned) rather than signifying trade origin.[35]

Despite the difficult issues surrounding merchandising and trade mark protection, as a practical matter art dealers, museums, galleries and artists are advised to consider carefully protecting their logos, names, and other brands through trade marks where appropriate and available.[36] Also any use made of their brands by others, for example for merchandising purposes, should be strictly controlled by a licence in the appropriate form in order to seek to preserve and maintain rights in the brand.

8.4 DOMAIN NAMES

Strictly speaking Internet domain names are not a species of intellectual property—they simply represent a unique Internet address, performing a similar function to a telephone number. Rights to use a domain name are governed by the contract made between the applicant and the relevant domain name registrar. Nevertheless domain names are often treated as if they were intellectual property. Furthermore there are frequently conflicts between domain names and trade marks (whether registered or protected at common law by passing off), as registrars generally register on a first-come first-served basis and no two domain names can be identical. Trade marks however are national in scope, so whilst there can be only one registrant of "art.com", say, "Art" may be a trade mark in various countries and in respect of a variety of classes of goods and services, each mark potentially being owned by a separate proprietor. This inevitably gives rise to conflicts between registrants

---

[35] See for example Laddie J in *Elvis* (at 550–4). For example the character of soap sold under the mark "Elvis" would be "Elvis Soap", hence the mark is descriptive of the goods in respect of which it is being used. The Elvis marks served merely to distinguish the products, not their producer, and would serve to describe the essential nature of the goods being traded (Elvis Presley memorabilia) but say nothing about their trade origins. However the whole point of a trade mark is to distinguish the proprietor's goods from similar goods marketed by competitors (see Simon Brown LJ in *Elvis* at 596). See also *TARZAN Trade Mark* [1970] RPC 450.

[36] Of course copyright protection may also be available for signatures, logos and designs. Note however that if a design itself were to be registered as a trade mark such a mark runs the risk of being held invalid, as use of a pattern as part of goods themselves rather than as a "badge of origin" is not genuine trade mark use (see generally Laddie (2nd edn.) at 23.6 and s.46(1), TMA). Nevertheless this risk may well be worth taking, given the uncertainties in the law here.

and trade mark proprietors. So it is worth briefly investigating this area from the perspective of an artist, dealer or museum.

A number of museums, art galleries, art publishers and artists have been the victims (or alleged victims) of "cybersquatting": unconnected persons have registered a domain name identical or similar to their name and have either sought money for its "return" or traded using the domain name in the hope of benefiting from the others' goodwill in their name. Such activities can amount to passing off or trade mark infringement in the UK.[37] In other countries the matter has been legislated against.[38] Increasingly cybersquatting is now dealt with by the aggrieved party making use of the Uniform Domain Name Dispute Resolution Policy (UDRP) established by ICANN,[39] a form of private arbitration, to which a number of domain name registrars have subscribed.[40] The UDRP is aimed at providing a swift remedy for "bad faith" domain name registrations.[41]

A number of museums, art galleries, art publishers and artists have used the UDRP.[42] These include disputes over the following domain names:

Samfrancis.com: Frederick M. Nicholas, Administrator, *The Sam Francis Estate* v. *Magdison Fine Art, Inc.*[43]

The complainant was the administrator of the estate of the abstract expressionist artist Sam Francis (who died in 1994). The respondent

---

[37] See for example the "One in a Million"case: *British Telecommunications and Others* v. *One in a Million and Others* [1999] 4 All ER 476.

[38] In the USA by the Anticybersquatting Consumer Protection Act 2000, for example.

[39] Internet Corporation for Assigned Names and Numbers, a non-profit corporation responsible for the Internet address system—see www.icann.org.

[40] All registrars in the .com, .org and .net domains must establish this procedure.

[41] To be successful the complainant must prove: (i) that the alleged cybersquatter's domain name is identical or confusingly similar to a trade mark or service mark in which the complainant has rights; and (ii) the cybersquatter has no rights or legitimate interests in respect of the domain name; and (iii) the domain name has been registered and is being used in bad faith by the cybersquatter (see para. 4(a) of the UDRP); the UDRP also gives in para. 4(b) non-exhaustive lists of the circumstances to be treated as evidence of registration and use in bad faith (for example, name acquired simply to sell back to the complainant at a profit, or use of the name by the respondent for commercial gain by attracting users to the respondent's site by creating a likelihood of confusion with the complainant's mark about the source, sponsorship, affiliation or endorsement of the respondent's website), and in para. 4(c) indicates how rights to and a legitimate interest in a domain name may be demonstrated.

[42] Decisions of the various arbitrators appointed to resolve disputes can easily be found from the ICANN website (www.icann.org). Case references are noted below.

[43] Case No. D2000–0673 (WIPO Arbitration and Mediation Center), 27 September 2000.

was an art gallery in Aspen Colorado, "a legitimate fine art gallery,. physically and virtually, exhibiting and selling modern and contemporary art masters of which Sam Francis is one".[44] The gallery had been operating for over 30 years in New York City and Aspen. On or about 14 April 1998 the respondent registered the domain name "samfrancis.com" in which it offered for sale lithographs, etchings and screenprints by Sam Francis. The complainant did not authorise the respondent to use the name or mark "Sam Francis" as its domain name or website. The complainant sent two "cease and desist" letters to the respondent requiring it to stop using the domain name. Then on 24 June 2000 the complainant invoked the UDRP. Interestingly the complainant failed. The Panel had no difficulty in finding that the complainant had a common law (i.e. unregistered) trade mark and service mark in SAM FRANCIS.[45] The majority of the panel of three arbitrators, however, held there was no bad faith registration and use of the domain name under the UDRP, although the presiding panelist dissented.[46] Because the respondent made clear on its website that it was *not* the artist's site, but a commercial gallery selling his paintings, and as there was no misleading assertion that it was sponsored or approved by the artist nor did it tarnish the reputation of the artist, the complainant was unable to show that the respondent had registered and used the mark in bad faith. "To use an artist's name as an informa-

---

[44] Decision at section 4.

[45] "The Panel finds that an artist may be entitled to a common law trademark or service mark without registering the mark with the appropriate authority. See *Julia Fiona Roberts* v. *Russell Boyd* (WIPO Case No. D2000–0120)" (29 May 2000). [This UDRP case concerned the bad faith registration of "juliaroberts.com" which the well-known actress of the same name successfully complained about, despite not having a trade mark registration for her name—instead common law trade mark rights in her name were recognised. A UDRP case where English law was applied also found that common law trade mark rights exist in an author's name (*Jeanette Winterson* v. *Mark Hogarth* (WIPO Case No. D2000–0235, 22 May 2000))—this was cited in support in *Julia Roberts*.] "The artist must show that his or her name has achieved sufficient secondary meaning or association with Complainant. Over the course of Sam Francis' lengthy and distinguished career, and continuing today, the public has come to recognize and associate the name 'Sam Francis' as a symbol that distinguishes the artwork produced exclusively by a single artist. The name 'Sam Francis' has become synonymous with the works produced by Sam Francis in the public mind. As a result, the name 'Sam Francis' has acquired distinctiveness and secondary meaning as a common law trademark and service mark when associated with works of art" (at section 6 of the decision).

[46] The dissenting panelist was of the view that because the domain name in issue was identical to the complainant's SAM FRANCIS common law marks, the respondent intentionally attracted customers by creating the impression that the website www.samfrancis.com was sponsored or authorised by the artist, hence there was bad faith (see para. 4(b)(iv) of the UDRP).

tional reference in the context of otherwise legitimately offering that artist's genuine work for sale to the public may well constitute a fair use under applicable law."[47] The Panel also concluded that in a difficult case such as this the scope of "fair use" is a matter best determined by the courts rather than the UDRP.

Gallerina.com: Gallerina v. Mark Wilmshurst[48]

In this case the award-winning British contemporary art gallery "Gallerina" was successful in having the domain name "gallerina.com" transferred back to it: the domain name was found to have been registered and used in bad faith by the respondent.[49]

Artnews.net: Artnews, L.L.C v. Ecorp.com[50]

The publisher of the well-known US monthly magazine, *ARTnews* (which also owned the registered trade mark "ARTnews") had no difficulty in obtaining a transfer of the "artnews.net" domain name back to it from the respondent who was held to have registered the domain name in bad faith.

Gettymuseum.com/Gettysmuseum.com[51]; *Brooklynmuseumofart.com/ Brooklynmuseumofart.org*[52]

The Getty Museum (which held a number of registered trade marks for "the Getty" and related marks) and the Brooklyn Museum of Art (which was held to have common law rights in its name) also had no

---

[47] Decision at section 6.

[48] Case No. D2000–0730 (WIPO Arbitration and Mediation Center), 16 August 2000.

[49] The Panel had no difficulty in finding that the complainant Gallerina, which had traded under that name for six years, had sufficient reputation and goodwill in its name to sustain a passing-off action in the UK to protect its name, despite not having a registered trade mark, i.e. it had a trade mark or service mark (albeit under common law) identical or confusingly similar to the domain name, hence para. 4(a)(i) of the UDRP was satisfied.

[50] Claim Number: FA0007000095231 (National Arbitration Forum), 22 August 2000.

[51] *The J. Paul Getty Trust v. Domain 4 Sale & Company*, Claim No: FA0007000095262 (National Arbitration Forum), 7 September 200.)

[52] *Brooklyn Institute of Arts and Sciences v. Fantastic Sites, Inc.*, Claim Number: FA0009000095560 (National Arbitration Forum), 2 November 2000.

difficulty in obtaining these domain names back from respondents who had clearly registered them in bad faith.[53]

---

[53] "When the name of a famous museum is registered as a domain name by anyone other than the museum itself, and the registrant provides no evidence of why the domain name was registered or what good faith use is proposed, the only inference is that the domain name was registered in bad faith". See the discussion in the *Brooklyn* case (*per* the Honourable Carolyn Marks Johnson, Panelist)).

9

Conclusion

THIS BOOK HAS sought to explore the scope and nature of the copy-right protection granted to artistic works under UK law. As well as setting out the applicable law with reference to the treatment of artistic works in certain other jurisdictions, a number of current and practical issues have been discussed. A number of recurring themes and issues occur. These are considered further in this conclusion.

9.1 CATEGORIES OF "ART" AND THE SUBSISTENCE OF COPYRIGHT

The confining definition of "artistic works" in section 4(1) of the CDPA means that the courts are increasingly having to determine whether works outside the boundaries of traditional art forms are protected by copyright.[1] In determining the subsistence of copyright issues such as the fixation/permanence of the work, its categorisation as a "graphic work", "sculpture", "collage", "film", etc, and its originality will arise.

In seeking to classify works within a specific category of "artistic work" it is clear from section 4 of the CDPA that, except for "works of artistic craftsmanship",[2] "artistic quality" should not be a relevant factor. Nevertheless a recent case suggests that where the court cannot easily fit a work into a specific category issues such as the intention of the creator and their status (as an "artist") are likely to be considered, despite both the express language of section 4 and the often-expressed reluctance of the courts to determine questions of aesthetics and subjective matters generally noted in Chapter 3.[3]

---

[1] See *Creation Records* v. *News Group Newspapers* [1997] EMLR 444; *Norowzian* v. *Arks* [2000] FSR 363.

[2] Also (arguably) for works of architecture (see Chap. 3).

[3] See *Metix (UK)* v. *G.H. Maughan (Plastics)* [1997] FSR 718: sculpture was defined as "a three dimensional work made by an artist's hand". In considering whether the plastic moulds concerned were "sculptures" Laddie J noted that their designers did not consider themselves to be "artists" when they designed the moulds (nor would anyone else have considered them to be) and their only consideration in making the moulds was to

"Works of artistic craftsmanship" remain an ill-defined category. Various tests have been used to determine whether a work falls within it.[4] These include considerations of the function of the work, the intention of the designer, whether the work appeals to the aesthetic senses, whether the designer is an artist-craftsman, whether the work is artistic or creative enough, that "works of artistic craftsmanship" be given its ordinary and natural meaning, and so on. Given the increasing importance of "craft" in artistic circles and the difficulties surrounding the protection of works as diverse as fashion designs, film sets and patchwork bedspeads,[5] it is submitted that a clear and consistent approach by the courts is necessary in this area.[6]

Moving on from the category of work, the issue of "fixation" remains a difficult one for artistic works. A leading text, Copinger,[7] is of the view there is no requirement of fixation for artistic works, and whether a work is intended to have a long or short existence should be irrelevant. However the cases on this issue appear to conflict.[8] It is submitted that some element of fixation is surely necessary to define the scope of what is protected by copyright.[9] In practice when considering whether the work in question is an "artistic work" the issue of fixation will be dealt with—the very categories of "artistic works" (graphic works, photographs, sculptures and collages) would seem to require such a determination.[10]

Originality remains wedded to the notions of "sweat of the brow" and of "authorship". Xerographic or similar reproductions apart, skill

---

achieve functional, as opposed to aesthetic, features. However artistic intent alone may not help if there is no fixation (see below and also *per* Lloyd J in *Creation Records* v. *News Group Newspapers* [1997] EMLR 444 at 450, discussed in section 3.2.1 of Chap. 3).

[4] As discussed in section 3.2.1 of Chap. 3.

[5] See respectively *Radley Gowns Ltd* v. *Costas Spyrou* [1975] FSR 455, *Shelley Films Ltd* v. *Rex Features Ltd* [1994] EMLR 134, and *Vermaat* v. *Boncrest Ltd*, *The Times*, 23 June 2000; [2000] EIPR N–151; *Intellectual Property Lawyer*, Issue 3, July 2000 (at 10)).

[6] Of course the whole area illustrates the various judicial approaches that can be taken to defining art and craft. See also Kearns, chap. 3.

[7] At 3–40.

[8] In *Metix (UK)* v. *G.H. Maughan (Plastics)* [1997] FSR 718 a sculpture made from ice was considered by Laddie J to be no less a sculpture because it would inevitably melt; contrast *Davis (J&S) (Holdings) Ltd* v. *Wright Health Group Ltd* [1988] RPC 403 and the other cases noted in section 3.2.4 of chap. 3.

[9] See for example *Tate* v. *Fullbrook* [1908] 1 KB 821, discussed in section 3.2.4 of chap. 3.

[10] See for example *Creation Records* v. *News Group Newspapers* [1997] EMLR 444 where the collocation of random unfixed objects was not a collage even if done with artistic intent.

and labour devoted to the visual expression of an artistic work will be sufficient to satisfy the threshold of "originality" in UK law; "creativity" finds no part in UK copyright law.[11] However as Lord Hoffmann recently noted, "copyright law protects foxes better than hedgehogs",[12] so whilst a simple artistic work may be protected by copyright, the protection afforded to the artist to prevent copying may well be limited.[13] Works must also have an "author" for copyright purposes—this is embedded in both the structure of the CDPA[14] and the very notion of "originality". So works of communal origin where there is "collective" authorship, as is often the case for indigenous art, may fail to be protected by copyright.[15]

Given the above features of UK copyright law, how valid is the criticism that UK law is inflexible in its categorisation of artistic works so that various forms of contemporary art will fall outside the ambit of copyright? It is submitted that whilst clarity would be helpful in certain areas (most notably for works of artistic craftsmanship), in light of recent cases the categories of protected work in section 4 of the CDPA appear to have a reasonable degree of flexibility in practice.[16]

What then will copyright protect?

---

[11] Although this may gradually change in the light of EU copyright harmonisation: for example, the Term Directive (Directive 93/98/EEC) states that "photographs which are original *in the sense that they are the author's own intellectual creation* shall be protected in accordance with Article 1 [extension of duration of copyright term to life plus 70 years] [emphasis added]. No other criteria shall be applied to determine their eligibility for protection. Member States may provide for the protection of other photographs." Kearns describes the criterion for copyright protection in England as "originality divorced from creativity" (at 83).

[12] *Designers Guild* v. *Russell Williams (Textiles) Ltd* [2000] 1 WLR 2416 at 2423E.

[13] See *Kenrick* v. *Lawrence* (1890) 25 QBD 93, discussed in section 3.2.1 of chap. 3.

[14] " '[A]uthor' in relation to a work means the person who creates it" (s.9(1), CDPA): this even appears for computer-generated works (s.9(3))—see Chap. 5.

[15] See generally section 3.2.2 of chap. 3, *Vermaat* v. *Boncrest Ltd*, *The Times*, 23 June 2000, [2000] EIPR N–151; *Intellectual Property Lawyer*, Issue 3, July 2000 (at 10)), and section 6.4 of chap. 6.

[16] For example there will generally be skill and labour expended in creating a ready-made and, following *Metix (UK)* v. *G.H. Maughan (Plastics)* [1997] FSR 718, it is difficult to see why such a work cannot be classed as "sculpture". Of course in *Creation Records* v. *News Group Newspapers* [1997] EMLR 444 the "assemblage" concerned was denied copyright protection but here (following *Metix* v. *Maughan*) the *purpose* of the work was surely central—if it had been created, not to be photographed for a clear commercial purpose and then immediately dismantled, but as a temporary installation to be exhibited, it is submitted a court would probably find some way of protecting the work. It is however admitted that exact reproductions by way of appropriation art *prima facie* appear to be cases of copyright infringement: see section 6.3 in chap. 6.

9.2 APPROPRIATING THE PUBLIC DOMAIN: IDEA VERSUS EXPRESSION

"Skill and labour" are the yardsticks used to class a work as "original" and it is the perceived need to prevent the unjust appropriation of an author's skill and labour that remains the chief judicial justification for copyright, a policy pursued by the courts with "almost evangelical fervour" in the words of one leading judge.[17] To state matters even more simply, "what is worth copying . . . is worth protecting".[18] Furthermore as copyright is a right of property, the infringement of that right is actionable without proof of damage.[19] As noted in Chapter 2, this "misappropriation" justification for copyright protection can easily be taken to extremes, absent any checks and balances in terms of what is protected. So, as discussed earlier in this book, both the courts and the legislature have sought to limit the application of this doctrine on public policy grounds through various mechanisms including:

(a) copyright protection is restricted to certain classes of works and is limited in duration;

(b) the functional aspects of works are in most cases given limited or no protection;

(c) copyright is infringed only if the whole or a substantial part of the work is copied;[20]

(d) Chapter III of the CDPA contains a substantial list of activities which may be done without infringing copyright, chief of which are the "fair dealing" provisions;[21]

(e) although the idea/expression dichotomy has no statutory basis in UK law, it remains a frequently applied, and appealed to, principle in cases of similar but not identical works;[22] and

---

[17] *Per* Laddie J in *Autospin (Oil Seals) Ltd* v. *Beehive Spinning (A Firm)* [1995] RPC 683. As noted in section 3.2.9, that the function of copyright is to protect the skill and labour of the author was noted by the majority of the House of Lords in the current leading artistic copyright case, *Designers Guild* v. *Russell Williams (Textiles) Ltd* [2000] 1 WLR 2416.

[18] *Per* Peterson J in *University of London Press Ltd* v. *University Tutorial Press Ltd* [1916] 2 Ch. at 610.

[19] Copinger at 22–42.

[20] S.16(3), CDPA.

[21] See in particular ss.29 and 30.

[22] See generally sections 3.2.8 and 3.2.9 of Chap. 3.

(f) by the use of judicial discretion in applying (a) to (e) above including a very limited public interest defence.[23]

So in looking at the cases one sees the courts being reluctant to protect the "mere style or technique" of a work such as pointillism,[24] either through copyright or the law of passing off.[25] However it is clear that wholesale appropriation of a work, even if done for the purposes of parody, is likely to amount to copyright infringement absent any permitted exception such as a fair dealing defence.

UK law does not have a general "fair use" defence to copyright infringement, so in difficult cases the courts have to rely on the above exceptions. Whilst notions of "fairness" and judicial common sense can do much to eliminate the harsher effects of the lack of such a general defence, it is submitted that the advent of the Internet makes the need for the development of a more general "fair use" defence pressing.[26]

9.3 THE DIGITAL FUTURE

9.3.1 The End of the Public Domain?

Artists and publishers are frequently under the impression that the Internet spells the end of copyright, unregulated piracy being the inevitable outcome of placing copies of their works on the Internet.[27] In fact we may be facing the end of the public domain.

The Digital Copyright Directive[28] strengthens the copyright protection afforded to copyright owners in the digital environment. It does so by,

[23] See chap. 3 at n. 9, especially *Hyde Park Residence Ltd* v. *Yelland* [1999] RPC 655, [2000] 3 WLR 215. Also see *Canon Kabushiki Kaisha* v. *Green Cartridge Co* [1997] AC 728 (PC).

[24] *Per* Nourse LJ in *Norowzian* v. *Arks* [2000] FSR 363 (CA); see also Morritt LJ in *Designers Guild* v. *Russell Williams* [2000] FSR 121 (CA); presumably examples of mere style or technique would generally fall within the second category of unprotected "ideas" noted by Lord Hoffmann in *Designers Guild* ([2000] 1 WLR 2416 at 2423D) as being "not original or so commonplace as not to form a substantial part of the work".

[25] There being no general tort of unfair competition in English law—see Chap. 8.

[26] See 9.3 below and also the discussion on Internet visual search engines in Chap. 6.

[27] Hence the practical trend to put low resolution (hence low value) images on websites and the use of digital watermarks—see Chap. 5.

[28] The latest published version as at 9 April 2001 is the Common Position (EC) No 48/2000 adopted by the Council on 28 September 2000 [2000] OJ C344/1. Some of the points raised in this section together with other issues are discussed at some length in Vinje.

among other things, introducing a new right of communication to the public, by limiting what is permitted by way of transient or incidental copying, and by effectively circumscribing the exceptions or limitations to copyright Member States may wish to maintain or introduce in the future. Whilst artists will potentially gain stronger copyright protection as a result, in the aim of harmonising the exceptions to copyright the Directive effectively sets in stone what Member States may do in this regard but fails to provide a set of mandatory exceptions. So Member States will be free to have different exceptions to copyright infringement regarding parodies, educational use, private use, etc. So there is no express, clear "fair use" type of doctrine enshrined in the Directive which *all* states must provide for in their copyright legislation. It is submitted this is a missed opportunity for a much-needed harmonisation.

Also the Directive will require the UK to make changes to a number of the exceptions to copyright infringement in Chapter III of the CDPA including the "fair dealing" exceptions. For example, one exception to the reproduction right in the Directive is that copying may be permitted by the Directive where "made by a natural person for private use and for ends that are neither directly nor indirectly commercial, on condition that the rightholders receive fair compensation which takes account of the application or non-application of technological measures referred to in Article 6[29] to the work or subject matter concerned".[30] At present "fair compensation" is not a concept recognised by the equivalent provisions in the CDPA permitting fair dealing for the purposes of research or private study[31] and the clarity and meaning of the whole exception can be questioned.

Other changes relevant to artists include the probable removal of the section 64 exception which permits artists to copy their previous work where the copyright is owned by someone else,[32] as well as the

---

[29] Technological measures means "any technology, device or component that, in the normal course of its operation, is designed to prevent or restrict acts, in respect of works or other subject matter, which are not authorised by the rightholder" (Art. 6(3)).

[30] Art. 5(2)(b).

[31] S.29.

[32] The Directive contains no such permitted exception (although see Article 5(3)(0) which may allow the UK to retain this for analogue as opposed to digital uses). As mentioned in Chap. 3, this exception applies only where the artist copies the prior work in making another artistic work where the artist does not "repeat or imitate the main design of the earlier work". There was a broadly similar provision in the Copyright Act 1956 (s.9(9). According to Copinger, in the course of the Parliamentary debates on this section it was said that the provision would, for example, allow an architect to reuse their designs elsewhere and to allow the painter of a group portrait to reuse sketches to reproduce individual portraits (at 9–92). Copinger also suggests it would allow a painter to

probable removal of "works of artistic craftsmanship" from the works which may be freely photographed if on public display.[33]

Furthermore the Directive will ensure that there is adequate legal protection against the circumvention of technical means to protect against copying (which must inevitably include preventing unauthorised access in order to view a work).[34] Whilst the Directive appears to recognise the public domain in the sense of allowing the permitted exceptions and limitations to override an attempt by the copyright owner to use, for example, encryption to deny access, it is very unclear how this will be achieved in practice, if at all.[35]

So once implemented the Directive will potentially severely restrict the fair use/fair dealing of copyright material. It is already a matter of debate to what extent the statutory exceptions to copyright infringement in Chapter III of the CDPA can be overridden by contract, such as a website licence and terms of use. The Directive appears to expressly allow this.[36]

9.3.2 The Future of Moral Rights

The Digital Copyright Directive is concerned only with the "economic rights" aspects of copyright.[37] As discussed in Chapter 1, the

---

reuse a "trade mark" object or motif in their work such as Magritte's *bilboquets*. Note that if, instead of assigning copyright in the prior work, the artist had instead granted an exclusive licence over it to a third party then in that circumstance the artist would not be able to benefit from this provision and their right to copy the earlier work will depend on the terms of the licence (see Copinger at 9–92). US law, for example, appears to contain no such express provision, and there have been cases where this issue has arisen. For example, see *Gross v. Seligman* 212 F 930 (2nd Cir.1914) where despite small differences a photographer was held liable for copying his earlier photograph; contrast *Franklin Mint Corp v. National Wildlife Art Exchange Inc* 575 F 2d 62 (3rd Cir.1978) where dissimilarities in the two paintings concerned were sufficient to constitute "a diversity of expression rather than only an echo" in comparing the later "copy" to the original (see DuBoff and King at 206, and Joyce at 120).

[33] S.62, noted in Chap. 3. The Directive is in fact much more restrictive than s.62: it states the exception as "use of works, *such as works of architecture or sculpture, made to be located* permanently in public places" (Art. 5(3)(h) emphasis added (although see Art. 5(3)(0) again)). S.62 simply requires the works to be permanently situated in a public place or in premises open to the public—they need not have been made for this purpose.

[34] See Chap. 5.

[35] See Art. 6(4).

[36] See para. 4 of Art. 6(4). See also generally H.L. MacQueen, "Copyright and the Internet" in Edwards and Waelde, chap. 9, for a discussion of whether the "fair use" and "fair dealing" type of exceptions to copyright infringement can be overridden by contract.

[37] It is justified on economic grounds on the basis that a high and harmonised level of copyright protection is needed to foster investment in, and guarantee rewards for,

justification for moral rights protection for artists on the basis of natural law, and in particular the "personality theory" of copyright, is a strong one. The lack of harmonisation of moral rights laws both across the EU and world-wide is a significant issue for artists. Artists are now finding their works displayed in virtual art galleries and a number are also using digital technology to create new works.

Whilst some argue that the application of moral rights to the Internet should be severely curtailed, if not excluded, it is submitted that the pragmatic UK approach to moral rights is a good model for the Internet. Where the artistic works concerned are created with commercial objectives in mind there is the possibility of a waiver of the rights of paternity and integrity; otherwise the artist will benefit from them.

As it will shape copyright law in Europe for years to come, it is hoped that the voices of artists and the public, as well as business, will be reflected in the implementation of the Digital Copyright Directive to the fullest extent possible. A strong public domain and the recognition of artists' moral rights in the digital environment in any future EU harmonisation are surely necessary if the wealth of visual information, not to say culture, in our society is to be maintained, criticised and developed.

creativity and innovation, etc. (see Recitals 2, 4, 9, 10, 22). It is stated that such a "rigorous and effective" system for protection of copyright will safeguard "the independence and dignity of artistic creators and performers" (Recital 11). However as the Directive expressly does not deal with moral rights (Recital 19) it is difficult to see how this will be achieved by it.

Index